KILLING GOLDFINGER

Also by Wensley Clarkson

THE CURSE OF BRINK'S-MAT
HASH
COCAINE CONFIDENTIAL
LEGAL HIGHS
SEXY BEASTS

KILLING GOLDFINGER

The Secret, Bullet-Riddled Life and Death

of Britain's Gangster Number One

WENSLEY CLARKSON

Quercus

First published in Great Britain in 2017 by

Quercus Editions Ltd
Carmelite House
50 Victoria Embankment
London EC4Y 0DZ
An Hachette UK company

A CIP catalogue record for this book is available
from the British Library.

HB ISBN 978 1 78648 485 7
TPB ISBN 978 1 78648 486 4
Ebook ISBN 978 1 78648 487 1

10 9 8 7 6 5 4 3 2 1

Text designed and typeset by CC Book Production

Printed and bound in the UK by Clays Ltd, St Ives plc.

I come to lead you to the other shore
Into eternal dark, into fire and ice

— Dante, Inferno

To ALL John Palmer's Victims – Dead or Alive.
Without them this story could not be told.

AUTHOR'S NOTE

In this book, I've delved inside John 'Goldfinger' Palmer's deadly world to reveal an extraordinary story built around a way of life; a mentality that was shaped by post-war Britain when bomb sites were playgrounds and dodgy spivs hung about on every street corner. John Palmer's bullet-riddled career is beyond most people's imagination and all the more terrifying because it really did happen.

My undeniable curiosity about John Palmer has been fuelled by a number of significant events over the past thirty years. The first one was back in the late 1990s when I investigated the activities of one of Palmer's closest associates and discovered that he had earned untold riches from the proceeds of one of the world's biggest ever robberies.

Then in 2001, I got a phone call from an acquaintance who'd helped me with a number of crime books and documentaries in the past. 'John Palmer wants to do his life story,' said my associate. 'You interested?'

At first I was shocked that someone as secretive as John Palmer would want a book written about him. Then his most likely motive for doing this dawned on me and I realized it would be a monumental mistake to get involved, so I politely declined.

And my connections to the real life story you are about to read do not just end there, either. In the summer of 2016, I was approached by Essex police and asked if I could help them with their inquiries into Palmer. I politely declined on the basis that it would not do my credibility inside the UK underworld any good.

Unpeeling Palmer's life has left me with myriad impressions of the man himself but as I began to write it, I realized some of my sources had shady, ulterior motives and my aim has always been to show Palmer in a balanced light, not a version warped by the evil intent of so many who knew him.

So the story you are about to read may not be the one that John Palmer would have preferred to be told. But it is the nearest to the truth about a man who left a 'mark' on everyone he met, from cold-blooded gangsters to one of the world's most deadly narco-terrorists.

During the course of researching this book I've been taken into the confidence of many people who, for obvious reasons, would prefer to remain anonymous. I have respected the wishes of those individuals, and I need only say that my decision to do so was more to protect the guilty than the innocent, as well as ensuring the safety of my family and myself. As a result, some of the scenes depicted here represent a combination of facts dramatically reconstructed to reflect Palmer's story.

Lastly, John Palmer used the term 'Clumpers' to describe the enforcers and henchmen who worked with him throughout his adult life. Put simply, they 'clumped' anyone who got in his way and I make no apology for using that term in the book you're about to read.

Wensley Clarkson, London, 2017

Remember the golden rule – he who has the gold makes the rules

– The framed words John Palmer kept on his office wall

CAST OF CHARACTERS

MISHA – Russian mobster with friends in high places

THE BLACK JUDGE – Law chief who wouldn't give up

GB – The richest money launderer in London

CAPTAIN BOB – The ultimate fraudster

CHARLIE BOY – Underworld legend who thought he was invincible

THE PROFESSOR – Coke baron with a secret Nazi past

PSYCHO BILL – American surfer-dude from hell

DIESEL – Smothered in baby oil and off his head on steroids

THE BIG CHEESE – TV detective who nearly ran out of breath

THE DEVIL'S ADVOCATE – Dodgy lawman living in legal hell

MAD MICKEY – Short-fused robber with gold chip on his shoulder

FLO – Bubbly mum who didn't watch her back

BILLY – Followed the money and paid the price

BILL AND BEN – The brothers from hell

TEL – The ultimate narco-terrorist

ELVIS THE EEL – Slippery entertainer who packed a punch

MANUEL THE MIDGET – Andalucian crime lord

KILLER KENNY – Psycho-villain with a deadly temper

CHRISTINE – Loyal partner and timeshare associate

MARNIE – Long-suffering wife who knew nothing

HOWARD THE PUFF – Legendary pot king who took no shit

SCOTTY BOY – Soft-talking henchman who ran out of steam

BOBBI – Fearless Bermondsey drag queen

LEM – Brummie scallywag who pushed his luck

SID AND NANCY – Sole survivors of a timeshare massacre

THE SHARKS – Latin heavies in a black limo

CONTENTS

PART THREE
THE CHILL FACTOR
2007–2015

INTRODUCTION

**PLAYA DE LAS AMERICAS RESORT, SOUTHERN
TENERIFE, CANARY ISLANDS, JULY 2006**

The pristine skyscraper headquarters of John Palmer's Island Village timeshare resort rose majestically above the tatty bars and scruffy one-euro shops that lined the long strip of sandy beach known as the Golden Mile. The temperature was close to one hundred degrees as I stood by the rear of this building next to a small entrance just wide enough for a car to enter. I'd been told by one of Palmer's oldest associates on the island that this led to a treasure trove most befitting such an immensely wealthy and secretive character, who'd plundered the wallets and lives of so many people over the previous thirty years.

Looking both ways in case Palmer's armed thugs at the main entrance to the building just thirty yards away saw me, I took a deep, nervous breath and headed down the steep slope. For three or four minutes it twisted and turned like a vast subterranean slide leading me further and further beneath ground level.

Occasionally I heard the shrill whistle of the strong breeze coming in off the nearby Atlantic Ocean or the echo of a car door shutting. At one time, this secret opening had provided

John Palmer's criminal associates with an escape route whenever unwanted visitors appeared at the double entrance doors
to his headquarters above.

Many who worked for John Palmer said they were amazed
the entire basement hadn't caved in from the weight of the
marble-encrusted walls and floors that covered every inch of
the ground floor of the main building.

As I reached the bottom of the ramp, strips of overhanging
neon lights suddenly flickered to life revealing one of the most
eerie sights I'd ever seen in my entire life. I hesitated for a few
seconds as I tried to take it all in.

There in front of me, caked in dust and cobwebs, was the
largest collection of classic sports cars I'd ever seen, probably
worth at least £10 million. Nearest to me stood an iconic 1960s
Ferrari Spider, its red bodywork barely visible through the dirt.

Then I remembered the words of one of Palmer's oldest associates a few hours earlier: 'You won't believe what you find
down there. It's incredible. They aren't just old bangers, either.
They're worth a fortune and JP's got just about every make and
model that matters.'

I waited a few more seconds, wondering if one of Palmer's
henchmen would show up and confront me. But no one appeared.

I quickly looked around and then approached the Ferrari, half
expecting to find some cobweb-covered human remains in the
driver's seat. Then it dawned on me that it was the cars that
were the skeletons in this bizarre scenario. They represented all
John Palmer's victims; left to rot in a hot, dusty underground
car park under the once thriving headquarters of his empire in
the sun.

My eyes panned from the Ferrari to a beige left-hand drive

vintage Mercedes convertible with Spanish plates. There was a right-hand drive James Bond Aston Martin DB5, its gold bodywork also barely visible beneath the dust and cobwebs. Next to that was the sort of Cadillac convertible you'd have expected to see Meyer Lansky driving down the Vegas Strip in the late 1950s. Alongside it was a Maserati and a Jensen Interceptor followed by a line of other carefully parked vintage cars.

But why had John Palmer stashed these vehicles away right under the headquarters of the criminal empire he'd built from so much fear and loathing? Surely he should have sold them years earlier?

My Tenerife informant had his own personal theory: 'I think JP liked being near them. They made him feel secure. Strange, innit?'

But there was a much bigger clue to all this hot metal staring me in the face. All the cars appeared to be very low slung. Their bumpers almost touched the tarmac, just like the getaway Transit van that scraped the road as it left an airport warehouse twenty-five years earlier packed with £27 million worth of stolen gold bullion, which had ignited the entire John Palmer story.

Back in the flickering neon light of that basement car park, these sad-looking vehicles reminded me of burnt-out old characters in hell's waiting room, unsure what was going to happen to them but no doubt certain that wherever they turned up, it had to be better than here.

These cars perfectly reflected Tenerife's troubled past. Located directly beneath the building where John Palmer had turned this sunshine holiday island into his very own, chilling one-man version of Crime Incorporated.

And it all finally came to a close on a warm summer's day in June 2015, that rocked the underworld to its foundations.

PROLOGUE:

LIVE AND LET DIE

SANDPIT COTTAGE, SANDPIT LANE, SOUTH WEALD, ESSEX, 24 JUNE 2015, 6.30 P.M.

A thin plume of grey smoke and the crackling sound of a bonfire were the only signs of activity in the grounds of the large, isolated detached house on the corner of dense woodland bordering a 500-acre country park.

CCTV security cameras lined the driveway recording every moment twenty-four hours a day. And through the late-afternoon drizzle, half a dozen bland red 'do not enter' signs could be seen nailed to trees on the perimeter of the same property.

From inside the house, the muffled sound of two Rottweilers barking furiously could be heard in the distance. They stood on hind legs pawing at the steamed-up double glass doors at the back of the house.

Just then a young man and woman in their early twenties appeared inside the house and tried to calm the dogs down.

Eventually, they dragged them into the sitting room and returned to open the double doors. Hesitantly, the couple crept out on to the patio shouting 'Dad'.

When there was no reply, the young man turned towards

the bonfire, still crackling noisily in the distance. Behind him, his girlfriend stopped as she saw something, arching her neck to get a better look.

Grabbing her boyfriend by the arm, she pulled him around and pointed.

The young man froze momentarily in his tracks, then rushed towards the crumpled body of his 64-year-old father, lifeless and contorted, lying spread across the ground. His torso was soaked in blood.

He straddled the body and started trying to give him CPR, frantically thumping his chest. The young man later said he could feel the life draining out of his father. With the body limp beneath him, he stopped and struggled back onto his feet. Breathing heavily, he then rang 999 on his mobile.

Within half an hour, paramedics arrived and were examining the bloody corpse. They immediately noticed very recent 'pre-existing wounds' to the body following recent major heart surgery and ruled out foul play. The victim had clearly died from natural causes after falling from his quad bike, slewed on the ground nearby.

'Are you sure it's his heart?' interrupted a young trainee paramedic, who was accompanying two senior colleagues.

'Yeah, it's his heart.'

Two young junior police constables, who'd also just arrived at the scene, didn't even bother examining the corpse after being told the man's wounds from his recent surgery had split open when he fell, causing him to bleed out. There was no point in even calling an inspector to the scene to confirm their assessment or check the man's antecedents on the police national computer. It was, as they say, an open and shut case.

If those two police officers had bothered to make the 'normal checks' they would have discovered that the UK's National Crime Agency and the Spanish police had had the victim under surveillance for the best part of twenty years.

Despite being assured he'd died from natural causes, the man's death was obviously heartbreaking for his family. It was something they'd all dreaded but hoped would never happen.

Police ordered an autopsy as a matter of course because the death would be recorded as sudden, even though there were no suspicious circumstances.

Less than an hour later, the corpse was gingerly loaded on to a gurney and taken away in a dark van with blacked-out windows to be stored in a nearby morgue.

It was an oddly muted end for a man feared and loathed throughout the underworld. Most had expected him to die in a hail of bullets after one feud too many. But instead, he'd keeled over in the middle of the grounds of his big house just like Marlon Brando's Don Corleone in *The Godfather*.

'Goldfinger's dead.'

The news spread like wildfire through the underworlds of the UK, US, Spain and Russia. Goldfinger's partner tried to keep a lid on the inevitable backlash. The couple had talked many times about this happening and had even made detailed contingency plans.

Thirty miles south of the death-scene, members of London's most feared crime family were stunned by the news. Goldfinger's death had just cost them tens of millions of pounds after a twisted financial deal had been agreed between the family and the victim, their most infamous criminal rival.

So, the king of crime had been cruelly taken from the world in his prime. Goldfinger had once told an associate that when he died he wanted to go out with a bang. 'I want everyone to know I was topped. That's the best way to go.'

Instead, his body was now in a deep-freeze unit awaiting an examination to confirm what everyone already knew; that he'd died from a congenital heart defect.

Five days later, the pathologist assigned the Goldfinger case returned from an early summer break. Less than two minutes after pulling open the drawer to the refrigeration unit containing the corpse, the medical examiner put down his instruments, walked to the phone attached to the wall in the corner of his laboratory, punched out a number and then waited for a response.

'I think you'd better get over here as quickly as possible,' he said.

What goes around, comes around.

PART
ONE

BORN
TO DIE
1950–1987

Train up a child in the way he should go,

And when he is old, he will

Not depart from it

Proverbs 22:6

CHAPTER ONE

HIT 'EM HARD

Almost two hundred years ago, in the area now known as Greater Birmingham, rich tradesmen bought properties which they then leased out to tenants safe in the knowledge that the Grand Canal was about to be built and would turn the area into a thriving metropolis. But a lot of the businesses never took up the challenge, so instead the canal district attracted bear-baiting rings, theatres, drinking dives and brothels where customers were often fleeced of all their hard-earned, yet modest incomes.

Often, criminals of the day would pickpocket and scavenge off the big crowds that wandered the canal's cobbled towpaths. The petty villains and dippers would then head back to their run-down homes in the dilapidated slum areas nearby. It was from these poorly lit ghettos that the scourge of the 19th century, cholera, sprang.

The canal itself was bleakly overshadowed by a handful of leatherworks and candle factories that filled the atmosphere with putrid smoke and an obnoxious stench, which many said smelt like death.

The arrival of the railways enabled Birmingham New Street station to help disperse the pockets of dire poverty and violence.

But the railway ended up having the same long-term effect as the canal by simply luring poor people to gather near these two transport hubs in the hope of casual work and easy criminal pickings.

Gang violence first erupted in Birmingham in the late 1800s when youths began claiming 'ownership' of certain districts such as Solihull, Small Heath and Cheapside. One of the most ruthless gangs at this time were known as the Sloggers, led by a gangly teen called John Adrian. They were known for their weapon of choice: a heavy-buckled belt used to pummel male and female victims so that they could then be robbed.

It wasn't until just after the end of the First World War in 1918 that a new crime gang called the Peaky Blinders emerged with the specific aim of crushing the Sloggers and taking over the reins of Birmingham's growing underworld. The name 'Peaky Blinders' was derived from the gang stitching razor blades into the peak of their flat caps, so they could use them as weapons.

The Blinders consisted mainly of disenchanted ex-soldiers who'd left the trenches of France behind at the end of the Great War, only to find themselves destitute and unwanted despite helping save Britain from the Germans.

The Blinders eventually evolved into a stylish bunch of fellows thanks to those same peaked caps tilted slightly to one side, cravats, bell-bottom trousers, jackets with brass buttons down the front and steel-capped boots. They even wore silk scarves tied around their necks.

Gang members often used their caps to swipe at their opponents' faces – cutting off an ear or a nose here and there. Legend also had it they would sometimes blind their opponents by head-butting them while wearing this lethal headgear. Even the women had their own distinctive 'uniform': flashy pearls and a carefully styled fringe of hair down almost to their eyes.

This was rounded off by a brightly coloured silk scarf wrapped around the throat.

The Blinders' main crimes were illegal betting, protection rackets and supplying Birmingham's ever-thriving black market. Court reports from the time refer to the gang's members as 'foul-mouthed young men who stalk the streets in drunken groups, insulting and mugging passers-by.'

Gangs like the Blinders were largely ignored by politicians and law enforcement agencies because few wanted to admit they were the direct result of Britain's complete inability to look after its former soldiers, still reeling from the horrendous sights, sounds and smells of the trenches.

As illegal bookies took bets on the towpaths that twisted alongside the rank-smelling canal, lowlifes roamed the narrow cobbled streets and frequented illegal dives, rat-holes consisting of dirty stinking mattresses and sackcloth curtains. In Birmingham's central streets, hustlers – some as young as five or six – tried their hardest to hawk their dodgy goods.

As one local policeman later recalled: 'Suicides were two a penny back in those days after World War One. And the canal was the place where most of them did it. We'd fish their stinking, rotting corpses out a few days later. Most of them unrecognizable to their loved ones.'

It's said that John 'Goldfinger' Palmer's father was one of the lucky ones, who took the identity of another man who'd committed suicide because he was wanted by the law and needed to reinvent himself. It was later claimed Palmer's father joined the infamous Peaky Blinders during the 1930s after recalling his 'exploits' during the First World War. In fact, he was talking about the background of the man whose identity he stole.

Life in Birmingham's underworld was very different from

most other areas of Britain at the time, thanks to the racial mix of its inhabitants. This was a truly multicultural society before the word had even been invented. Chinese, African, Eastern European were all there.

Of course the traditional racial prejudices of this time existed but inside the heart of the Birmingham underworld there was an acceptance of people's colour, which would have surprised many outsiders. In later years, this attitude was passed down to John Palmer himself, who would often say: 'I don't care what colour anyone is as long as they don't try to screw me over.'

The opening title sequences of the BBC TV drama *Peaky Blinders* perfectly sums up the sort of world which John Palmer's family inhabited in those tough, barren, poverty-stricken years between the two world wars. In the programme, the lead character – Blinders gang boss Tommy Shelby – tours his 'territory' riding bareback on a horse. Like Shelby, it is said that John Palmer's father was part gypsy. As one associate later said: 'You can see the gypsy in JP's eyes. They were dark and soulless and his father's were just the same.'

It's claimed that John Palmer's father 'graduated' from gypsy cattle rustling to being an enforcer for the Peaky Blinders. He is said to have 'had more fights than hot dinners'. Palmer's father's other speciality was bullying people into giving him money if he was in need of a drink. But in later life, Palmer's father is said to have ended up a tramp on those very same seedy streets close to the canal.

This was a world with no tarmac on the streets, although the cobbles proved much more lethal when it came to smashing someone so hard they fell flat on their face. They left indentation marks on faces and those scars became like a calling sign for many of Birmingham's villains. If they walked into a room, a pub or a shop, everyone would know within seconds who they were once they saw the marks on their faces.

And that was how the term 'Clumpers' came to be used by many criminals in Birmingham. It referred to the noise that could be heard when a body hit the cobbles. Being a Clumper was probably the highlight of John Palmer's father's criminal career.

And of course in the middle of this heady mix were the police. Poorly paid like everyone else but well aware that in order to survive they needed to let the local 'faces' buy them a drink now and again. It's said that when the police came across John Palmer's father in the 1930s, they tipped their hats as a mark of respect. John Palmer himself always found that amusing. He told one old associate: 'My old man wasn't worth the air he breathed and yet those snivelling, arse-licking coppers still gave him respect. Says it all about the cozzers. You can't trust any of 'em an inch.'

John Palmer only ever had one positive story to tell about his father in later years. 'The old man treated us all like shit. But you know what? He always gave money to tramps in the street. Maybe he knew all along that one day he'd end up there with 'em?'

The Second World War wasn't too hard on Olton and neighbouring Solihull because Birmingham city centre was a far more tempting target for the Luftwaffe, thanks to munitions factories and other strategically important buildings.

After the war, many from the disease-ridden canal-side areas were encouraged to turn their backs on the cobbled streets and start afresh in nearby Olton, on the edge of the bigger community of Solihull. John Palmer's family could only afford to make such a move by accepting the help of a charity, which paid for their move into a rundown Victorian house in Olton.

Many greeted the 'scum' inhabitants from the canal district with disdain because they were seen as interlopers, who'd lower the 'tone' of the area.

There had been a steady influx into Olton and Solihull thanks, in part, to the development of the nearby Rover car plant. There was also a planned expansion of what was then Elmdon Airport which would go on to become Birmingham International Airport. But perhaps most significant was the release of large tracts of land for housing development attracting inward migration of new residents from across the UK, not just the centre of the city.

It was into this environment that John Palmer was born in September 1950. That made him a member of the so-called Baby Boomer generation. It was supposed to be the beginning of a decade of hope for Britain but for John Palmer it was far from easy as his only parent was his mother. No one in his family ever referred to his father's departure except to say it was sudden and without remorse.

Being one of seven children meant that there was little affection and attention given to John Palmer and his siblings, although their home in Richmond Road, Olton did become something of a hub for local villains, who used to pop round at all times of the day and night. They hid their stolen goods under the children's mattresses and in the rusting bomb shelter in the rundown back garden. John Palmer looked up to these colourful characters and became fascinated by them from an early age.

The streets of Olton where the young John Palmer spent his early years were dominated by impoverished Irish immigrants at this time. Hard-working womenfolk just like his own mother, struggling around the clock to feed and care for their ever-increasing broods of children. With no playgrounds and few parks in the area, kids like John Palmer ended up in nearby bombsites and on desolate wasteland. Local rubbish tips often provided the raw material to make everything from box carts to wooden swords and toy guns.

Palmer and his siblings were roaming free from the age of three or four. His mother didn't worry because she was just relieved to get them all out of their tiny home. Occasionally, the family managed a trip to a local picture house to watch a typical 1950s film like *The Lavender Hill Mob*. John Palmer later said he wasn't impressed by the comic portrayal of criminals, headed by so-called mastermind Alec Guinness.

Children weren't allowed in pubs back in those days, so John and his siblings loitered outside the local taverns whenever their older relatives had time for a half of stout. If they were lucky, John and his siblings would be offered a bottle of pop to share while they hung around on the pub steps.

John's mother couldn't get a job because she had seven children to look after. His father had gone, so it was often left to the kids to bring some money home to enable them all to survive.

Food and clothes were always in short supply. The Palmers didn't even have any heirlooms to pawn in exchange for cash. At Chapel Fields Primary School in Olton, John and his brothers and sisters were provided with boots to wear by the local council because they were so poor. These often came complete with holes punched in the side as a makeshift 'trademark' so they couldn't be sold off.

One of Palmer's classmates later recalled: 'John never had any money and he often came to school without socks. In fact, the teachers kept a bag of clothes at school to make sure he was properly dressed for lessons.'

In later life, John Palmer spoke openly about the effect such dire poverty had on him and how he grew to loathe those so-called 'council shoes' because they labelled him and his siblings as 'scum' in the eyes of many. He told one associate: 'Those shoes were like an advert telling all the other kids we was smelly, crummy people without a hope in the world. Even the teachers treated us different. Those shoes helped ruin my childhood.'

And John Palmer *never* forgot the bad things that happened to him.

Slum-dwellers like John Palmer always insisted later in life that they were obliged to commit crimes. It was all about survival of the fittest. And he already looked up to the criminal 'faces' – many of whom had begun their lives of crime in the 1930s as members of gangs like the Peaky Blinders. The Blinders had proved to the poor that organized crime was the only way to go.

Being a member of a gang guaranteed you real power and influence out on the manor where you were brought up. The only golden rule was, don't steal from your own. The rich and the flashy and the well insured were the legitimate targets. Palmer later said he greatly admired his mother's determination and strength in keeping them all together. But where had all that honest, hard work got her? Nowhere. From a young age, John – the apple of his mother's eye – hatched a plan in his head to help his beloved mother escape the slums for ever.

No one to this day knows how Palmer's mother managed to cover the rent and family food bill. It's believed that local gangsters helped the family out in exchange for using the children to 'run a few errands'.

Many of John Palmer's childhood friends' fathers worked long hours of overtime at local factories or on the public transport system in order to provide for their families. But Palmer's family did not have such a lifeline. Their cramped terraced house was close to an enormous, stinking rubbish dump filled with rotting garbage and abandoned items which Palmer and his siblings regularly 'raided' for all sorts of household essentials from cutlery to furniture. Palmer and his six siblings and mother had electricity but the only hot water came from a smelly gas boiler in the kitchen. An old tin bath was brought out no more than twice a week and everyone in the family was expected to share the water to save money.

Olton and Solihull in the 1950s was a confused environment; new homes had been built at a blistering pace while at the same time there also remained clusters of drab streets lined with rundown terraced houses – most of which had been built more than half a century earlier for the servants who worked on the big country estates in nearby Warwickshire and Staffordshire.

When unemployment and the Depression had swept the country less than twenty years earlier, many firms had laid off their workforces and very few industries had replaced them in the so-called optimistic post-war years of the 1950s. Britain was in dire economic freefall. The war had cost billions and food rationing was still in place for the first five years of John Palmer's life.

Palmer later told one associate that he never tasted fresh meat or fresh eggs until his seventh birthday. As queues grew increasingly long outside labour exchanges, clothes became even more threadbare than during the war. With money so scarce, it was hardly surprising that Palmer and many of his schoolmates were up to no good from a very early age. He quickly appreciated the thrill of grabbing a bar of chocolate from the corner-shop counter and dashing out the door. It was a buzz he'd spend the rest of his life trying to replicate.

John Palmer's bedroom – which he shared with three brothers – was at the rear of the family home, so he'd often slip out of the back of the tiny house by climbing down a drainpipe, then hopping over the back fence and running down a dimly lit alleyway that led to the nearest road.

During those grey post-war years, policemen and local youths in Olton and Solihull were frequently involved in clashes which often ended in a severe beating from the local coppers. The police station at Solihull was a familiar and much-loathed place to young scallywags like John Palmer and his pals. It's been said that Palmer had his collar felt for the first time by his local constabulary when he was just seven or eight years old. His irate mother showed up at the local police station to take her young son home with a face like thunder.

Vicious prejudice against the Irish seeped into every aspect of John Palmer's childhood. By the age of ten, he'd found himself in numerous scraps with other children, many of whom had been brought up to hate the 'bogtrotters'. Most of them – including John's mother – had only moved to Birmingham in the early 1930s because of the famine in Ireland. They'd grown used to being looked down upon as stupid because they didn't speak with the same Brummie accents as everyone else.

As a result of this, John Palmer speedily developed a broad Midlands accent because he didn't want to have any hint of Irish in his voice, in case it sparked trouble.

This was just the type of 'self-education' that helped inject John Palmer with supreme confidence, even from a very young age. He believed he was brighter and more cunning than any of his contemporaries.

Palmer later said he understood why he deserved to be nicked by the police, but what upset him the most was that the officers wouldn't ever explain to him what he'd actually done wrong. By the age of ten, John Palmer was out and about so much that there was little or no communication between overstretched parent and son. Palmer had never been much of a talker but now he didn't like to open up, in case it upset his beloved mother. She forbade all her children from swearing and as a result Palmer never used profanities, even throughout his criminal career.

At school, Palmer was often absent. He'd had such a struggle trying to learn to read and write because of dyslexia that he saw little point in formal education. On the rare occasions when he actually attended class he didn't fully understand most of what was being said.

One old associate explained: 'It hurt him because it made him feel inferior to other people and that led to anger and outbursts of temper.'

Palmer's main sideline back then was extorting money from his classmates in exchange for protection from the bullies, who dominated classrooms in those days. Palmer wasn't popular but few had the courage to stand up to him. 'Even then he had this fuckin' scary way of challenging you. He seemed capable of anything,' recalled one old classmate.

Most people wrongly assume that the ability to learn is determined by such things as basic intelligence, whether you pay attention or whether you stick at something when the going gets tough. But John Palmer's mind was more like that of a creative instrument, which veered off in certain directions depending on his surroundings.

The confidence and pride his mother showed in her son probably single-handedly helped turn Palmer into a sociopathic mastermind. It was all driven by a need to earn money and get revenge on the bullies who'd laughed at his council shoes.

Older brother Malcolm took on the role of father-figure to his six siblings as they grew into their teens. John Palmer's mother was a deeply religious woman – a Catholic – but she soon gave up forcing her boys into church because they all had a more important duty: to provide for the family.

John Palmer even got himself a 'straight' job – delivering newspapers – from an early age. But he got fired when it was discovered that some of the houses he delivered to had been burgled. The implication was that Palmer had become a 'tipster' to a gang of older child thieves.

John Palmer's narcissism developed early because of his power over other children, his over-generosity to certain people plus his undoubted need for admiration and, finally, his complete lack of empathy towards those outside his own crooked world. Palmer also had a sprinkling of obsessive-compulsiveness thrown in for good measure: a preoccupation with orderliness, perfectionism and control. Palmer was developing into what one might call a born leader and undoubtedly his stocky build, cunning, confidence and handsome appearance helped.

Naturally, every youngster out on the streets in those post-war years was fascinated by guns. Most had their own toy pop guns and a few had even managed to find real weapons through fathers or grandfathers who'd fought in both world wars.

There was even a black market on the streets of nearby Solihull where guns could be bought and sold with relative ease. It's said that Palmer worked briefly as a runner for one gun dealer and that taught him the power of weapons.

Palmer later admitted that he shot his first gun at the age of eleven or twelve. It undoubtedly gave him a taste of what the future held.

CHAPTER TWO

BABY BOOMER FROM HELL

John Palmer undoubtedly possessed a self-destructive split personality. As a child he hadn't received the sensory stimulation he required from his family, so increasingly found it hard to establish a boundary between himself and the world beyond his caring mother and siblings. Palmer had already become an all-encompassing individual, seeing things from his own perspective and no one else's.

Other family members noticed how fearless Palmer became even before he reached his teens. He also often seemed incapable of realizing when he'd hurt other people's feelings. He rarely felt remorse and certainly had little sympathy for his victims.

But beneath the hard-nosed, tough-guy façade lay an undoubted inner sadness, which meant Palmer struggled to enjoy any so-called 'normal' activities such as team sports. His development had its own twisted symbology, steeped in terror of some unpleasant memories and fears that had permanently scarred his mind. An image of those ever present 'council shoes' with holes punched in them was lodged in his memory bank, constantly fuelling his inner sense of detachment.

23

Just a few days before John Palmer became a teenager in September 1963, the Great Train Robbery was added to the adventures of Robin Hood and Dick Turpin in British national mythology as details of this supposedly dastardly crime emerged. The gang had got away with millions of pounds and most of the nation hoped they'd never be arrested. The Great Train Robbery probably did more to help the underworld's recruitment drive than any other single crime.

John Palmer had little need for any further education. He was a bright, quick-witted child with an eye for the main chance. It was around this time in the early 1960s that Palmer first heard about two London families who'd carved up most of the smoke (London) between them. The Kray Twins ran everything north of the River Thames while the mighty Richardsons were kings of south London. These cockney criminals charged protection money to every business on their 'manor' and claimed to have detectives from Scotland Yard's Flying Squad in their pocket. Palmer saw himself running a similar operation in the Birmingham area one day. He'd already got himself a 'crew' of big 'Clumpers' (henchmen) who went everywhere with him.

One time, Palmer organized his gang to target the marketplace in the centre of Olton, which he knew was full of people 'armed' with wads of cash. He stationed five or six of his Clumpers at different corners of the market. Minutes later they ran through the crowds, knocking customers flying and even pulling a few stalls down on the way.

In the ensuing chaos, Palmer strolled calmly through the crowd like a poverty-stricken orphan pulling a tatty wooden cart on wheels behind him. Meanwhile, his pals grabbed everything they could lay their hands on and threw it all into the cart. By the time anyone realized what had happened, Palmer and his gang had long gone.

All the stolen goods were quickly taken to local barrow boys to be sold off at knockdown prices, although this sometimes kicked off fights when the two parties did not agree on the 'valuation' of the loot. And that's when John Palmer first came to appreciate the need for violence. His Clumpers didn't hesitate to hit back. And Palmer himself even developed a menacing stroll, which acted as a warning sign to a lot of his rivals.

John Palmer's 'soulless exterior' was already extremely focused on one thing: money. He didn't tell jokes or smile much, which bothered his competitors even more. They couldn't work out what was really going on inside his head and that made everyone even more wary of him.

Behind Palmer's blank looks lurked a razor-sharp mind as his dark brown eyes snapped around in all directions, constantly on the lookout for opportunities and enemies. Palmer proudly told one associate many years later that he didn't get any pocket money throughout his childhood. Instead, he went out and 'earned' it by thieving.

Palmer and his Clumpers often travelled around the Birmingham area by bus. In the daytime (most often on Saturdays), Palmer oversaw shoplifting 'raids' on the big department stores in the city centre. Their favourite target was Debenhams. Often, Palmer would hide shirts under his jacket while one of his Clumpers grabbed ten or fifteen ties and ran out of the store in the opposite direction. By the time Palmer caught up with his gang further up the street, they'd often already sold the ties for ten bob each to a local stallholder.

Birmingham's favoured tools of the criminal trade at this time weren't very different from when the Peaky Blinders ruled the roost thirty years earlier. Weapons included razors, broken bottles, revolvers, hammers, hatchets, coshes and knuckle-dusters. The city's main hospital employed a special staff of medical seamsters to deal with the gaping wounds made by many of these weapons. Victims seldom complained but harboured an urge to get even with their attacker. One detective from that era later recalled: 'One well-known tearaway who was "chivvied" had a beautiful "curvature" of the face that stretched from one ear right round his chin to the other ear. He had to have ninety-nine stitches inserted to draw this gaping wound together.'

John Palmer reflected an attitude that prevailed at that time. He wanted money and believed that it would create happiness – something his absent father had never managed to bring to the table. Palmer watched the older villains out and about, wheeler-dealing in everything from stolen jewellery to car parts. No wonder he understood the potency of money from such an early age. It meant the young John Palmer could get himself some decent shoes, a jacket and trousers. No more council shoes with holes in them for him.

The capture of the Great Train Robbery gang in 1964 and the long sentences handed out to them further fuelled the 'them and us' world that John Palmer and other young criminals occupied at this time. One later explained: 'We all saw those sentences as fuckin' outrageous. It made a lot of villains very angry and even more determined to go out and cause mayhem.'

John Palmer quickly concluded that school had done nothing for him. He hadn't even learned how to read and write, although no one had said he had dyslexia because it was not commonly known about at that time.

By the time Palmer quit Lyndon High School in Olton in

1965, he knew the police were already keeping an eye on him. Palmer's older brother Malcolm insisted he work for his roofing company at first in the hope it might keep young John 'on the straight and narrow.' Palmer then sold paraffin oil off the back of a lorry before moving. He then moved to a used car business as a 'washer', quickly impressing his boss so much that he was allowed to park the vehicles back in their right positions in the car lot after test drives, even though he wasn't old enough to legally drive. Palmer later paid a criminal associate to take a driving test for him as he would not have passed because of his illiteracy.

The only hint of John Palmer's alleged gypsy 'blood' was when he attended illegal bare-knuckle boxing bouts in fields, well away from the prying eyes of the police. Carloads of villains would turn up with their favourite fighter to take on an equally fearsome-looking opponent. One time, Palmer witnessed a fight to the death between two notorious 'pikeys' (gypsies). The two men smashed each other to pieces for a £500 prize while more than ten times that amount changed hands in bets.

While still in his mid-teens, Palmer was a familiar face at Birmingham's fairgrounds, where he often handled stolen goods for the gypsies who ran the sites.

And for the first time, John Palmer discovered the importance of 'greasing palms'. One old associate recalled: 'Back then, we all had to pay backhanders to coppers at New Street nick. Twenties here, tenners and fivers there.'

This type of blatant bribery and corruption undoubtedly affected Palmer's attitude towards the police later in life. His argument was simple: 'How can you trust a copper if most of them want a backhander? They're the enemy and some of them are less honest than we are.'

As John Palmer climbed the criminal ladder on the streets of Birmingham, he didn't recognize *anyone* in authority – apart from perhaps the occasional underworld 'face'. He believed policemen, judges and Home Office officials were meaningless characters who deserved no respect.

Back home in Olton, Palmer continued to resent his father for abandoning his family and breaking his wife's heart in the process. As a result, he never completely trusted men and in later life this may well have cost some their lives.

Even as a young tearaway, Palmer steered clear of heavy drinking and drugs so he always had his wits about him. He looked at least two or three years older than his real age, thanks to chiselled facial features rounded off with those piercing dark brown eyes, which narrowed menacingly whenever he met anyone new. John Palmer the young hood didn't shout or swear. He'd just look people in the eye 'long and hard' if they ever tried to cross him.

Palmer was already disconnecting from mainstream society, floating along in his own bubble, calculating the next deal and constantly thinking about how much money he had in his wallet at any one time. Palmer used pubs in order to make deals, rather than get drunk. He prided himself on never avoiding the rough and tough neighbourhoods because he wasn't afraid of anyone, even at that young age. But then it helped that Palmer already had a team of Clumpers who went everywhere with him providing protection.

Palmer's illiteracy did not hold him back. He had other 'unique' skills, including an extraordinary memory for things that people said to him during the course of his life. He'd often quote back entire conversations he'd had many years earlier.

Palmer's pinpoint memory undoubtedly fed into classic

sociopathic tendencies when it came to 'getting revenge'. One old associate recalled: 'If someone really pissed off JP, he'd clinically work out a way to get revenge on that person. He wouldn't leave it alone until he'd done something. It was a matter of extreme pride.'

It's said that Palmer had a brief encounter with his long-lost father during his mid-teens and this had a profound effect on him because his father belittled him and tried to borrow money. Afterwards Palmer is alleged to have said that as far as he was concerned his father no longer existed after that day. One associate said: 'JP said he'd make sure his father went to hell and he never saw him again.'

John Palmer – now aged around fifteen or sixteen – then made a conscious decision to move full-time into handling stolen goods rather than committing actual crimes. Palmer realized he could earn more money as a 'fence' handling the proceeds from dozens of other people's crimes at any one time.

Palmer's primary aim was to earn enough money to open a jewellery business, which he could then use as camouflage for all the stolen goods he'd be handling.

Young John Palmer carefully watched and learned from the old-time professional villains, who still dominated the underworld back in the mid-1960s. They were smartly dressed mobsters, who bankrolled robberies and often lived in expensive-looking detached houses. These characters were feared and respected by entire communities and their names whispered reverentially in the local pubs and cafés.

Palmer's crime 'heroes' at this time were those two notorious south London criminals, the Richardson brothers, Charlie and Eddie, who ran their empire from a scrap-metal yard on the south shores of the River Thames. The two brothers were said at their 1966 Old Bailey trial to have run a Crime Incorporated that used torture to control their enemies and terrify their friends.

Palmer was fascinated by how torture could be used as a powerful weapon to instil fear and trepidation in his enemies. Not long after hearing about the Richardsons' 'exploits', John Palmer and his Clumpers 'detained' a couple of down-on-their-luck young crooks, who owed Palmer some money. The two petty criminals paid up within minutes of being threatened with torture by Palmer.

Just before his eighteenth birthday in September 1968, John Palmer rented his first jewellery shop, which opened twelve hours a day because many of his customers preferred to bring their stolen goods to him in the evening. Palmer soon became renowned as a tough bargainer when paying for stolen items, which he'd then sell on, often for more than ten times what he paid for them.

Crime in the UK was heading for epidemic proportions at this time. Tens of millions of pounds' worth of stolen property changed hands illegally every week. Violent offences were up by more than 10 per cent each year from 1965 and the number of drug convictions doubled between 1960 and 1970.

Politicians and the police believed that the jailing of the Krays and the Richardsons in the late 1960s would destroy the menace of organized crime. They couldn't have been more wrong. New, better-organized crime networks often run by cold-blooded individuals like the up-and-coming John Palmer, rather than families, began emerging.

Palmer earned his first £100,000 in one year before he'd even reached twenty years of age. That amount of cash in the late 1960s – which equates to at least £2 million today – undoubtedly helped fuel Palmer's confidence as well as greatly enhancing his reputation.

Armed with all this cash, Palmer bought his mother a new home in the countryside outside Birmingham as a thank you for all the sacrifices she'd made for him.

Meanwhile his 'jewellery business' was going from strength to strength. The majority of Palmer's criminal transactions took place round the back of the store, located in a narrow lane. With two Clumpers often on duty outside, visitors gave a secret knock on the rear door and then waited for Palmer to invite them in.

When one of Palmer's neighbours told him he was being 'leaned on' by another criminal to pay protection money to avoid having his shop firebombed, Palmer stepped in and made sure it stopped. Then he offered protection to all nearby store owners, undercutting his rival criminal's demands. Palmer also developed a new sideline lending money to people with extortionate interest rates. Those who didn't pay Palmer would get a visit from his Clumpers.

John Palmer deliberately remained low key and avoided flashy cars, sticking to a rusting two-door Ford as his main transport. He knew only too well that envy would breed contempt among his peers, just like it had with his own father.

Palmer never used banks, so he hid most of his cash in carefully located stashes spread around Birmingham and the surrounding countryside, something he would continue to do for the rest of his life.

Palmer once admitted that he got his biggest thrill from knowing he had more money than most other people. That was how he measured life and his own sense of happiness.

Just turned twenty years of age, John Palmer was a handsome, well-built fellow with a fashionable haircut and a penchant for natty dark suits and crocodile shoes. Many women were intrigued by his brooding good looks and liked the way he talked constantly about his dear old mum.

One woman who met Palmer at that time explained: 'He wasn't like most other villains who were awkward in front of women and seemed to only want us for one thing. No, John was relaxed in the company of women and they appreciated him for it. His mum must have done a good job on him.'

Palmer put those early girlfriends to the test by taking them out for a spin in his 'rustbucket' Ford. If they looked disappointed when they saw it, he'd rarely go on second dates with them. Although he loved money, he didn't want to be used just because he had loads of it.

However, he showed a different side when it came to men. Some believe Palmer's mother smothered him with so much love and attention when he was younger that he hadn't learned the proper art of conversation. As a result, Palmer didn't do small talk. One old associate explained: 'This often made men quite nervous. They didn't enjoy the long awkward silences and it made JP seem charmless and cold.'

The long arm of the law finally caught up with John Palmer when he was arrested for fraud at the age of twenty-three. Few details are known about this offence but Palmer was locked up without bail in Winson Green prison, in Birmingham, to await trial. He later claimed he was framed by a policeman to whom he'd failed to pay a bribe. But whatever the truth of the matter, Palmer found himself in Birmingham's notoriously overcrowded main prison, which had been built in the 1840s for 350 inmates. By the time Palmer arrived there in the autumn of 1973, it was holding nearly 800 inmates and almost half of them slept three to a cell.

Palmer's new home in Cell Block B had housed some famous names from the past including one of his Great Train Robber heroes, Charlie Wilson, whom he would meet later in life, and much-loathed Russian spy Gordon Lonsdale. Palmer kept his head down and his prison file description read as follows: 'Fresh complexion, dark-brown hair and brown eyes. No visible scars and a dimpled chin, with thin lips.'

But while awaiting trial, Palmer picked up one prison habit for which he would be eternally grateful. He threw all his pent-up anger into an obsessive keep-fit regime, which involved exercising at least three times a week in the prison gym. It was the start of a keep-fit regime which he would keep to for the rest of his life.

Palmer later claimed his stay in Winson Green fuelled his hatred for the Establishment because he didn't like taking orders from petty prison officers. The light in his shared cell was kept on night and day. Today, this would be called sleep deprivation. Back then it was considered entirely acceptable.

Not long after arriving at Winson Green, Palmer had a confrontation with another inmate on the prison's first floor. 'The screws left 'em to it and the geezer ended up in a crumpled heap on the ground,' one of Palmer's associates later recalled. Within seconds, Palmer had brushed down his prison uniform and returned to his cell as if nothing had happened.

Palmer used his stay in prison to plan more criminal enterprises because he picked up a lot of ideas from big-mouthed inmates.

One old-school professional criminal he got to know was from the Bristol area in the West Country. Palmer was amazed to hear how relatively untapped that part of England was.

Then just before his fraud trial, Palmer was visited in prison by a criminal he'd known since his school days. The man calmly informed Palmer that while he'd been inside, his jewellery business had been 'taken over' by one of Birmingham's oldest crime families. Palmer knew only too well what 'taken over' meant. In his underworld, the strong could simply walk in and take over any business they fancied and that was precisely what had happened. They'd noticed Palmer had been earning good money before his arrest and they'd decided they wanted it for themselves.

After hearing the news, Palmer shrugged his shoulders nonchalantly, stood up and walked back towards his cell without uttering another word. He knew the name of the game. He wasn't strong enough to hit back at the crime family, so he decided that when he got out he'd start afresh away from the gangsters of Birmingham. But he also pledged to himself that the villains who'd invaded his territory would never be forgotten.

A few weeks later, just before his twenty-fourth birthday, Palmer appeared in court on the fraud charges and was given a suspended prison sentence after pleading guilty. The magistrate had decided to give young John Palmer a second chance in the hope he might learn from his mistakes and stay on the straight and narrow.

Back in the real world, John Palmer swiftly moved his life lock, stock and barrel down to the Bristol area, following that earlier recommendation from his fellow prison inmate. Just before he departed, Palmer heard a rumour his long-lost father had encouraged that notorious crime family to take over Palmer's jewellery business. Palmer later told one associate that if he hadn't pulled out of the city then and there, he would have been tempted to get revenge on his father.

CHAPTER THREE

THE WILD, WILD WEST

BRISTOL, SUMMER 1974

John Palmer quickly set up a new jewellery shop in Bristol city centre. The local police weren't interested in him at first because they didn't even know who he was.

Palmer moved into a scruffy rented flat, which helped him maintain a low profile, although many were soon intrigued by why such a cocky Jack-the-lad Brummie boy *never* swore in public. This was seen as a sign of weakness. But Palmer later said he liked the way it threw the other villains he came across.

Some local criminals pretended to befriend Palmer when all they really wanted to do was to keep an eye on him and make sure he didn't invade their territory. But Palmer wasn't bothered. He'd seen a whole lot worse back in Birmingham.

Palmer's suspicious nature – especially when it came to men – made it hard for him to make any real friends in Bristol. But then he was introduced to a beautiful 21-year-old beauty queen called Marnie Ryan. Palmer was immediately 'bowled over'. She was attractive, stylish and extremely down-to-earth in a typically blunt West Country sort of way. A breath of fresh air compared to the women Palmer had dated back in the Midlands.

Marnie later said she found Palmer very attractive and liked the way he didn't waste his words. However he was very careful not to mention his 'business interests' to her. Only a few days after their first date, Marnie and Palmer were sat talking over a drink in a pub when Palmer suddenly leaned closer and whispered in her ear: 'You gonna marry me one day?'

Marnie laughed and tried not to say yes but she knew it was destined to happen. For the following couple of weeks, Palmer took Marnie out every night because he didn't want to let her out of his sight. That's when Palmer decided to make his move to the West Country permanent.

But Palmer's 'activities' soon started to get in the way of their relationship. He'd take her out to an expensive restaurant and then spend half the evening talking in a nearby phone box, leaving Marnie all on her own. When she asked Palmer why he'd been on the phone, he told her not to concern herself with his business.

Within six months, Marnie was pregnant, which was the perfect excuse for Palmer to press ahead with his much-talked-about marriage plans. Guests at their 1975 wedding later recalled a working-class bash consisting of lots of smiling and proud faces. Few, if any, of the people who attended the wedding ceremony that day knew what John Palmer did for a living, apart from the fact he was a 'businessman'.

The couple initially moved into a small house on the outskirts of Bath, a graceful city whose four-storey Georgian terraces and neatly laid-out gardens and squares couldn't have been more of a contrast from gritty Birmingham. Palmer promised Marnie he'd eventually buy them a 'proper' house once his 'businesses' in the West Country were fully up and running.

Palmer even worked part-time at his new in-laws' fruit and

vegetable stall on the outskirts of Bristol in a bid to convince Marnie he was an 'honest broker'.

Even when the police came calling at the couple's small terraced house in Bath, Marnie didn't realize what Palmer was up to.

And all Palmer would say was: 'Don't worry, luv.'

Palmer did make an attempt to 'go straight' by opening a second-hand car business in partnership with a local hard-nosed 'businessman' called Garth Chappell, a real-life version of TV's classic spiv, Arthur Daley, played by George Cole in *Minder*.

By this time, Palmer had begun using a handheld tape recorder at 'business meetings' because he couldn't read or write. One old associate recalled: 'It didn't go down well with other villains but JP claimed the tape recorder was the equivalent of a pen and notebook.'

Later, back at his new office above the used-car lot, Palmer would play back the recordings to confirm details of deals he'd made. He often challenged other criminals by playing tape recordings of them saying certain things. One old associate recalled: 'That tape recorder did a lot of people's brains in. Villains don't like evidence like that floating around but JP was insistent on using it at all times.'

Palmer and his new West Country business partner Garth Chappell eventually opened another business selling second-hand car spares. In fact, the two men were running a huge fencing operation. Soon they were earning so much money from handling stolen goods that they had to open another 'straight business' – a furniture shop – just to help launder the proceeds of their highly lucrative criminal activities.

By this time, John Palmer was living two entirely separate lives in the West County. By day he was running at least three lucrative criminal enterprises. Then he'd go home to Marnie and play the role of loving, generous husband to his beautiful young wife and newly born daughter Ella.

About a year after joining forces, John Palmer and Garth Chappell went into partnership with another local 'face' called Terry Patch, so it was no surprise when the police began taking a much closer look at Palmer, already rumoured to be one of the richest fences in the West Country.

Bristol detectives mounted a big surveillance operation on all three men but came away with little or no actual concrete proof of their criminal activities. The detectives concluded that Palmer and his associates might have some friends in the local police, who'd tipped them off about the operation.

Meanwhile Palmer continued to switch hats and go home to his family each evening. Marnie always made sure her husband had a tasty meal waiting for him after a tiring 'day at the office'. Palmer later said he really appreciated this 'normal' side of his life because he needed this type of 'down time' to cope with the stress of his criminal activities. And of course he wanted the outside world to believe he was just an ambitious, hardworking businessman.

Back at 'work', Garth Chappell introduced Palmer to a notorious Bristol criminal family, who began supplying much of the stolen loot they were now fencing. The family was led by a gruff father and his two well-built sons. They were feared and admired in equal measure in the area.

The city of Bristol was a heaving metropolis with a very active underworld, so it was imperative for Palmer to have this local crime family on his side.

When a young Bristol gangster was shot dead in a small Caribbean drinking club in the city centre and detectives were told he was an 'associate' of John Palmer, it was the crime family who helped Palmer avoid problems with the police. No one accused Palmer of direct involvement in the killing but jealous local gangsters had pointed out Palmer's links to the dead man because they wanted him off 'the manor'.

The Bristol crime family told Palmer they'd take care of it but warned him that detectives in Bristol would most likely step up their surveillance on Palmer, Chappell and Patch so they needed to watch their backs.

Besides pubs, clubs and scrap-metal yards, the same West Country family ran transport companies specializing in perishable goods, which were often used as cover to import drugs from Spain and Morocco. Palmer studied these operations very closely and learned a lot from being close to the family. He was struck by the way the family had fingers in so many pies. They owned many pubs and restaurants, which were run as genuine businesses in order to ensure they had a legitimate income to camouflage their illicit activities.

Palmer was also impressed by the way the family had bought up large amounts of land on the perimeter of Bristol's then-modest airport. The airport would eventually double in size as package holidays and low air fares became more popular over the coming years.

Palmer was told that the family had their own aircraft hangar in the far corner of Bristol airport where they stored smuggled and stolen goods, which had either just arrived by air or were about to be picked up. The family gained access to the airport land via an innocent-looking farm gate, which meant they did not have to deal with airport officials in order to move around on airport property. There were rumours back then that the family were even running arms via cargo planes that landed at Bristol airport. All this would eventually become highly relevant to Palmer's later criminal activities.

However, for now John Palmer's rapid rise – first in Birmingham, and now in the West Country – was earning him some potentially dangerous underworld enemies. They began tipping off Bristol CID whenever Palmer took delivery of stolen goods he was fencing. After a few close shaves with the police, Palmer began to feel insecure in the Bristol area; something he'd already experienced back in Birmingham and he didn't want to deal with ever again. So Palmer issued a few warnings to his enemies about what to expect if they ever crossed him.

One old Bristol criminal began feeding detectives with information about 'young upstart' John Palmer's nefarious activities. When Palmer heard, he and his Clumpers took the man out on a small fishing boat into the Bristol Channel. He was then bundled into a fishing net, which was cast into choppy waters, trapping the man under the weight of the heavy nets.

The man was eventually hauled in, dried down and let free. The message from Palmer was loud and clear: 'I mean business.'

Palmer's show of strength worked well. Local gangsters who heard what had happened came to him first with their loot and 'business' boomed even more.

Palmer – together with Garth Chappell and Terry Patch – eventually opened a gold and jewellery dealing company called Scadlynn Limited, in Bedminster, near Bristol. Within months all three men had agreed they could make even bigger money by concentrating more on smelting stolen gold. So they purchased a smelter and installed it in the basement of the shop.

Now they could melt down all the stolen gems and turn them into unrecognizable pieces that could never be traced back to their original owners.

By now John Palmer had realized that friends were not important in his world. They got in the way of business. Palmer preferred having associates because they just wanted to do deals. They didn't want a piece of him.

Palmer was also super-careful about whom he mixed with when it came to his family. He avoided socializing with neighbours, because he didn't want people gossiping about him. Palmer couldn't stop Marnie mixing with some local housewives of a similar age but he kept well away from them all.

Palmer admitted to one associate that he preferred animals and cars to people 'because they don't do you over'. And it was around this time John Palmer first began his lifelong love affair with classic sports cars. He purchased a Jensen Interceptor in Bath and kept it in a lock-up garage. Palmer only ever took the vehicle out on Sundays and stuck to quiet country lanes in case anyone decided he was being flashy. He adored the power and deep purring sound of the Jensen's V12 engine. He'd also been told by one associate that the Jensen would be a very good long-term investment. With John Palmer it was always ultimately about money.

Meanwhile Palmer was beginning to think that his overt use of a tape recorder at every meeting was perhaps 'a little clumsy' even though he needed to use it because of his illiteracy. So he decided not to openly use the machine at meetings. Instead he kept it switched on in his pocket. That meant he still had the tapes 'for a rainy day'. He later told one associate: 'You never know when they might come in handy.'

*

The UK underworld during this period was dominated by proactive young villains on one side – many of whom came to Palmer to fence their loot – and equally youthful police detectives on the other. Few were over forty years of age and smooth, well-dressed John Palmer sat back and watched them all chasing each other around the west of England safe in the knowledge that he was well removed from such activities.

Robbery was a young man's game, or so the underworld presumed. Most gangs were far from sophisticated but they remained highly effective and were collectively getting away with an estimated £1 million a month in wage snatches, bank heists and security van hold-ups.

But it was already clear back then that informants – otherwise known as 'grasses' – were playing a significant role in helping the police try to retake the streets, or so it seemed to villains like John Palmer. Informants infuriated Palmer because in his mind he was a 'businessman' with no direct involvement in actual crimes, so why should he be put under the police spotlight by a double-dealing 'grass'?

Meanwhile the level of corruption inside the nation's police forces in the mid 1970s had reached such epidemic proportions it was said that detectives in London had been involved in a robbery at the *Daily Mirror* newspaper offices in Holborn Circus, during which a guard had been killed and £200,000 stolen. Officers were also connected to an earlier payroll snatch at the *Daily Express* offices in Fleet Street, during which £175,000 was stolen. Then there was a £225,000 robbery at Williams & Glynn's Bank in the City in 1977.

Strategically placed police officers would, for a fee, ensure bail was granted, hold back evidence and details about past convictions from a court, or pass on to a person under investigation details of a case being made against them. The police were even accused of providing warnings about covert operations in which they could be compromised. Corrupt officers also held on to a proportion of whatever valuables they recovered during an inquiry.

For the John Palmers of this world, police corruption was further evidence that the old enemy occupied the same moral ground as the very people they were supposed to be bringing to justice.

So back in the West Country, John Palmer was collecting a select band of crooked policemen in much the same way other people collect vases or stamps. Palmer later told one associate he liked moving from cop to cop because they always got too greedy.

One of Palmer's favourite detectives at this time was an officer who later retired after years of 'feeding' Palmer information and then bought himself a country pile with all the proceeds he'd 'earned' from the underworld.

One of Palmer's oldest associates later explained: 'This old copper was shameless. He took tens of thousands, maybe even hundreds of thousands, off JP and others over many years and then he rubbed it in by buying himself a mansion and even a boat.'

At one stage, the same crooked policeman offered to run Palmer and other villains back and forth from the coast to Europe in his sixty-foot cruiser. This retired detective went on to become the go-to character for any gangster who wanted to travel incognito in and out of Europe for the following thirty years.

As Palmer's empire expanded, Marnie often found herself home alone. As one old friend later explained: 'Marnie looked after the house and the family while Palmer was out at meetings late into the night.' Palmer even pledged to himself that once he'd got enough money together he'd quit his 'dodgy' work and stick to 'legit' businesses. Meanwhile Marnie made a determined effort to enjoy riding horses and be thankful for small mercies.

By now Marnie could see her husband was under pressure at 'work', and tried to help him relax when he got home. But Palmer could never quite shut those demons out altogether. In some ways, they were an important part of who he was and he didn't want to lose that cunning and energy, which had contributed to his speedy rise to the top.

But the two sides to Palmer's character did sometimes clash with potentially explosive consequences; one time he took his family out to a funfair near their home and ended up accusing a fairground gypsy of looking inappropriately at his young daughter. One old associate explained: 'JP could turn on a sixpence, especially if anyone disrespected his family. I heard he later sent a couple of his Clumpers to the fair to beat up that gypsy.'

Others recall that when he was upset, Palmer's eyes would glaze over while he silently studied anyone who'd dared to offend him. One old associate later explained: 'He'd just stand there watching them without saying a word. Then he'd slowly mutter something chilling like "okay", which usually had the required effect of terrifying everyone in the room.'

CHAPTER FOUR

TIMESHARE BECKONS

ORLANDO, FLORIDA, SUMMER 1977

With his new-found fortune, John Palmer could afford to splash out on luxuries he'd missed out on as a child. Holidays in the sun were a classic example. He and his family regularly began jetting off from nearby Bristol airport.

One trip to Orlando, Florida, with Marnie in 1977 got John Palmer thinking about new business opportunities. He wanted something through which to feed his criminal fortune that was not illegal. He'd dabbled in a bit of property in Birmingham when he was younger but it hadn't been as lucrative as he thought it would be. He was also wary of investing any more cash in the UK because of the ongoing police interest in him.

While the family were in Florida, Palmer stumbled upon a new property sales concept called Timeshare, where holiday homes were shared between owners. Palmer soon discovered that timeshare developments had already been launched on a modest level in Britain in the 1960s. But they hadn't taken off in the UK and Palmer had no doubt that was down to the lousy weather.

In Florida, however, customers were queuing up for a chance

to buy their own place in the sun. Palmer visited three or four timeshare complexes to get a feel for the business. He concluded that such timeshare developments would go down a bomb in somewhere sunny like Spain.

The attraction of the timeshare business to someone like Palmer was that by selling access to the properties in blocks of one week at a time, the cumulative amount made from all the weekly bookings added together would be much greater than the actual real-estate value of the property.

During the 1970s, more and more Brits were travelling to Spain and the Canary Islands thanks mainly to a huge drop in the cost of so-called package holidays. And of course credit cards had come on to the scene. John Palmer licked his lips with anticipation. This could turn into a veritable gold mine.

So Palmer persuaded Marnie that their next sunshine holiday should be on the Costa del Sol, in southern Spain. Just before their first visit in 1978, the extradition agreement between Spain and Great Britain collapsed and that had focused the UK underworld's attention on Spain. The agreement had broken down because Spain felt Britain was making it too difficult for the Spanish to retrieve their fugitives from the UK.

Virtually overnight this turned all Spain's territory into an ideal safe haven for criminals wanted in the UK; close enough for the family to come out and visit, yet far enough away to avoid the attentions of the police. Soon at least one hundred old-school UK professional criminals on the police's wanted list had settled on Spain's southern coastline, unsurprisingly nick-named the Costa del Crime by the British tabloids.

Just a short hop across the Straits of Gibraltar was Morocco, where vast quantities of hashish could be obtained for smuggling into Britain at a huge profit. And across a far wider stretch of water – the Atlantic Ocean – were plentiful supplies of cocaine, the marching powder of South America that many criminals believed could provide them with much bigger profits than anything they'd previously imagined.

While in southern Spain, Palmer earmarked a cluster of potential property deals near the resort of Estepona, west of Marbella, where he believed he could build a timeshare resort. Palmer decided to start his business on a small scale because he was concerned that some of the on-the-run UK criminals might try to swoop in and steal his operation just like they'd done to him all those years earlier in Birmingham. The newly dubbed Costa del Crime had already turned into Europe's California – sunny, spoiled, decadent and dangerous.

Not long after this, Palmer and Marnie went on holiday to the Spanish island of Tenerife, which enjoyed even more year-round sunshine and higher temperatures than the Costa del Sol. Tenerife was much more 'off the radar' than the Spanish mainland, thanks to a four-hour flight from the UK and its location far closer to the West African coastline than mainland Spain.

Tenerife's new resorts in the south-east of the island were crammed with neat English-run tourist bars and restaurants serving plain old-fashioned food and even slap-up Full English breakfasts. The beaches were mostly man-made with imported sand from Africa due to the darkness of the volcanic sand found on the island.

But most importantly there were no familiar criminal 'faces' lurking in the neighbourhood and many of the holidaymakers looked to Palmer like just the sort of people who'd love to own a place in the sun. John Palmer and his young family stayed in Playa de las Americas, sandwiched between the other popular resorts of Los Cristianos and Costa Adeje.

Las Americas' once-tired streets were being gradually replaced with designer-label stores and bougainvillea-lined walkways. This meant the resort was being reshaped to appeal predominantly to families and couples. These were the sort of people who were the prime market for timeshare holiday home ownership.

John Palmer needed a conduit to push all his money through and the lack of an extradition treaty between Spain and the UK at the time meant transferring money between the two countries was relatively easy. Palmer also hoped that Tenerife's distant location from Spain meant it would be relatively 'untouched' by all the usual governmental interference such as policing and customs.

And then there was also Tenerife's close proximity to West Africa. Palmer knew from his associates in the jewellery trade back in the UK that there were countries in that area where you could buy an entire 'blood diamond' mine for the cost of a small house.

John Palmer eventually convinced Marnie the family needed a sunshine holiday home and bought a penthouse apartment in Tenerife, which looked down on the resort of Las Americas and its picturesque 'Golden Mile' beach front. However, Marnie told her husband she would never live there full-time because she wanted to be near her family in the West Country. Palmer was as pragmatic as ever. He recognized that a holiday island like Tenerife wasn't exactly the best environment for a long-lasting marriage and as a place to bring up children.

But back in the UK, John Palmer discovered that Bristol police had earmarked him for some 'special attention'. In 1980, Palmer and his business partner Garth Chappell were arrested for fraudulently obtaining credit on furniture they were selling by providing false references. Both men received six-month suspended prison sentences. Palmer later claimed the police had 'fitted them up' because they couldn't prove anything more serious against the pair. The police were infuriated that Palmer and Chappell were not given custodial sentences.

It seemed to John Palmer that sharp-eyed young detectives were trying to crack down on organized crime after years of ignoring it. Police surveillance operations were becoming commonplace, which resulted in many older criminals being rounded up. John Palmer wanted to find a place where no one could touch him and he'd have total control of everything.

His ability to plan ahead had always been second to none . . .

Back in the West Country, John Palmer – already the ultimate workaholic villain – decided to step up his gold smelting in the basement of his shop. Palmer had heard on the grapevine about a clever scheme to avoid paying VAT on all newly smelted gold, while at the same time claiming the VAT back, which would bring in another 15 per cent return on every deal.

Palmer and Garth Chappell also began smuggling gold into the country, selling it to reputable dealers and then pocketing the 15 per cent VAT on it. Another scam was to draw up documents showing that the gold had been exported immediately after its arrival in Britain, which meant it was not liable for VAT. The honest trader, meanwhile, would still have to pay the 15 per cent VAT to the 'company' selling him the metal. That 'company' would be based in short-let office accommodation and then close down within a matter of months without registering any VAT returns.

Gold was particularly suitable for these scams because its high value meant large returns with a minimum of delay. It also had an official price, fixed twice daily by the London gold market, so the smugglers did not have to worry about commercial competitors undercutting their prices. And of course it was also extremely compact and easy to transport.

VAT frauds in general had one further major advantage – in the early 1980s the maximum penalty for indulging in such a racket was just two years' imprisonment, making it immensely popular among professional criminals like John Palmer.

But it wasn't all plain sailing; Palmer knew that the true origin of ingots of gold had to be disguised which meant removing identification numbers and assay marks. Many ingots carried their own individually designed hallmarks to signify their purity and, in some cases, a serial number. Absolutely pure gold did not exist. Some contamination was always present, however expertly the metal has been refined.

But bars with the number 9999 meant they were 99.99 per cent pure, the highest level to which the metal could be refined. Then there were 999 bars, known in the trade as ten-tola bars (a tola being an ancient Indian unit of weight) which were only marginally less perfect.

As well as removing the identifying marks, Palmer and his associates disguised the purity. Failure to do so would have risked legitimate traders quickly becoming suspicious that the quantities they were about to buy were either smuggled or stolen gold bullion.

John Palmer's specialized smelting equipment was crucial to the entire operation. Not surprisingly, he was soon getting requests to smelt down gold from criminals based all over the UK. Most of them had to deliver the gold to a middleman who would then bring it to Palmer in the West Country.

Now John Palmer had worked out how to make a *real* fortune from crime.

CHAPTER FIVE

FENCING FOR GOLD

John Palmer had been honing his criminal instincts since an early age. He liked to check people out before going into business with them. A classic example of this came when he chartered a Bell helicopter and pilot to take him from Kent's Biggin Hill airfield to an airstrip near his home in Bath. Just after takeoff, Palmer passed the pilot a scribbled note with the co-ordinates of a location in the nearby Kent countryside.

Palmer wanted to check out the home of a criminal called Kenneth Noye, who'd been pressing him, Garth Chappell and Terry Patch to agree to handle some of his stolen gold. A few minutes later, the helicopter pilot announced they were descending to about 200 feet above Noye's property, which was a substantial house standing in five acres of land.

'Now that's what I call a decent house,' said the pilot, as Palmer studied the spread of buildings below him.

Just then a man emerged from the main house and stood in the driveway looking up at the helicopter. Palmer watched as the man then produced a shotgun from under his arm and panned it up towards the aircraft.

51

'Shit,' exclaimed the pilot as he pushed the throttle forward and the helicopter rose rapidly.

Palmer laughed as he looked down at the matchstick figure below, who was still aiming the gun right at them. Palmer liked the look of Kenneth Noye and decided there and then he was definitely someone he could do business with.

A few days later, Palmer told Noye it had been him in the helicopter. Noye tilted his head slightly to the left and said in a deadpan voice: 'If I'd thought you was the cozzers I would have pressed the trigger. You're a lucky man.'

Notorious south London criminal Kenneth Noye was immensely proud of his isolated detached house near the sleepy village of West Kingsdown, in Kent. Many other villains would later claim Noye was a police informant. But this sort of rumour was typical in the UK underworld at that time, so impossible to verify.

Initially Kenneth Noye came to Palmer with substantial amounts of stolen high-end gold jewellery for him to smelt down. Palmer, 28, and Noye, 32, were only four years apart in age and they seemed to have the same workaholic tendencies, as well as a particularly sharp eye for the main chance.

So it was no surprise when they joined forces after Prime Minister Margaret Thatcher – who'd come to power in 1979 – inadvertently created a further opportunity for fraudsters by scrapping VAT on gold coins, such as Kruggerands.

Palmer and Noye immediately began buying Kruggerands from banks, melting them down and selling the ingots back to the banks as gold bullion, charging 15 per cent VAT in the process – having avoided paying it out in the first place.

British Customs and Excise eventually plugged this loophole with new legislation but by this time shrewd operators like

Palmer and Noye had simply sourced their gold sovereigns from the continent, where VAT was low or nonexistent and then just carried on as before.

Over the following eighteen months, Palmer and Noye earned a small fortune from their VAT gold scam. And the two men became renowned in the underworld as the go-to team when it came to handling dodgy gold.

But then Palmer and Noye both made a classic but uncharacteristic mistake: they started flashing around evidence of the enormous amounts of cash they were making.

Palmer bought a large detached villa in Tenerife to add to his penthouse apartment on the island and even opened an estate agency.

Meanwhile Kenneth Noye purchased at least half a dozen properties in the suburbs of south London. Noye bought his wife Brenda a £10,000 fur coat, as well as a house for one of his mistresses who lived nearby. Between them the two men now owned six cars, including top-of-the-range Jaguars and Range Rovers plus Palmer's classic Jensen Interceptor.

The same influx of cash also helped John Palmer purchase a property that would become his family's long-term, permanent home. After months of house hunting in the Wiltshire and Avon countryside near Palmer's 'businesses' in Bristol, Palmer and Marnie came across a detached Georgian coach house called Battlefield, seven miles outside Bath. It had been designed and built by the renowned Bath architect John Wood the Younger and nestled on the edge of a sleepy hillside village called Lansdown.

Battlefield – built in distinctive grey brick and containing five bedrooms with a vast courtyard and numerous outbuildings – was ideal in every way for John Palmer and his family.

He liked it because it was isolated and could be reached only by a single driveway from the main road a quarter of a mile away. The house overlooked rolling hills and Palmer told many associates he could now see all his enemies coming before they got near him.

Palmer immediately purchased three horses for Marnie to ride, which she kept in the stables attached to the main house. She later said she felt like the luckiest person in the world when John Palmer scooped her up and carried her through the front door on the day they completed the purchase of the house.

John Palmer began to consider himself a cut above most other villains. He developed an interest in fine French wines and also encouraged Marnie to buy expensive antiques to furnish Battlefield. As one old associate who visited the property later explained: 'It wasn't exactly oozing with class but it was a lot more tasteful than you would expect. For starters, JP had bought himself an old coach house, not some brand new red-brick monstrosity complete with shining wrought-iron gates and ten-foot-high walls, which was what most criminals seemed to prefer.'

Palmer even made sure the driveway to Battlefield was gravel rather than brick or tarmac and he admitted to one old associate he liked living 'the real country life'. Not long after moving in, Palmer began dressing like a country squire with a penchant for tweed jackets and flat caps, while Marnie toned down her beauty queen look with twinsets and pearls, jodhpurs and neat jackets.

To villagers in Lansdown, the couple seemed pleasant if not over friendly. Palmer was said to be a wealthy businessman and no one questioned the source of his wealth.

'It wasn't a bad life,' Palmer told one associate many years later. 'In fact it was a fantastic life. But as ever I wanted more.'

John Palmer saw Battlefield as his palace, a property where

he could duck and dive to his heart's content without anyone else being any the wiser. The moment he drove through the imposing gates on to the long driveway he felt a sense of relief because this was his territory and no one was going to take it away from him.

Meanwhile Marnie had stopped riding horses in order to get through the final weeks of her second pregnancy and in late 1980 she gave birth to another daughter, Sarah.

Many of John Palmer's associates were shocked because until this period he'd always been so low key. Now he had a posh manor house and even splashed out £100,000 cash on a huge outbuilding constructed in the grounds to house an even bigger and more efficient gold smelter.

Over in deepest Kent, Palmer's partner-in-crime Kenneth Noye had become so flush with cash that he'd knocked down his original detached country house and built a new property in its place, complete with a swimming pool and secret underground compartments where he could hide stashes of stolen items. Noye even kept a few wild animals such as tigers and wolves in the grounds of the property.

With all this extravagance in their lifestyle, it was little wonder that people started talking about them.

Yet despite this enormous influx of cash, neither man was renowned for his generosity when it came to buying a round of drinks. 'The pair of 'em were bloody tight-fisted and avoided putting their hands in their pockets for a pint in the pub,' remembered one associate.

But John Palmer and his Kent associate Noye were about to stumble on an opportunity to make more money than either of them could have ever imagined.

CHAPTER SIX

OTHER PEOPLE'S MONEY

SECURITY EXPRESS DEPOT, SHOREDITCH, EAST LONDON, MONDAY 2 APRIL 1983

In 1983, two historic robberies were carried out in Britain which threatened for the first time to overshadow the exploits of the Great Train Robbery. The first one was the Security Express heist on Easter Monday, 2 April 1983, when armed robbers struck the supposedly impregnable Security Express depot in Shoreditch, east London. Palmer later told associates he'd been offered an opportunity to finance the robbery, but pulled out in the early stages because he believed one of the gang was a police informant. Almost £6 million was stolen of which only a small amount was ever recovered, despite Security Express offering a £500,000 reward.

Then just a few months later at 6.25 a.m. on 26 November 1983, a gang of south-east London robbers – largely unknown to John Palmer – raided a Brink's-Mat security warehouse near Heathrow airport, disabled the alarms and headed for the unit's vault where they found a carpet of drab grey containers, no bigger than shoeboxes, bound with metal straps and labelled with handwritten identification codes. There were sixty boxes in all, containing 2,670 kilos of gold worth £26,369,778. There were also hundreds of thousands of pounds in used bank notes locked in three safes. One pouch contained traveller's cheques worth $250,000. In the other was a stash of polished and rough diamonds worth at least £100,000. They'd expected a million pounds' worth of gold at the most but nothing like this.

The Brink's-Mat robbery, brilliant in its conception and ruthless in its execution, had just landed a team of professional criminals with the biggest haul of gold in British criminal history. But the police were soon hot on the trail of the robbers, so the gang put out the word that they urgently needed to start turning all that gold into cash.

Kenneth Noye knew two of the robbers indirectly, so in the aftermath of the Brink's-Mat heist he made contact with them and let it be known that he and Palmer could handle all the gold for them. Palmer had just installed that new improved gold smelter in the Battlefield barn and both men had the perfect criminal network through which to launder the bullion.

The fact the two main robbers were on the verge of being arrested made it even more appealing to both Palmer and Noye because that would enable them to take over complete control of the gold. So with the tabloids calling the Brink's-Mat heist 'The Crime of the Century', John Palmer and Kenneth Noye rubbed their hands with glee in expectation of their biggest ever payday.

One day, two 'associates' of the main Brink's-Mat robbery gang turned up unexpectedly at Battlefield to inspect Palmer's smelter and discuss terms. Palmer was immediately wary of the two men, who turned out to be brothers whom we will call 'Bill' and 'Ben'. Palmer told one old associate many years later: 'I didn't like the way they just showed up out of the blue.'

Bill and Ben headed the most feared crime family in London and even accused Palmer of having a 'crap smelter'. When he snapped back at them, they laughed and said they were only testing his reaction to see how he handled them. Palmer later commented: 'They was evil bastards and I should have kept away from them.'

Bill and Ben claimed they were acting as 'agents' for the Brink's-Mat robbers because they'd financed the raid in the first place and had a 'duty' to try and get the best possible deal for themselves and the gang.

The brothers said they'd pay Palmer and Noye 25 per cent as a handling charge on every penny they got back from selling the gold by whatever means they could manage. It was too good an offer for Palmer and Noye to turn down.

And of course that handling charge didn't even include the 15 per cent extra that Noye and Palmer intended to earn through their favourite VAT scam.

All this put John Palmer and Kenneth Noye in the driving seat, even though they'd had nothing to do with the robbery itself.

Kenneth Noye turned out to be the natural 'front man' of the pair. He was later described by one of Palmer's oldest associates as 'a charming, but evil guy. He spotted everything, and I mean everything. Nothing got past him.'

But inside that scheming criminal mind, Kenneth Noye nursed a massive dose of paranoia. He didn't trust anyone, especially his supposed new friend John Palmer. One associate described meetings between the two as 'a jousting competition' after they'd agreed to handle the Brink's-Mat gold bullion.

As an old associate of Noye's explained: 'JP and Noye were extremely alike in some ways. But JP liked to avoid most of the head-on aggravation. He preferred it when people backed off without having a fight. But Noye was the opposite. He'd hammer anyone who got in his way – and that included his friends.'

A few days after Palmer and Noye had agreed to handle the Brink's-Mat gold, three of the original robbery gang members were arrested and held in custody. It was rumoured on the underworld grapevine that the police had them 'bang to rights'. This included the ringleader's brother-in-law, who worked at the bullion warehouse and had been their inside man. He'd told the police all they needed to know.

As one ex-robber explained more than thirty years later: 'Those lads had pulled off a brilliant robbery. But then they went and got nicked so quickly they'd lost control of the system to smelt the gold down and turn it into hard cash.'

Those two 'lads' were 'Mad' Mickey McAvoy and Brian Robinson and they were now under lock and key awaiting trial. They were certainly not the sort of characters you fucked over.

Two meetings at London's swish Savoy Hotel followed between the two brothers Bill and Ben from the London crime family and Palmer and Noye. Palmer was so impressed by the Savoy that in later years he began using it regularly for London meetings. Palmer laughed when the two brothers told him that Savoy staff expected £50 tips. They even showed Palmer the best place to sit in the restaurant to ensure that anyone meeting him would be blinded by the sun glistening off the nearby Thames.

At the Savoy meetings, the brothers coolly informed Noye and Palmer that the operation to collect the gold bullion and then smelt it down would need to be done under the utmost secrecy. Noye and Palmer assured Bill and Ben they had an airtight masterplan to ensure it was all done well away from the watchful eye of Scotland Yard's Flying Squad.

*

Approximately a month after the Brink's-Mat heist, a couple reported to the police in Bath that they'd seen a smelting crucible operating in a building in the grounds of John Palmer's house, Battlefield. Two local constables visited the property to be greeted by a beaming Palmer , who welcomed them into the outhouse, showed them the smelter and then gave them both a cup of tea before sitting down and explaining to the officers that this was the professional tool of his trade as a metal smelter. The two uniformed officers concluded that there was nothing suspicious going on and no one to this day knows if that visit was ever reported to Scotland Yard's Flying Squad.

Meanwhile detectives hunting the rest of the Brink's-Mat gang announced to the media that they believed there were at least fifteen other people involved in the heist.

Over at his Grade II listed manor house, John Palmer was preparing to handle his first consignment of Brink's-Mat gold with a wry smile on his face as he hung a framed quotation on the wall of his smelter outhouse. It read:

'He who has the gold, makes the rules.'

CHAPTER SEVEN

THE ODD COUPLE

BATTLEFIELD, NEAR BATH, JANUARY 1984

It sums up the crafty nature of both John Palmer and Kenneth Noye that neither of them was prepared to admit to London crime family brothers Bill and Ben, or indeed the Brink's-Mat robbers themselves, that they intended 'nicking' another 15 per cent off the gold bullion cash by fraudulently claiming VAT on it.

As one old south London villain explained many years later: 'The pound signs registered in their eyes every time they talked about the Brink's-Mat gold. It was a win-win deal for JP and Kenny Noye. They were like the Terrible Twins with the key to the castle, only this castle was made of solid gold. They knew that if they played their cards right then they'd easily make more money out of the Brink's-Mat robbery than the poor bastards who nicked it in the first place.'

The key to the success of the operation was to spread all the gold bullion around various locations in southern and western England, where it could then be picked up and delivered to Palmer's smelter near Bath. It was made clear to Palmer and Noye by Bill and Ben that if any of the bullion went missing then they'd be held personally responsible. In other words, it would cost them their lives. This veiled threat prompted nothing more than a shrug of the shoulders from both Palmer and Noye. Palmer wasn't worried because he could always hot-foot it to Tenerife if any problems kicked off.

With the gold-smelting operation at Palmer's house about to start, Noye and Palmer agreed not to meet unless it was an absolute emergency. Palmer had insisted on this because he'd heard from his own sources that Noye was often under the watchful eye of the Flying Squad.

When Noye quietly admitted to Palmer that some of the gold bullion was hidden in an underground bunker beneath his house, Palmer told Noye it was bloody risky if the police decided to pay them a visit. Noye ignored Palmer's request to move the gold and for the first time the two men almost came to blows. Noye didn't like being told what to do by someone who wouldn't even be on the job if it hadn't been for his recommendation.

Noye and Palmer's so-called 'middleman/courier' was to be another old-school south London criminal called Brian Reader. His job would be to pick up the bullion in small loads from wherever it was stored and then deliver it to Battlefield. Reader had known Noye since they were youths growing up in the suburbs of south-east London.

A few days after the operation began, John Palmer told Noye that once they'd started smelting the gold it made sense to transport small amounts of the 'new version' of it abroad on a private jet from nearby Bristol airport. Palmer informed Noye and Reader he had access to a private hangar in the far corner of the airport, which would enable them to not even have to go through security checks. Palmer had secured this access through the local crime family he had befriended since arriving in the West Country.

Some of the reconstituted gold bars would also end up being smuggled out of the UK in the Tupperware lunchboxes of dozens of lorry drivers, who worked for a haulage company owned by one of Kenneth Noye's oldest friends in the south-east of England. The gold was then brought back into Britain from Holland and that's when the VAT was claimed on it.

From their prison cells, Brink's-Mat robbers McAvoy and Robinson kept a close eye on developments through their own underworld associates. No one completely trusted Palmer and Noye, who were considered outsiders. However, the two professional robbers had little choice but to use their 'services'.

They even ordered the rest of the gang to steer clear of Palmer and Noye in case the police were on to them. This conveniently left Palmer and Noye to their own devices.

Back in his Battlefield outhouse, John Palmer found himself thoroughly enjoying the entire smelting process. He later said there was something magical about watching the gold melting into liquid and then cooling down in a completely different shape from what it had looked like originally. Palmer said he also liked the sweltering heat and intensity of the whole process.

Palmer soon earned the nickname of 'Goldfinger' from Noye and Reader because he was the one who got his fingers dirty smelting the actual gold. At first, he revelled in the name because it reminded him and many others of the infamous James Bond villain, who'd presided over the biggest fictional gold bullion robbery of all time. But Palmer would eventually grow to loathe the nickname when it attracted the *wrong* sort of attention.

Middleman Brian Reader later admitted driving between Kent and the West Country on at least thirty occasions, spread out over much of 1984. Usually, he'd head west on the M4 motorway to John Palmer's home near Bath in a modest Vauxhall saloon or one of the many other cars he owned.

Inevitably, rumours about Palmer and Noye's links to the Brink's-Mat gold bullion began to circulate. And eventually a handful of envious villains happened to mention it to some of their close 'friends' at Scotland Yard's Flying Squad.

Then, in late 1984, police received a tip-off that a man had been seen a few months earlier in London's Hatton Garden jewellery district trying to buy an industrial-sized gold smelter. Less than a week after the tip-off, undercover detectives in Worcestershire watched the same man loading a smelter into the back of a gold Rolls-Royce following a routine service. 'He was easy to follow because the smelter was too big for the Rolls and the boot wouldn't close,' one of the detectives later explained. 'So we followed him all the way to Kenneth Noye's house in Kent.'

Flying Squad detectives stayed outside Noye's property all night and then followed the driver when he returned to his car the next morning. But within five minutes they had lost him. By the time the police returned to Noye's house later that same day the smelter had also disappeared.

The driver of the gold Rolls-Royce was a man called Mickey Lawson who happened to be a close friend of Noye. Despite its ostentation, the Rolls had been used to transport the smelter because it had the biggest boot.

It was obvious to the police that these characters must be involved in smelting down the Brink's-Mat gold bullion. But detectives decided to be patient because they wanted cast-iron evidence that would not only imprison the handlers but also help them nail the robbers, only two of whom had been arrested for their part in the original heist.

While Palmer, Noye and Reader were busy transporting and

then smelting the stolen gold bullion, these same characters from the gang who seemed to have got away scot-free decided they wanted their share of the loot ASAP.

Noye and Palmer needed this type of problem like the proverbial hole in the head but they were powerless to stop it happening. Sizeable amounts of cash were quickly handed over. Within weeks, those other gang members had purchased large detached houses mainly in the English countryside. It was a clumsy move, which alerted the Flying Squad and greatly irritated the hard-working trio, who were ultimately responsible for turning the stolen gold into cash. As one Flying Squad investigator later explained: 'They should have just sat on it but in the end they couldn't resist spending the cash.'

Despite a pledge never to be seen together, Kenneth Noye ended up visiting John Palmer's home near Bath with a car boot filled with gold bullion at least three times towards the end of 1984. Other meetings were held in isolated laybys of A-roads mainly near the Kent town of Gravesend, which was handy for the motorway in both directions.

One evening, John Palmer and his old West Country sidekick Terry Patch visited Noye at his house in West Kingsdown to discuss how to speed up the transportation and smelting process.

Palmer later told one associate how 'glitzy' Noye's home was compared to Battlefield. The house had gold-leaf wallpaper and the sitting room was filled with clocks that chimed constantly, much to the irritation of both Palmer and Patch as they discussed the progress of the gold-smelting operation. Kenneth Noye even gleefully announced he'd named his two Rottweiler puppies 'Brink's' and 'Mat'. Palmer rolled his eyes but said nothing.

*

Just a few days later, in December 1985, Brink's-Mat robbers Brian Robinson and Mickey McAvoy were sentenced to twenty-five years after waiting more than a year for their trial to take place.

It may be no coincidence that within weeks, John Palmer – who had by this stage smelted at least £10 million worth of the stolen gold bullion – was coolly informed by Kenneth Noye that they'd both just been put under round-the-clock Flying Squad surveillance. Noye's friends at the Yard had given him the nod but he told Palmer there was no need to worry. He believed they'd set up such a well-organized 'shipment' system for the gold that it would be impossible for the police to pin anything on them.

Palmer thought about their situation and then nodded reluctantly in agreement. Noye could sometimes be a reckless type but Palmer could see his point. If they suddenly stopped their routine, it would probably cause more suspicion than if they just carried on as they had been doing for almost twelve months.

So, while Brian Reader and Kenneth Noye amused themselves sometimes leading their police shadows down a few 'dead ends', John Palmer got his hands as dirty as ever by living up to his nickname 'Goldfinger'. Out on the motorways and A-roads between Kent and Wiltshire, gold courier Brian Reader set up 'dummy runs' during which he'd change cars three times over a twenty-mile journey just to confuse watching detectives. That would then enable one of Noye's other associates to slip out of his Kent house with another load of gold heading off towards the M4 motorway and Palmer's house.

One day John Palmer took time off from his West Country gold-smelting duties to drive to London. He was unaware that the police were following. They watched Palmer meet up with a gold dealer called Christopher Weyman, who ran a business called Lustretone Ltd, in Greville Street, just around the corner from London's infamous diamond district of Hatton Garden. Palmer had been a regular visitor to the area over the previous five or six years and was on first-name terms with Weyman and other gold dealers. The visit in itself proved nothing, so the police switched their attention back to Noye's house in deepest Kent.

Specialist Scotland Yard C11 undercover detectives moved into position in a row of bushes by the public road in front of the entrance to the long driveway leading to Kenneth Noye's home. Just opposite its high wrought-iron gates, a video camera disguised as a nestbox was placed in an overhanging tree.

Meanwhile over in a street close to Brian Reader's large detached house in Grove Park, south-east London, unmarked police vehicles kept watch as Reader arrived home from a trip he'd also made to Hatton Garden earlier that same day.

Many years later, Palmer told acquaintances that he believed Noye and Reader had made a lot of 'elementary mistakes' while transporting the Brink's-Mat gold to and from the West Country. But the biggest of all those mistakes was about to come crashing down all around Palmer and his two associates.

CHAPTER EIGHT

CASUALTY OF WAR

It was freezing cold when Brian Reader arrived at Kenneth Noye's house for yet another gold exchange. John Palmer by this time was refusing to travel outside the Bath and Bristol area because the police were tailing him constantly and he didn't want to take any chances. Within a few minutes of Reader's arrival, both men heard Noye's dogs making a commotion outside so Noye went to investigate.

As Noye passed his Ford Granada parked on the driveway, he grabbed a torch from it and took a knife he'd been using earlier to clean the car's battery tops. A few moments later, Noye spotted a hooded figure dressed all in black just four or five feet away. The two men got into a scuffle and Noye plunged his knife into the intruder.

The man tried to escape but ended up collapsing nearby. Noye threatened to attack the man again if he didn't say who he was. The intruder mumbled 'SAS' and then passed out. Undercover police officer John Fordham died within minutes of the attack. Noye later claimed he thought he was dealing with a rapist or a peeping tom.

Just beyond the perimeter fence, policemen could be heard talking loudly after encountering Fordham's partner, who'd just managed to scramble over the back wall when Noye had appeared in the garden. Moments later a police car smashed through the wrought-iron gates to Hollywood Cottage.

Kenneth Noye and his wife Brenda were immediately arrested and taken to a local police station. Brian Reader was also detained and then made a very uncharacteristic mistake. He admitted that he and Kenneth Noye had been discussing the Brink's-Mat gold earlier that evening. Whether Reader did that deliberately in order to 'water down' his involvement with the death of the undercover policeman we will never know.

Police forensic examinations at Hollywood Cottage quickly connected Reader and Noye to the stolen bullion through globular fragments of gold discovered on the boot mat of Noye's Ford Granada and Reader's Vauxhall. Police also discovered a further eleven gold bars wrapped in red-and-white cloth hidden in a shallow gully beside Noye's garage wall. Detectives also claimed they'd found paperwork with telephone numbers that proved a definite link between John Palmer and Noye.

Brian Reader, Kenneth Noye and his wife Brenda Noye were all charged with the murder of undercover policeman John Fordham. Reader and Noye were also charged with conspiracy to handle stolen bullion.

Years later, Brian Reader said that he believed if Noye hadn't discovered Fordham in his garden that night then he, Noye and Palmer would have got away with it all. 'The death of that copper was a disaster,' Reader told one associate. 'It made the Old Bill go crazy and they were never going to let us out of their sights after that.'

The killing of an undercover policeman in the grounds of Noye's home completely overshadowed all other professional criminal activities at the time. It was the final straw for John Palmer. He finished smelting the gold he had at Battlefield and immediately dispatched it from his house in case the police came calling.

Then he booked himself on the first available flight to his beloved Tenerife.

Palmer needed to distance himself from the Brink's-Mat job as quickly as possible and it was essential that he switched 'hats' to concentrate on other businesses further afield. The British police had no jurisdiction in Tenerife because of the collapse of the extradition treaty between Spain and the UK, so Palmer believed he was safe as long as he kept away from Blighty.

Just hours after John Palmer flew off to Tenerife, a team of Flying Squad officers turned up at Battlefield with a warrant for his arrest. A cleaner who opened the door to the police later said detectives brushed past her, demanding to know if Palmer was inside. Minutes later – after a thorough search of the premises – the detectives emerged with tails between their legs because Palmer was nowhere to be found. Detectives later stated they found two 'warm' gold bars at Battlefield, as well as two hand-guns. Palmer always claimed these items had been planted there by detectives – but then he would say that, wouldn't he?

When Palmer heard from Tenerife what had happened, he insisted that Marnie and their daughters be immediately 'pro-tected' by two Dobermanns who were encouraged to roam the grounds of Battlefield at night. Marnie wasn't keen because the dogs scared her beloved horses. Palmer told her it was non-ne-gotiable.

Over in nearby Bristol, Garth Chappell and Terry Patch – John Palmer's partners in their original West Country metal smelting business, Scadlynn Ltd – were arrested in connection with the Brink's-Mat gold bullion smelting operation.

Chappell had clumsily withdrawn £348,000 from Scadlynn's company accounts at Barclays Bank, red-lighting his activities. It later emerged a total of £11.5 million had been deposited and then withdrawn in cash through that same bank. The Bank of England later claimed they had to personally issue Barclays with more brand new cash notes because it had literally run out of money.

Chappell and Patch admitted the company had been processing millions of pounds' worth of gold, but claimed it was gold they'd purchased themselves. The company's books stated that they were selling the melted-down gold for virtually the same amount as they had purchased it for, which didn't make sense, unless the records were false. Confiscated documents also showed that Scadlynn had been evading tax, and the company was immediately ordered to pay £80,000 in unpaid tax.

The numerous transactions involving Chappell and Patch sparked a furious response from associates of Brink's-Mat robbers McAvoy and Robinson, fearful that others were stealing their money.

Then, in Kent, more gold was found at Kenneth Noye's house while he awaited trial for killing the undercover policeman. There were even rumours in the UK underworld that some of the bullion had been shipped to Tenerife and hidden under Palmer's new villa.

Many in the London underworld accused Palmer of being a 'Judas' who'd agreed to help the Flying Squad in exchange for immunity from prosecution. None of this was true but Palmer's residency in Tenerife gave the clear impression he was untouchable, fuelling the rumours in the first place.

John Palmer picked up the phone in his penthouse apartment overlooking Las Americas and spoke to a man who in turn spoke to one of three Spanish police officers Palmer had nurtured on the island. Palmer asked them to let him know if there were any official police plans to look more closely at his 'business interests' on Tenerife.

The Tenerife police were poorly paid and neglected by their bosses back in Madrid. Spanish police equipment was antiquated, as were the wages they were paid and many detectives happily ignored the criminals who British authorities were so desperate to arrest, because they were bringing money into Spain. This meant jobs for the locals and big bribes for some individual officers to boot.

Back in his Las Americas penthouse apartment above the Golden Mile, John Palmer sat back and tried to assess his situation. He was loaded with cash but urgently needed something new to invest in. Then he remembered that the nearest land to Tenerife was across the Atlantic Ocean in West Africa.

Palmer had heard a few months earlier that the cheapest place to buy diamonds was in the war-torn nation of Liberia, where a prominent civil servant called Charles Taylor controlled the diamond trade while his associates took hefty kickbacks from anyone who sought out the country's gems. Later Taylor would set up a rebel group backed by Libya that within a couple of years would spark a vicious civil war. This eventually led to Taylor taking over the presidency of the country.

Palmer made contact with Charles Taylor's associates through a South African diamond dealer who paved the way for a visit to a country where child soldiers were said to rule the streets and life was notoriously cheap. Many of these child soldiers would eventually serve under the notorious Charles Taylor but John Palmer wasn't interested in the politics. His only priority was money.

CHAPTER NINE

DIAMOND HUNTING

ROBERTS INTERNATIONAL AIRPORT, LIBERIA,
APRIL 1985

John Palmer arrived at Liberia's only international airport to be met by an old-fashioned Mercedes limousine. One of Palmer's oldest associates later recalled: 'Taylor ensured the red carpet was rolled out for JP, even though Taylor himself was still officially at this time nothing more than a humble civil servant. As such, Taylor was careful to avoid any direct contact with characters like John Palmer.'

But Taylor did send along a couple of bodyguards to protect Palmer. These included a Lebanese ex-soldier, who'd been recruited by Taylor when Taylor visited Libya at the invitation of Colonel Gaddafi. This character immediately hit it off with Palmer, who nicknamed him 'Tel' because he looked a bit like Telly Savalas, star of TV's *Kojak*.

Tel's bald head and pock-marked face made him look terrifying to most people he encountered. One source later said his deep, matt black, cesspool eyes were like a shark's.

Tel's background was a world away from Palmer's. He came from a wealthy Muslim family that had at one time led a militia unit during the Lebanese civil war which had started in 1975 and was still going strong. Tel's family had originally been traders and they'd made a fortune from all the opposing factions during the war by smuggling arms into Lebanon, mainly from Syria.

Tel had originally gone to Libya to lie low for a while after trying to double-cross Hezbollah on an arms deal. Then, following a personal recommendation from Colonel Gaddafi, Tel had been recruited to work unofficially for Charles Taylor's criminal associates in Liberia.

Tel, who was almost exactly the same age as John Palmer, openly admitted to Palmer he was virtually penniless following the collapse of a recent 'business' deal. Palmer later said he liked Tel because he was 'as hard as nails'. Tel had no connections whatsoever with criminals in the UK or Spain, which greatly appealed to Palmer.

Tel also boasted to the Englishman that he'd personally killed many enemy soldiers in battle in the Lebanon. Palmer was impressed because this meant Tel would not hesitate to shoot anyone who posed a threat to them while Palmer was in Liberia.

Palmer had no inkling of Tel's former close links to the Syrian-backed Hezbollah terrorist group, who'd been supported and encouraged by Syria's despot President Assad throughout the ongoing war in Lebanon.

In war-ravaged Lebanon, Tel had even organized shipments of Lebanese black hashish, which was the most popular form of cannabis resin in the world at that time. Tel used money provided by terror groups such as the IRA and his old friends Hezbollah to finance such drugs deals in exchange for getting them a big return on their cash. This made Tel a sort of unofficial 'investment manager' for terror groups. And of course he was greedily skimming off big chunks of their profits for himself.

*

In Liberia, Tel escorted Palmer to various diamond mines and even drove him across the border to neighbouring Sierra Leone to view other potential business investments. Palmer appreciated the power of a Kalashnikov for the first time and later told his associates that 'No one takes you on when you've got one of them slung over yer shoulder.'

Travelling in a convoy of three heavily armed vehicles, John Palmer started to appreciate the security of 'owning your own territory' for the first time. He liked the freedom of movement best. Tel told him how Charles Taylor and the rest of Liberia's rich and powerful didn't even have to go through passport control to enter and leave the country.

Palmer eventually bought hundreds of diamonds through Charles Taylor's criminal associates in Liberia. He intended cutting them all down and selling them on the open market back in Europe.

Palmer's main concern was getting the diamonds safely to Tenerife, so he persuaded Tel to escort him back to the island. En route, he suggested to Spanish-speaking Tel that he should stay in Tenerife where he could help him start developing some new 'business interests' on the island.

Tel later told one associate that southern Tenerife was not so different from southern Lebanon before the war had ripped it to shreds. As a result, he soon felt at home on the island.

John Palmer now reckoned he had most of the people on Tenerife he needed deep in his pocket. He felt relatively safe and secure on the island for the time being but he needed to press ahead with his plans to build some timeshare resorts in order to 'wash' his Brink's-Mat gold cash, as well as all his other illicit income.

By this time, John Palmer's eyes and ears were everywhere on Tenerife. He needed this sort of knowledge in order to avoid being dragged back to the UK to face any charges connected to the Brink's-Mat gold.

In London, Scotland Yard officers teamed up with British security services and started looking into Palmer's overseas money transactions and offshore banking. Huge amounts of money were involved but Palmer had cleverly cleared his offshore accounts of cash just before he left for Tenerife. So the money trail soon went cold.

Not surprisingly, Palmer became very security conscious. He began using an electronic scanner to pinpoint listening devices in landline phones and hidden in rooms he frequented. Before any meeting, either he or one of his Clumpers would always insist on silence until the scanner had been tested.

Back in London, Kenneth Noye and middleman Brian Reader were about to appear at the Old Bailey in a case that had been dubbed the crime trial of the decade: the alleged murder of John Fordham in the grounds of Noye's house.

A few weeks before the trial, a senior Brink's-Mat police investigator called Brian Boyce interrogated Noye about his involvement in the robbery. Noye tried a Masonic handshake on Boyce followed by an offer of a £1 million bribe if Boyce would help Noye get off the murder charges. Boyce immediately reported the approach to his supervisors at Scotland Yard.

There were rumours that Noye and a number of other professional criminals had 'infiltrated' the Freemasons after being supported for membership by certain crooked police officers. No one knows to this day if John Palmer also worked his way into the secretive organization. If he did, then it might well explain how he came to have so many tame police contacts.

*

John Palmer had no doubt he was a marked man and that Scotland Yard's Flying Squad had made him their number one target since Kenneth Noye's arrest.

He told Marnie to stay put in England with their two daughters while he decided how best to deal with 'some business problems'. Palmer had been told by a police informant he was on a list of twenty wanted men whose names had been supplied to the Spanish government in a bid to get them to waive their non-extradition rules.

With his recently hired secretary Christine Ketley by his side in his penthouse apartment overlooking Las Americas, Palmer sat down and began making a masterplan to cover all eventualities, including his imminent arrest. He told Ketley, an accountant by training, to work out a business strategy so they could turn their planned timeshare resorts into big 'legitimate' earners.

Palmer later claimed that if it hadn't been for him having to flee to Tenerife, his timeshare empire and criminal activities might never have taken off so lucratively. He'd turned from an astute West Country gangster into a crime lord with a booming legitimate business in a very short space of time.

It was during this period that Palmer and Ketley began a relationship. He kept the romance secret at first and criminal associates who flew out to see him said most visitors were not even aware she existed at that time.

Ketley later recalled the moment they'd 'sparked' their romance. She said: 'I was expecting some sort of London crook in a heavy camel-haired coat and rings on his fingers. But he was a gentle and lovable person.'

Christine Ketley was obviously well aware of Palmer's wanted status back in the UK but as far as she was concerned the timeshare business was completely legitimate. As a result, she tried her hardest to relax Palmer who was growing increasingly anxious about the Brink's-Mat ringleaders and his police pursuers.

Palmer financed his first two timeshare resorts in Las Americas with money from the Brink's-Mat gold bullion plus some sizeable loans from local banks, who'd been encouraged by Tenerife's tourist authority to help Palmer because they believed his development plans would encourage more visitors to come to the island. Newly recruited henchman Tel acted as translator for Palmer during most of his negotiations with the banks and local authorities.

Sometimes Tel complained he couldn't understand what Palmer was saying because of his thick Brummie accent. But eventually the Lebanese ex-militiaman grew accustomed to Palmer's mumbling tones and the two began operating very effectively together when it came to nailing down deals.

John Palmer's flagship timeshare resort Holiday Village was constructed on what had once been a two-acre plot of wasteland in the heart of Las Americas. It had no direct legal connection to Palmer himself because his 'financial advisors' had insisted he should not be the registered owner of any property on the island.

A promotional film made by Palmer's property company at the time showed palm trees at the entrance to the resort's tower-block headquarters with lots of smiling salesmen accompanying not so happy-looking 'punters' sitting at rows of desks, where so many holidaymakers would end up signing away their pension money in the deluded belief that they were about to own their own piece of paradise.

Over on the Costa del Sol, in southern Spain, Palmer pushed ahead with another smaller timeshare development.

He instinctively preferred Tenerife but wanted to keep his hand in the mainland, just in case Tenerife did not take off as he expected.

John Palmer decided that if he got through all this he was going to buy himself a private jet, which would give him the freedom to travel anywhere he wanted without state interference, just like Charles Taylor and his cronies back in brutal, war-torn Liberia. Palmer even began researching makes and models and their ranges, so that he could pick the perfect aircraft for his purposes.

Palmer later described this time on Tenerife as his 'rebuilding period'. As the timeshare resorts were completed, he took personal control of their launch, choosing everything from his first teams of staff to deciding with his lawyers the wording on the contracts he wanted potential home buyers to sign when they bought into his crime-funded property empire.

Initial approaches were made to holidaymakers by Palmer's small army of touts who patrolled the streets and nearby beaches most mornings. The touts were officially known as OPCs and gave away free scratch cards to the tourists, which almost certainly guaranteed they won a prize, usually a bottle of cheap imitation champagne. The tourists were then told by the tout that the only way for the tout to get a commission was if they agreed to go into the Holiday Village headquarters; the vast majority of holidaymakers immediately agreed.

In the main reception area a middle-aged woman called Flo Robinson usually ran the front desk together with her two Jack Russell terriers called Sid and Nancy, who'd growl menacingly whenever people came in through the double-door entranceway.

On the ground floor were banks of desks where Palmer's so-called executives sat down with the holidaymakers and began their high-pressure sales tactics. Potential customers would be left with virtually no choice but to buy into one of Palmer's timeshare resorts.

Palmer then hit on a plan to also get his sales staff to press existing timeshare owners to buy shares at a second holiday home on the basis that their old timeshare would be sold for a huge profit. They were promised a better apartment and substantial profit at no financial risk and told that the timeshare they were buying would be rented out and that the rent would cover the cost of the entire deal.

But Palmer's staff simply banked their money from these deals and made no effort to either sell the original property, or rent it out on their behalf. When victims realized they'd been duped, Palmer's complex web of companies even made it impossible for them to get a refund.

Holidaymakers even found that the paperwork they'd signed committed them to paying instalments to a finance company. Those who cancelled would lose whatever money they had already paid. It was only later they'd realize they could never resell their timeshares at the prices promised by Palmer's salesmen.

The first two timeshare resorts took off so quickly that Palmer decided to immediately construct five more, even though he was technically still on the run from UK police. And at every meeting, Palmer still secretly recorded everything on a small handheld tape recorder inside his pocket while asking everyone else present to speak up because he was hard of hearing, to make sure he got everything down on tape.

Palmer's timeshare scheme relied on people preferring to have their own apartments and villas for just one week or month of the year than not at all. Holidaymakers were soon coming in to sign on the dotted line in droves. Few worked out they were buying into one of the biggest confidence tricks the world has ever seen.

Palmer had worked out a way to sell the same property ten or twelve times over. His yield was at least five times the real value of each property. As he once said: 'Not bad for a kid from the slums of Birmingham who can't read or write, eh?'

Buyers paid a relatively small amount of cash upfront to give them part-time ownership of a property plus an annual fee for the running of the resort. All they had to do was give their name, address and bank account details. Few bothered to read the small print. Customers later described leaving the Holiday Village headquarters feeling elated with their decision to buy a piece of Tenerife.

Based on an average £3,000 for a lifetime ownership of one week a year on the complex, initial sales of the 180 villas on that first Holiday Village site would net more than £500,000 for each week, or well over £20 million a year. A further 'mantainence fee' of £100 a week was even bringing in another £1 million a year.

Back in the UK, things were not going so well. Those two Brink's-Mat robbers in prison had been informed that a 'significant quantity' of what they considered to be their gold bullion had gone missing during the period John Palmer was involved with smelting it down. As a result, at least two criminals involved with the handling of the bullion had been gunned down in broad daylight. No one could be certain the killings were linked to the stolen gold but it seemed highly likely.

Palmer soon became worried he might end up a victim of what people in the London underworld had already dubbed 'The Curse of Brink's-Mat'.

The UK seemed like a distant and dangerous place to Palmer at this time. Here he was on the sunshine island of Tenerife on the run but already making more money than he had ever done before in his life, thanks to timeshare. He'd struck gold and wished in many ways he'd never even touched the real stuff in the first place.

OLD BAILEY CENTRAL CRIMINAL COURT, LONDON, NOVEMBER 1985

Kenneth Noye and Brian Reader's trial for the murder of detective John Fordham temporarily took the heat off John Palmer. The hearing dominated the media for weeks. At the request of the defence, other proceedings relating to the handling of the gold and VAT fraud were deferred to a later date.

After twelve hours and thirty-seven minutes of jury deliberation, not guilty verdicts were returned against both Reader and Noye. The jury accepted that the killing had been in self-defence.

Back in Tenerife, John Palmer must have felt a strange combination of relief and anger. He was relieved because he didn't like seeing any fellow villains go down, but was angry because he knew only too well that the police would be spitting blood about the acquittal and that would inevitably mean they'd try and come down even harder on him.

But worse was to come. In May 1986 Noye and Reader strolled back into the Old Bailey to face gold smelting and VAT fraud charges. Alongside them in the dock were five other fellow Brink's-Mat-connected conspirators, all of them known to Palmer.

The loss adjusters handling the Brink's-Mat insurance claims were so concerned that the accused men might be acquitted, they'd already launched a civil action against them. In a High Court action, a judge agreed that the assets of all seven – including Noye and Reader – should be frozen pending an outcome of any civil hearings.

Noye was eventually jailed for fourteen years for VAT fraud connected to the stolen Brink's-Mat gold. He was so annoyed to have been finally convicted of something he turned to the jury after their guilty verdict and said: 'I hope you all die of cancer.'

When John Palmer saw this on the TV news he didn't know whether to laugh or cry. Noye was a vindictive character and Palmer sensed that this was *not* the last he would ever hear of him.

CHAPTER TEN

A BIT ON THE SIDE

SANTA CRUZ, TENERIFE, MAY 1986

John Palmer had recently noticed another seismic change in the criminal underworld. Cocaine had overtaken robberies as the most lucrative source of income for most of Britain and Europe's professional criminals. Initially, Palmer had presumed that the 'drugs game' was full of nasty, trigger-happy Colombians and he'd carefully sidestepped it.

But when Palmer heard about the immense amounts of cash being earned on the back of cocaine he started to wonder if he should grab a piece of the action. With US law enforcement cracking down heavily on shipments flooding across the border with Mexico, Spain was about to become the new gateway for the majority of the world's cocaine.

John Palmer knew two criminals who were part of a British cocaine gang in Spain, who claimed to be riding high on the European-wide multimillion-pound drug industry. They told Palmer the profits from drugs were phenomenal. Cannabis, for example, cost £250 a kilo in North Africa and could be sold in the UK for upwards of £4,000. An investment of £20,000 in a shipment of cocaine would bring a return of £160,000.

Usually, four investors worked together to buy 100 kilos at a time.

John Palmer's biggest problem with drugs was that he was not the type of character to get personally hooked on them. Palmer sneered at his fellow villains who put almost as much up their noses as they were selling. Not only were they damaging their health but to him they were also wasting their hard-earned money. One of Palmer's oldest criminal associates later said: 'JP just didn't *get* the attraction of actually taking drugs. He was all about control and people like that never want to lose control with drugs.' The increasing use of cocaine by many of Palmer's associates was having another ominous knock-on effect; he'd found himself sometimes doing deals with highly erratic characters with hair-trigger tempers fuelled by their consumption of cocaine.

However, Palmer was tempted by a deal involving a Colombian gang that was based entirely in Tenerife – rather than mainland Spain – because there was a long stretch of choppy Atlantic ocean between himself and Europe. Sure, Palmer was already starting to claw in huge amounts of money from time-share, but he couldn't resist the additional 'hit' of excitement that came with a criminal enterprise like this.

In the Tenerife capital of Santa Cruz, Palmer met up with a Colombian cartel rep who outlined how they often used light aircraft to parachute cocaine drops of up to 600kg a time to waiting boats. Smaller speedboats would then take the produce to shore. Ocean-going yachts and other larger vessels in the Caribbean, Venezuela and South Africa were often used for long-haul journeys. The Colombians boasted about using a highly sophisticated computerized Global Positioning System to organize yacht-to-yacht drug transfers called 'coopering'. These transactions could take place off any coastline. The 'coopering' process also meant drugs gangs could dodge customs checks whenever their transatlantic vessels arrived in port.

Palmer told the rep that Tenerife was a perfect first stop-off point for their yachts sailing across from Central America and the Caribbean, as well as their aircraft. With his newly developed contacts on Tenerife, Palmer could guarantee the Colombians that their shipments of cocaine would come safely in and out of the island without any law enforcement interference.

Eventually Palmer agreed a deal that meant he took a percentage of every cocaine shipment, without ever having any direct contact with either the smugglers or their cargo. Palmer simply made the necessary arrangements to guarantee the police and customs would look the other way. Palmer also knew that by paying public officials he would have them eating out of his hand for any other criminal activities on 'his' island.

A lot of the staff working at Palmer's resorts discovered cocaine around this time and soon it was so prevalent on Tenerife that the island earned an unwelcome nickname – 'the white island' – among partygoers. In the middle of all this, Tenerife police arrested a 24-year-old drug mule who was carrying almost a kilo of cocaine in his stomach. A female smuggler was caught a few weeks later with a kilo of 'marching powder' in the shoulder pads of her dress, which greatly amused many because it was such an iconic fashion accessory in the 1980s.

But these arrests suggested that many more such mules were getting on to the island undetected by police. John Palmer never mentioned that his 'deal' with the Colombians was most likely responsible for that 'white island' tag.

Palmer's deal with the Colombians also introduced him to the cold, hard reality of money laundering for the first time. He soon began using 'financial institutions' in mainland Spain to convert the dirty money he was paid each month by the Colombians as well as a lot of his timeshare cash.

Palmer discovered there were banks in Tenerife where he or one of his people could turn up with half a million pounds and no one cared. Back then, the Spanish authorities unofficially encouraged a so-called black market because they needed the spending power of the rich to help their economy. In any case, the Spaniards had always been very suspicious of banks and many citizens still kept cash under their mattresses. It was also very easy to buy any property in Spain with cash at that time.

This then enabled Palmer to reinvest his money into yet more timeshare deals in Tenerife. He even deliberately laundered some of his criminal earnings through smaller enterprises such as selling second-hand luxury cars from Germany. Mercedes, Audi and BMWs were traditionally a great deal cheaper there than in Spain – especially on an isolated island like Tenerife where a tariff was also added to each vehicle. Palmer's men would go to Germany, buy three or four cars perfectly legally and then transport them back to Tenerife before selling them on for a healthy profit.

As Palmer's power and wealth grew in Tenerife, a number of old-school criminals came to talk to him about 'new business' that nearly always involved drug smuggling. Palmer turned them all down because he knew the Colombians wouldn't appreciate it if he set up a separate operation. In any case, no one could ever match the money he was making from them and his timeshare operation.

John Palmer was by all accounts a superstitious character who liked to do things certain ways. He had favourite suits, lucky shoes and most important of all, a scruffy brown leather briefcase that rarely left his side. Many presumed he carried cash in it, as well as his prized tape recorder.

But when it came to making conversation, John Palmer continued to pride himself on a 'less is more' philosophy. Associates recalled that many meetings with Palmer were filled with long periods of awkward silence as he contemplated what he was going to say or how to respond to other people's conversations. 'It was unnerving,' recalled one old associate. 'JP would make a bland statement about something and then say nothing more while he waited for others to respond. He rarely volunteered information. Even when he was asked a question he'd often ignore it completely.'

In June 1986, eighteen months after fleeing the UK following Kenneth Noye's arrest for murder, John Palmer received a call from one of his lawyers in the early hours of the morning.

The lawyer said that the UK government's ongoing pressure on their Spanish counterparts had *half* paid off; the Spanish were on the verge of introducing a new law stating that fugitives could only remain in their country with a valid passport. Palmer's passport had run out a year earlier.

Palmer was warned he would be declared an 'undesirable alien' and kicked off the island as a result.

'How long have I got?' asked Palmer.

'A few hours.'

Palmer was stunned.

He put the phone down and walked out on to the balcony of his penthouse apartment overlooking Las Americas' Golden Mile of sandy beach. Palmer glanced at the deep blue Atlantic Ocean as the sun slowly rose above the horizon to the east. Then he decided to do something he'd never done before; he was going to run for his life.

Palmer immediately rang two of his most trusted associates

and told them to oversee all his interests while he was gone. Neither of them attempted to dissuade him from going.

Palmer, along with millions of other Brits, had followed the antics of runaway Great Train Robber Ronnie Biggs for many years and he'd decided to join Biggs in South America.

Palmer then made a series of frantic calls to try and charter a private jet with the range to take him across the Atlantic immediately. But the only two planes available at the local airport didn't have the capacity to fly nonstop. Palmer slammed the phone down, grabbed a bag which had been hastily packed for him by Christine Ketley and headed out of the door.

Within an hour, Palmer was taking off in a private jet en route to the Portuguese capital Lisbon, where he then caught a connecting Varig commercial passenger flight to Brazil.

Back in Tenerife, police turned up at Palmer's penthouse to find him missing and Christine Ketley insisting she had no idea where he'd gone. In fact, she was telling the truth because Palmer had refused to tell her anything because he knew the police would come knocking.

No one knows to this day who told the authorities, but someone tipped them off that John Palmer was on that flight to Brazil, which was by now halfway across the Atlantic.

Three hours later, a Varig Lockheed Tristar carrying John Palmer landed with a sharp bump on the pot-holed tarmac of Recife International Airport, in northern Brazil, for a refuelling stop en route to Rio de Janeiro.

Palmer looked out of the porthole as the aircraft taxied towards its gate and immediately saw a welcoming party of police vehicles. He glanced around the cabin and realized there was no way out. He'd been hoping to get to Rio, sweep through customs using his fake passport and then head for an isolated resort a hundred miles south, where he believed he could stay in luxury and take advantage of Brazil's lenient attitude towards foreign criminals, perfectly illustrated by Ronnie Biggs.

As four uniformed officers walked on to the aircraft, Palmer closed his scruffy old brown leather case. Then he stood up and handed them his own passport. They studied it and pointed out it had expired. So Palmer closed his wrists together and, with a wry smile on his face, offered them to be handcuffed.

Hopefully, Palmer no doubt thought to himself, I'll be let free within hours thanks to a well-oiled lawyer and a few bribes paid in the right direction.

As Palmer was unceremoniously hauled off the aircraft and down the steps to the waiting police van, he began to sense something was wrong. The police were rough and uncompromising. He was pushed to the floor of the van, which smelt of urine and vomit, and the doors were slammed shut behind him.

John Palmer had just entered a faraway country where police brutality ruled.

Within minutes of arriving at the notoriously rundown Curado prison complex, in Recife, Palmer found himself being jeered and spat at by inmates in their cells as he was pushed down a greasy corridor towards the so-called 'gringo wing', where foreign inmates were afforded such luxuries as running water and holes in the ground to use as toilets.

Back in London, news of John Palmer's detention in Brazil made all the front pages. Inside their jail cells, Brink's-Mat robbers McAvoy and Robinson rolled their eyes and regretted the day they'd ever agreed to hire Palmer and Noye to turn their gold into cash. 'Those two clowns have fucked us royally in the arse,' one of them told another inmate. 'Fuckin' bastards. Where the fuck have they put our gold?'

Meanwhile John Palmer was trying his hardest to avoid eye contact with other prisoners and guards. However, he was 'advised' to pay out bribes for everything from a toothbrush to a guarantee he would not be forced to give the unit's richest drug baron a blowjob. Palmer was appalled. At one stage – just a few hours after his incarceration – he'd almost been knifed by a Chilean hitman after refusing to answer the man's questions about who he was and whether he had any cash to pay the man to ensure his personal safety.

Palmer later said he genuinely believed he wouldn't survive more than a couple of days inside that prison. Everyone had been told he was a rich gringo and they all wanted a piece of him.

The morning after his detention, Palmer was given what he presumed was a scumbag lawyer. The man immediately insisted Palmer sign a bank draft which would guarantee the lawyer a $10,000 down payment, irrespective of whether he could get him out of jail. Palmer was lucky. The lawyer proved as good as his word and negotiated Palmer's release with one condition: he was to get on the next flight back to London and never return.

Palmer had been stitched up by an unlikely collusion between the Brazilian, Spanish and UK authorities. The Brazilians had decided they didn't want Palmer because his presence could end up being much more embarrassing to them than that of Ronnie Biggs, who had after all fathered a child by a local woman. By this time, Brazil was trying to prove to the world it was a safe, honourable democracy and British criminal John Palmer reminded them of their troubled past.

*

So the Brink's-Mat job had finally come back to bite John Palmer squarely on the backside. Palmer was outraged that they were still after him because he didn't even consider himself a criminal. To him, he'd simply been helping move a bit of gold around. Sure, he knew it might be a bit 'dodgy' but, he'd later claim, he didn't want to know where it came from because none of that was his problem.

So after spending four 'horrific' nights in that Brazilian prison cell, John Palmer flew back to Heathrow, where he was immediately arrested and taken in a heavily guarded police convoy to Brixton Prison, in south London, to await a hearing.

CHAPTER ELEVEN

THE THINKING FACTORY

BRIXTON PRISON, SOUTH LONDON, JUNE 1986

Brixton Prison had been used for trial and remand prisoners in London since 1896 but it must have seemed to John Palmer like a holiday camp compared to that sweatshop in Recife, Brazil. The average population of Brixton Prison was around 1,000, but by the time Palmer arrived it was down to around the 600 mark. As one former inmate put it: 'We call Brixton the thinkin' factory because it's where the inmates lie on their bunks, hands behind their head thinkin' about who put them away, who they want revenge on and how the fuck they'll get out without serving loadsa bird.' John Palmer was given a single cell – measuring twelve feet by six feet – in Brixton because, as a remand prisoner, he was allowed a cell to himself.

Palmer was philosophical about his incarceration which he saw in terms of being part of his 'job'. He was confident that he wouldn't end up being found guilty, so it made his time in prison less troubling. He'd been refused bail on the basis he was a 'flight risk' but now he was biding his time.

Palmer's wife Marnie coped well with prison visits because she believed her husband was innocent. Marnie was allowed to bring in food such as sirloin steaks because he was a remand prisoner not yet found guilty in a court of law.

Palmer also sent three letters every week to Christine Ketley, his young mistress in Tenerife. He advised her to stay on the island and monitor the progress of their timeshare business. But Palmer was always very careful not to incriminate Ketley in any criminal activities.

Palmer's reputation as a 'respected professional criminal' ensured that most Brixton inmates and staff steered clear of him, apart from the bigger name criminals who were intrigued by the prisoner many said was one of the richest gangsters in the world. Palmer slipped into tough-guy-in-prison mode with ease. Eyes down, shoulders rounded, chewing gum. Palmer even applied for classes to try and help ease his lack of reading and writing skills but was told he wasn't eligible because he was a remand prisoner.

Palmer consistently denied to detectives that he knew anything about the original Brink's-Mat robbery, referring to it as the 'Matts Brink' job during interviews at Brixton Prison. He also had regular meetings with his then-solicitor in the lawyer's area at Brixton.

'Brixton is like a picnic compared to that jail in Brazil,' he told one associate. 'There were five murders a bleedin' day in there. Five murders, can you believe it?'

Other prisoners later said that Palmer was charming and very generous to his fellow inmates. 'He wasn't scared of anyone but he had a lot of sympathy for the no-hopers because he knew he could so easily have ended up like them,' explained one.

Palmer tried to help other inmates with their defence statements and cases because, as he later told an associate, 'Without any money in here you've had it, even if you're innocent.'

Palmer eventually recruited two of the country's best-known barristers to defend his case. Palmer then set about turning the defence case into a full-time job inside Brixton, bombarding his legal team with suggestions about how to approach the case. They weren't used to this level of interference but acknowledged that a lot of what Palmer suggested made complete sense.

Palmer also secretly helped finance the legal defence of three fellow inmates and paid out for a number of other prisoners to get help with their illiteracy. As he later told his associate: 'Just cos I can't read or write proper doesn't mean I want anyone else to suffer like me.'

In some ways, John Palmer was a walking contradiction. He was a greedy, cunning, deceitful villain yet there was a side to him that wanted to help people who were not as fortunate as him.

Palmer listened intently to everything the police told him when they came to see him in Brixton Prison, computing the long-term implications in his head and then telling them: 'No comment.' Palmer aimed to extract all the details of the case against him without actually helping the police with their inquiries.

One of Palmer's contacts inside the Metropolitan Police conveyed messages to the effect that detectives were struggling to come up with any concrete evidence that could directly link Palmer to the Brink's-Mat robbery itself. The Flying Squad's pride had been dented because they'd only ever managed to convict three members of the original Brink's-Mat gang, including the inside man. Yet half of the London underworld seemed to know the names of the other robbers who were never prosecuted.

As a result of this, the police had focused in on the criminals who handled the gold in the hope it might enable them to find a 'weak spot', thus enabling detectives to bring the rest of the actual robbers to justice.

From his prison cell in Brixton, Palmer authorized one of his associates to contact a police officer who had direct access to information ranging from car registration numbers to actual witness statements. Palmer wanted the names of witnesses in the case against him. No one knows to this day if he got hold of those details.

A few days later, a new member of staff joined John Palmer's wing at Brixton Prison and decided to do something about the TV set Palmer had in his cell. Palmer remained calm and in control, informing the prison governor he'd been watching an episode of *Rumpole* – a hit TV series at the time about a criminal defence barrister – when a couple of 'screws' had walked into his cell and taken the set away.

The governor knew as well as everyone else that professional criminals like John Palmer could get just about anything they wanted in prison if they paid enough for it. Palmer apologized for having the TV but refused to tell the governor which member of staff had supplied it, insisting that 'grassing' was something he never did.

Palmer suggested to the official that TVs should be allowed in every cell because they helped give inmates a diversion and relieved the boredom and frustration felt by so many, which often resulted in jailhouse violence. Funnily enough Palmer's words proved prophetic: the UK prison service later allowed TV sets in cells for that very same reason.

Meanwhile in another prison cell more than a hundred miles away, John Palmer's gold bullion associate Kenneth Noye was thinking a lot about Palmer. His attitude towards him was extremely ambivalent; he had his suspicions that Palmer might have done a deal with the police to guarantee he got an acquittal in his coming trial. But for the moment Palmer's incarceration on remand in Brixton seemed to imply he was keeping his mouth shut.

Just before Palmer's Old Bailey trial for the gold bullion smelting operation, a notorious old-school career criminal called John Fleming was extradited back to Britain from Florida. Fleming was accused of handling cash from the Brink's-Mat gold bullion robbery but eventually ended up spending just two minutes in the dock after a magistrate threw out the charges.

'What a great result,' said Palmer when he was told what had happened. He saw it as a good omen for his forthcoming trial.

Far from being dejected by a long stay in Brixton awaiting his trial, Palmer had been planning and scheming for what he now saw as his 'time' in court.

On the first day of the hearing in the spring of 1987, a number of jury members reported they'd been followed home. Palmer and his supporters later insisted it was the police trying to keep an eye on the jury in case anyone tried to interfere with justice. The police denied it.

Alongside Palmer in the dock was his old business associate Garth Chappell, who faced similar charges, although the evidence against him was more concrete because he'd been caught 'bang to rights' depositing those large sums of money in that local bank near Palmer's West Country home.

During the trial itself, prosecutors implied that Palmer was 'close' to Kenneth Noye because of a note of Noye's phone number which had been allegedly found scribbled on a telephone area-code directory in Palmer's house when police raided the property just after he'd fled to Tenerife.

Palmer denied such a note existed and later implied that the police wrote the number on his phone book to ensure they had sufficient evidence to link him to the stolen Brink's-Mat gold. Palmer's defence team even called a handwriting expert to give evidence during the case. Under careful examination in the witness box, the expert conceded that Noye's number might have been added later to the scrap of paper it was found on.

The expert also pointed out that they couldn't compare Palmer's handwriting with the number because Palmer couldn't write.

Palmer smiled as he heard the evidence, convinced that it showed the police in their true light.

Throughout the trial, Palmer and his defence team insisted he was nothing more than an innocent gold smelter, who'd been wrongly dragged into the Brink's-Mat inquiry. Palmer never denied melting down the bullion, but he claimed he did not realize it was stolen.

Palmer then told the jury that his timeshare business in Spain was worth £2.8 million so as to further convince them of his innocence. Why would a man worth so much money risk smelting a load of gold if he knew it was stolen? In actual fact, Palmer knew that his timeshare empire was already worth at least ten times that amount.

When the jury came back from their deliberations and announced that Palmer was 'not guilty' he leapt in the air with a broad smile on his face and blew a kiss in their direction. Then he tried to stifle his response because others in the dock with him had not been so lucky. Among them, Palmer's West Country business partner Garth Chappell was found guilty and jailed for ten years. The police and media were outraged by Palmer's acquittal. Everyone seemed to know Palmer was involved but his claims that he didn't know where the gold came from had won him an extraordinary reprieve.

Palmer later said he felt very sorry for Garth Chappell but felt that Chappell had not remained as steadfast over his lack of knowledge of where the gold had originated from and that had cost Chappell his liberty.

Unknown to John Palmer at the time, insurance investigators for Brink's-Mat – undeterred by the lack of criminal convictions connected to the robbery – had assembled a massive file on Palmer which proved to them he was involved and they intended to force Palmer to pay back some, if not all, of the value of the gold he'd smelted.

A few minutes after his acquittal, John Palmer appeared on the steps of the Old Bailey kissing and cuddling Marnie in front of a pack of reporters and TV cameras. Palmer milked the crowd and then headed to the nearby Ritz Hotel with his wife.

The couple stayed in a £500-a-night suite overlooking Green Park and Buckingham Palace. Marnie knew about his mistress Christine Ketley back in Tenerife.

The following morning John Palmer put on a bullet-proof vest under his shirt before he left the Ritz Hotel because he feared that a number of people wanted him dead, especially following his acquittal. Wearing that bullet-proof vest would become a habit for Palmer for the rest of his life.

PART
TWO

PALMER'S KINGDOM

1987–2007

It's my island and nothing and no one comes in and out of here without my sayso.

– John Palmer

CHAPTER TWELVE

ISLA LOCA (MAD ISLAND)

BRISTOL AIRPORT, SPRING 1987

As the crew busily prepared the private charter Learjet for takeoff, crates were placed in the aircraft's hold which it's rumoured contained small gold bullion bricks that John Palmer was intending to hide in Tenerife.

Minutes later, Palmer fastened his seatbelt as the Lear took off from Bristol airport. Palmer liked this aircraft immensely and decided that to celebrate his release and the ongoing success of his timeshare empire he was going to stick to that promise he'd made to himself to get his own Learjet very soon.

Then he picked up a copy of the *Sun*, saw his photo on the front page and handed it to one of his associates to read the headline and opening paragraph to him.

It began: *'Bullion dealer John "Goldfinger" Palmer walked free from the Old Bailey yesterday – to make a choice between the two women chasing his heart.'*

Meanwhile Palmer's long-suffering wife Marnie was facing a pack of reporters outside their seventeenth-century Battlefield home.

One journalist pointed out to Marnie that Palmer had told the press after his acquittal the previous day: 'I've got no mistress and I'm staying with my wife.'

A chorus of other journalists then yelled: 'Is that true, Marnie? D'you believe him? What about Christine Ketley?'

Marnie grimaced at the mention of her name but then smiled and responded: 'Of course, I believe him.'

Behind the smiles, Palmer had already agreed to give Battlefield to Marnie. It was said to be worth £2 million, not including her beloved horses.

John Palmer knew it was time for him to accept the inevitable and make a life for himself in Tenerife.

Sipping champagne as the chartered Learjet headed south towards the Bay of Biscay, Palmer told himself that he didn't need to take any more risks like the Brink's-Mat smelting job ever again. He could finally kiss goodbye to the dangerous end of criminality, thanks to Tenerife.

At the island's airport later that same day, Palmer was greeted by Christine Ketley and soon slipped back into his hard-nosed Tenerife persona. The Mister Big with his finger on the pulse. A chilling character who was starting to run an entire holiday island as if it was his own personal fiefdom.

The contrast between Palmer's now-estranged wife Marnie and Christine Ketley summed up the way Palmer's criminal career had evolved. Blonde, down-to-earth, working-class Marnie had always insisted on riding her horses and bringing up their two daughters in a safe, almost 'normal' environment.

Christine Ketley on the other hand came from a classically secure middle-class background in the suburbs of Essex and even spoke with a clipped English accent. She had a neat hairstyle and dressed very conservatively, although beneath that Middle

England exterior was the mind of a meticulous, highly trained accountant.

She'd helped run Palmer's timeshare empire as its profits soared while he was languishing in Brixton prison before his trial. Ketley also oversaw the reinvestment of the huge amounts of cash being earned through the timeshare business. Other, less legitimate businesses on the island were dealt with directly by Palmer. Ketley had no involvement in them.

Throughout all this Christine Ketley managed to avoid the limelight and keep her head down. She didn't have any interest in the 'bling' accessories adored by most gangster's molls. Her biggest expense was riding horses in the mountains above Las Americas, which meant she had more in common with Palmer's wife Marnie than either of them would have ever cared to admit.

Ketley was described by those who met her at the time as very cool, detached and efficient. One former neighbour later said: 'She's not like one of those [gangster's] dolly birds you see on TV. She dresses discreetly and speaks nicely. You wouldn't really notice her.'

Now he was back in Tenerife, it was business as usual for John Palmer. Besides the cocaine shipments and the timeshare empire, his gang of associates were also involved in money laundering, bribery, as well as firearms, falsifying passports and credit cards. Timeshare was without doubt the biggest earner but Palmer liked to keep all his other interests ticking along, just in case the timeshare bubble exploded. Palmer even used some of his new-found fortune to buy a couple of hotels, a few restaurants and a bowling alley on the island.

Meanwhile Palmer's money-laundering activities provided him with some unexpected 'bonuses', including a classic wood-framed yacht that was given to him in lieu of a large debt connected to money laundering. At first, Palmer didn't want the yacht since he was not exactly the nautical type; unable to swim and prone to extreme seasickness. But then it was pointed out that it would make a nice property for him to stay on when it was moored in the local marina. It was even renamed the *Brave Goose of Essex* in memory of Ketley's home county upbringing. Palmer didn't mind. He quite liked telling people he had a yacht and even encouraged them to think it was worth about £6 million, so it could soak up more of his dirty money. In fact it was worth about £1 million.

Back in the UK, old-school professional criminals were still spitting blood over Palmer's Old Bailey acquittal. Many were convinced he'd informed on his associates in exchange for his freedom. No one could understand how Palmer got off, despite all his blatant connections to the Brink's-Mat gold.

Palmer heard all this via one of his oldest and most trusted henchmen, who had close links to the London crime scene. But, typically, he chose to ignore it all.

Palmer intended pushing ahead with expanding his timeshare business into an even bigger empire. While he'd been away the business had brought in more than £30 million in revenue without, apparently, a law being broken. As Palmer told one of his timeshare executives at the time: 'This is the future.'

Palmer saw himself embarking on a fantasy lifestyle consisting of luxuries beyond his wildest dreams: private jets, the yacht, expensive cars, properties. It was going to be a never-ending cycle of money, money, money. Palmer immediately bought himself three classic sports cars through his UK car dealer and ordered them to be housed in a hangar on the edge of Bristol airport that was owned by the crime family he had befriended when he was working in the West Country. His intention was to eventually ship the vehicles over to Tenerife where he and Christine could take them out on Sundays for a spin in the mountains.

Palmer's financial associates advised him to continue spending his money because the Brink's-Mat insurance investigators looked to be on the verge of coming after him for compensation for the stolen gold. There were also the Spanish tax authorities to contend with.

Unknown to John Palmer, a young and ambitious Madrid-based lawman called Judge Baltasar Garzón Real was taking an interest in the British criminal after hearing worrying reports about rip-off timeshare property deals in Tenerife and Palmer's role in turning the island into his personal territory.

Garzón decided to set up a secret squad of investigators briefed with the task of nailing Palmer, however long it took. John Palmer represented everything that Garzón loathed about the foreign criminals who'd tainted his beloved nation with their drugs and vulgarity over the previous ten years. But for the moment, Garzón's operation would remain a heavily guarded secret.

Meanwhile John Palmer had other problems on his plate. He needed to 'iron out' some of the troublemakers in the UK and on the Costa del Sol who were still insisting Palmer must have done a deal with the police in order to get off the bullion-handling charges.

Palmer sent a couple of his Clumpers over to visit the two London crime family brothers Bill and Ben, who'd been Palmer and Noye's middlemen with the Brink's-Mat gang. The brothers assured Palmer's Clumpers that no one was angry with him and wished him well on his Tenerife business enterprises. 'He must be fuckin' loaded. Lucky bastard,' one of them said. It seemed that Palmer's timeshare bonanza had already been noted by the entire London underworld.

Palmer feared it was only a matter of time before Bill and Ben came knocking on his door. He considered getting all the big faces together for a meeting in Tenerife to explain himself, but then changed his mind.

'Sod 'em all,' Palmer told one associate. 'They're just jealous that I've found a way to make millions without robbing a bank.'

Palmer also insisted he hadn't used any of the Brink's-Mat gold smelting money to fund his timeshare expansion in Tenerife.

John Palmer's timeshare empire was rapidly cutting a swath across vast areas of the southern coastline of Tenerife; by this time, he was already developing a total of eleven resorts. Operating under the banner of 'The Palmer Group', all the resorts were either completed or in the process of being constructed. But the headquarters of the entire empire would always be the Holiday Village tower block located in the middle of Palmer's first resort in Las Americas.

With the timeshare business growing faster than anyone expected, John Palmer told Tel and the Clumpers to keep a close eye on any rival timeshare operations opening up on his territory. He didn't want them chipping away at his profit margins.

Meanwhile Madrid-based Judge Garzón had been in contact with Scotland Yard to start planning a pincer movement on Palmer. Garzón and Flying Squad chiefs named it Operation Beryk and it would focus entirely on Palmer's timeshare empire. Only a handpicked group of officers were even told about its existence. The Yard knew Palmer had some London detectives on his payroll and they wanted to ensure he didn't get wind of their plans. Investigators believed that eventually even a criminal as artful as John Palmer would make a mistake and they wanted to be there when he did.

In early 1987, John Palmer decided to outsource his southern Spain-based timeshare resorts through myriad companies, having ensured they were all virtually running themselves. He had plenty to do in Tenerife.

Palmer felt very safe on the island. It was self-contained and he could control every aspect of what was happening at any given time.

John Palmer even refused an invitation to the wedding of Security Express robber Ronnie Knight in Marbella because he so preferred it on Tenerife. There were too many informants and coke-addicted old-time villains loitering with intent along the fifty-mile stretch of coastline popularly known as the Costa del Crime.

Knight's wedding proceedings were watched by unmarked cars containing members of Scotland Yard's Flying Squad who photographed all the guests coming in and out of the bar where the wedding reception was held. Tabloid newspaper photographers spied with long-range telephoto lenses from motor launches and an overhead helicopter whirled away as it constantly circled the reception area.

Meanwhile, other forces were beginning to circle Palmer.

CHAPTER THIRTEEN

SENDING IN THE TROOPS

LAS AMERICAS, TENERIFE, JUNE 1987

By this time, and behind his back, John Palmer was already known to many of Tenerife's Spanish residents as 'El Capo'. There was a palpable fear of Palmer spreading across the south of the island. He was seen as a malignant force for evil, a man with a criminal background who'd leapfrogged to the top of the property ladder using money from criminal enterprises and intimidatory tactics to get people to buy into his timeshare empire.

When holidaymakers dared to complain about Palmer's sales team's heavy-handed tactics, senior henchmen like Tel would appear from a back office in the main resort headquarters to sort out any 'problems'.

Tel employed two South American criminals whom he'd first recruited while Palmer was in prison in the UK awaiting trial. The Latin pair known as 'Pedro' and 'Jaimie' drove around Las Americas in a black limousine and were nicknamed the Sharks by Palmer's timeshare staff.

'They were there purely to intimidate the timeshare moaners, as we called them,' one of Palmer's former timeshare executives later explained. 'The idea was to send a message to JP's time-share victims not to complain and it seemed to work because everyone knew who those guys were and what they were cap-able of doing.'

One time the Sharks visited a bar run by a couple who'd stupidly bought one of JP's timeshare apartments as a present for a relative. The Sharks strolled in, pulled out a knife each and began slashing at the blinds on the windows. It was a very unsubtle message but it did the trick because the couple imme-diately stopped complaining about their timeshare deal.

Despite the ever-increasing rumours of intimidation, Tener-ife's public officials and politicians were reluctant to criticize Palmer because he was a big employer, even though the majority of his workforce was British. Palmer tended to employ drifter-type Brits, many of whom were under the age of thirty and had arrived on the island as holidaymakers and then decided to stay on for the promise of big commissions.

Throughout this period, John Palmer portrayed himself as a hard-working family man who was simply trying to get his life back on track after being wrongly accused of involvement in the Brink's-Mat robbery. However, Palmer's day-to-day life in Tenerife summed up his own personal paranoia when it came to the criminals back in the UK who were 'after his blood'. Palmer rarely slept in one place for more than a few nights. He told associates he preferred to live that way and never openly admit-ted his fears for his life as he considered such a confession to be a sign of weakness. He also continued to wear a bullet-proof vest most of the time.

Occasionally, Palmer even slept at a special show villa in the heart of Las Americas, which was being used to tempt time-share customers into parting with their hard-earned cash. Sales staff were supposed to be told through a special series of secret codes if Palmer was in residence in the showhouse. They would then avoid showing any potential customers the property until Palmer had departed.

One former timeshare worker explained: 'But one time, we didn't get the message that JP was in residence and I walked into the villa with a bunch of tourists and found him in bed with a woman. He went ballistic. We all had a laugh about it behind his back but he sacked the manager who was responsible that very morning and I was lucky to escape any punishment.'

Palmer also had one top-secret property – a huge detached villa – built specially for him up in the mountains behind the island's capital, Santa Cruz. Even Christine Ketley was discouraged from visiting the villa because it was supposed to be for Marnie and their daughters whenever they came to the island from the UK.

In the main staff office on the first floor of the Holiday Village skyscraper in Las Americas, Christine Ketley ran a small army of accountants who spent much of their time counting the cash that was pouring in from the timeshare business. Not even John Palmer could believe how much money was being made without having to break the law. However, there were also other huge injections of cash Palmer kept secret from Ketley and his timeshare staff. These came via his other more nefarious criminal activities on the island, ranging from money laundering to drugs to arms smuggling.

All this cash brought with it immense power for John Palmer. He was the self-proclaimed leader of the southern half of a sunshine island more than two thousand miles from the UK.

At the entrance on the ground floor of the Island Village headquarters, John Palmer encouraged receptionist Flo Robinson to run a tight ship. Palmer also employed Flo's husband Billy as a Clumper and there was even a vague rumour that Palmer had a soft spot for Flo, who resembled Elizabeth Taylor as she looked in middle age.

The lobby of the Holiday Village building was the hub of Palmer's entire timeshare empire and Flo Robinson witnessed everything from fights to threats to tears. 'But it all seemed to go right over Flo's head,' explained one former timeshare salesman. 'Flo's husband Billy was a tough-looking fella but he always had a smile on his face and actually turned out to be one of life's true optimists. Both of them got on incredibly well with JP. They used to go out for dinner with him sometimes.'

If ever anyone on the staff complained about Flo's short-tempered Jack Russells Sid and Nancy, Palmer laughed it off and said he liked having the dogs around. Billy Robinson even often took Sid and Nancy with him when he went out on 'Clumping Business'.

One of the couple's friends later recalled: 'Billy loved to eat and drink and he'd buy you a meal and booze all night the first time you met him. But you could know him a year and he'd hardly speak two actual sentences to you. Flo was an angel though, a real mother figure who made everyone feel welcome and she couldn't stop talking.'

So while characters like Flo and Billy Robinson may well have considered themselves to be John Palmer's friends, the feeling wasn't mutual. Palmer continued to struggle with the entire concept of friendship as such. One old associate said: 'If it wasn't about a deal then JP wasn't interested in you. End of story.'

Flo Robinson was described by many who knew her as a bubbly brunette with a real appetite for life. 'Everybody loved Flo,' recalled one of her former colleagues in Tenerife. 'She used to love doing tarot card readings and said that one day she wanted to give up the timeshare game and become Tenerife's Mystic Meg.'

Flo and Billy regularly hosted poker nights at their house behind Las Americas and sometimes the stakes were said to be 'sky high'. Husband Billy was eventually promoted from Clumper to being a senior timeshare salesman and quickly became one of Palmer's top performers when it came to the art of a timeshare deal. Billy later boasted to one colleague that he had more than £600,000 in the bank.

'What I don't understand,' said that same colleague, 'is why the pair of them didn't just fuck off back to north London with all that money. They were getting very flashy with their cash and it certainly rubbed some people up the wrong way.'

By this time, around four million tourists were visiting Tenerife each year. And despite the rumours of timeshare intimidation, few holidaymakers seemed to realize that behind the sunshine image lurked an underbelly of crime and violence mainly fuelled by one man – John Palmer.

Palmer believed he could retain power and influence on Tenerife as long as his staff didn't step out of line. He encouraged all of them to socialize only with each other and even got his main henchman Tel to tour the bars of Las Americas some nights to check out what his staff were up to.

'It certainly had the desired effect,' one timeshare staff member later recalled. 'We stuck together like glue. But part of the reason was because everyone else hated our guts! It was a very closed world. We worked together, socialized together, even the sons and daughters married into other timeshare executives' families. But tread on the wrong man's patch or shag the wrong man's wife and you'd soon know about it. You'd be threatened, beaten and most likely ordered to leave the island.'

John Palmer would hear about it all. He'd learned from that West Country family and the brothers Bill and Ben from the London crime family that knowing everything was the key to controlling an empire.

In Tenerife, few police officers dared to point out the way that Palmer had been allowed to ride roughshod over most of the south of the island without any real interference. When one of Judge Garzón's detectives from the National Police in Madrid turned up on the island to take a closer look at Palmer's timeshare empire, he was ignored by some individual officers. The mainland detective soon realized that a combination of lawlessness, fear and corruption had been spread throughout the southern half of the island very effectively by Palmer and it would take a lot of time and effort to win it back from him.

The same investigator also studied reports about tourists being conned by Palmer's timeshare staff.

It was clear that scams perpetuated by Palmer's staff trod a thin legal line by getting the timeshare owner to come to Tenerife to meet a potential buyer, but then selling them another package, cruise or holiday, with the promise that this would help seal the deal.

It seemed that John Palmer didn't care what his staff did as long as it brought big helpings of cash flowing in.

Back in the UK, many inside the underworld were continuing to claim that not only had John Palmer stitched up other gangsters in exchange for his freedom, but he'd used all that Brink's-Mat gold money to turn himself into a multimillionaire timeshare mogul.

Palmer hit back once again by insisting his timeshare empire was already a success before the Brink's-Mat robbery. He claimed his chain of West Country jewellery stores and other business interests had provided the money he'd needed to launch the timeshare business.

Then Scotland Yard detectives also began openly saying that Palmer had ripped off his Brink's-Mat colleagues. Palmer believed this was just another example of detectives trying to get him killed because they'd been so humiliated by his acquittal.

John Palmer's workaholic personality was already having a serious impact on his relationship with Christine Ketley. She and Palmer rarely went out together because he was usually exhausted when he arrived back at whichever home they happened to be staying in that night. Palmer would often then cocoon himself inside the bedroom and hardly exchanged a word with Ketley.

One day, realizing he was in danger of turning into a hermit, Palmer announced to Christine Ketley they were off for a weekend in Las Vegas. But, as ever, he had an ulterior motive.

CHAPTER FOURTEEN

BANDITS THREE O'CLOCK

NEVADA DESERT, 100 MILES EAST OF LAS VEGAS, MAY 1988

After a night out on the Vegas Strip, Palmer drove Ketley one hundred miles out into the Nevada desert to view a 1985 Learjet which was being sold for $3 million by an American gangster who specialized in selling second-hand executive aircraft. It was a bargain price at a time when there was a slump in the market. Palmer paid for the plane with cash.

John Palmer knew the Learjet would wind up his enemies on the Costa del Crime and in the UK but he was sick of hiding his wealth away. As he told one associate many years later: 'Bollocks to 'em. I earned the right to buy that plane because I worked my arse off.'

Naturally, news of the purchase did soon reach the underworld. One old associate later explained: 'Yeah. They was green with envy. Here was JP, lording it up earning tens of millions and most of them were down to their last few grand. And not many of them could accept that JP had earned it through hard graft, either.'

The other reason why Palmer had bought the Learjet was

that estranged wife Marnie wanted her husband to see more of their daughters back at Battlefield, in the West Country. The girls were growing up without a father and Marnie wanted Palmer to step up to the plate more. Some of Palmer's oldest associates later claimed that Marnie may also have been trying to win her husband back from the clutches of Christine Ketley, whom she loathed.

The Palmer plane had eight seats, six windows and a 3,000-mile range, which meant Palmer could get between Tenerife and the UK in one hop. One associate who later flew regularly on Palmer's Learjet described it thus: 'It wasn't exactly roomy but the convenience of having your own air transport was obvious. JP was in control of his own destiny, literally.'

Palmer's decision to purchase his own aircraft had also been greatly influenced by his associates, the West Country crime family, who guaranteed he could enter and leave the perimeter of Bristol airport using their nondescript farm gate on a quiet country lane. It led to the hangar where Palmer intended to keep the jet whenever he was in the UK.

Palmer himself described the Bristol airport set-up as 'the perfect scenario'. One associate who flew many times with Palmer later explained: 'Custom controls back then were not what they became after 9/11. JP agreed to pay a big rent for the hangar and in exchange he was given virtually the free run of the airport. It meant he and his crew only had to write their names in a log when they arrived and did not even have to show their actual passports.'

Palmer insisted on keeping one of his now-obligatory bullet-proof vests in a cupboard on board his Learjet at all times. He believed he was particularly vulnerable to an 'enemy' bullet when he got on board and disembarked the aircraft either in that deserted corner of Bristol airport or at Tenerife South-Reina Sofia airport, where he would also have access to a hangar away from the main terminal. After each flight, Palmer paid his pilot and co-pilot with an envelope containing £50 notes. The fee varied, depending on how long the crew had had to wait around in Tenerife or Bristol. As far as the crew were concerned, Palmer was a timeshare tycoon, who paid them out of the vast profits from his legitimate business.

'JP would burst into the cockpit just after landing with a smile on his face and say "Good job, lads" and drop those envelopes in their laps,' added one source.

But Palmer's 'arrangements' with the customs at each airport came at a price. One source explained: 'Tenerife was the most expensive. JP had to splash out about £100,000 a year to make sure he wasn't bothered by any standard passport checks. But he told me it was money well spent.'

Palmer was soon using his Learjet as often as other people use a taxi. Palmer later admitted to an associate that things got so hectic at one stage that he'd find himself waking up in his Learjet, after a brief shuteye, having forgotten where he was heading.

Palmer often joked that having the Learjet at his disposal was 'worth its weight in gold'. This was a deliberate dig at the Brink's-Mat villains who continued to slag him off for his role in smelting down the bullion.

Each flight between Tenerife and Bristol cost approximately £5,000 in fuel so if Palmer had a full flight – six people – it really wasn't all that expensive.

Before every flight Palmer insisted that one of his Clumpers use an electronic monitor to check for bugs being planted on the plane. Palmer had started hearing rumours that some judge in Madrid had joined forces with the police in London to try to nail him.

The crew never saw any weapons being taken on board the Learjet. But there is no doubt guns were sometimes carried by Palmer and his associates. One source later claimed that Palmer provided a wooden box, which was produced inside the hangar and used to store all weapons before any passengers were allowed on board.

Back at this time, customs officials in both Tenerife and Bristol never made inspections as long as the so-called 'GenDec' flight-plan forms had been filled in ahead of takeoff. One who travelled on the plane explained: 'That form was signed off and left with customs hours earlier and sometimes even the previous evening if it was an early morning flight. That flight could take off without anyone knowing who or what was on board.'

The source added: 'JP once said that he wished he'd bought a plane ten years earlier. It gave him complete and utter freedom. He could go anywhere and do anything and no one could keep tabs on him.'

Palmer also made a substantial additional income by leasing out his aircraft to other criminals and sometimes even law-abiding business folk.

Back in the UK, Palmer was constantly adding to his burgeoning collection of classic sports cars, some of which he obtained from people who owed him large sums of money. One associate later said: 'JP was like a glorified pawnbroker in some ways. He loved doing a deal. He'd lend out money and take some of these cars as collateral in case the debts were not repaid and then often keep them.'

Palmer never tried to sell the vehicles on and began storing them in the same Bristol airport hangar where he now parked his private jet. One old associate explained the thinking behind this decision. 'JP was a clever speculator. He knew that classic cars like Ferraris, Maseratis and Mercedes would eventually shoot up in value so he sat on them, safe in the knowledge they were going to pay him back a lot more interest than a high-street bank.'

One time Palmer showed a rare public glimpse of his temper when he caught one of his Learjet staff sitting in one of his classic cars – an old convertible Cadillac – inside the hangar at Bristol airport. One source later revealed: 'Palmer crept up behind him and went ape-shit. The pilot nearly jumped out of his skin with fright.'

The hangar where Palmer housed his Learjet plane when he was in the UK was run with almost military precision. One of them had a handlebar moustache and greatly amused Palmer with his clipped accent and dated appearance. Palmer told the man he looked like a Spitfire pilot from the Second World War. Palmer even occasionally used 1940s fighter-plane phrases like 'bandits three o'clock' once they were airborne just as they had used during the war. Other times Palmer yelled 'Dive Dive Dive'. The pilots responded in a typically professional manner by laughing politely and then completely ignoring all Palmer's quips.

Palmer's crew eventually christened the Learjet 'The Battle-field Express' in honour of Palmer's manor house where wife Marnie now lived alone with their two daughters, although his visits to see them had greatly increased since his purchase of that private jet.

Back in Tenerife, John Palmer launched an 'offensive' to try to improve his image and reputation among residents in the south of the island. Palmer began making donations to local charities and organizations and appearing at charity functions, frequented by the island's rich and famous. At one such event, Palmer came face-to-face with Judge Garzón, on the island getting updates from his investigators who were secretly probing Palmer's affairs.

The two men exchanged pleasantries. It was only afterwards that John Palmer realized this was the same judge who was trying to nail him. Palmer even had a secret nickname for Garzón. He called him 'The Black Judge'.

In Las Americas, John Palmer felt safe surrounded by his Clumpers and with enough money to bribe anyone who had something he wanted. Palmer was immensely proud of his henchmen – although he tried to avoid calling them 'Clumpers' in public.

One of Palmer's all-time favourites was an American ex-soldier called Psycho Bill who'd been recruited by Tel. One of Palmer's oldest associates later recalled: 'We all only knew him as Psycho Bill, which tells you everything. He'd been shot to shit in Vietnam where he'd been a sniper. Tel met him when he was working as a mercenary in Liberia.'

Psycho Bill had turned up in Tenerife after hearing the beaches had huge Atlantic waves which were ideal for surfing. He talked like a stoned hippy with a southern drawl and used the word 'man' in every sentence. Psycho Bill also had a cannabis spliff hanging out of his mouth at most times of the day and night.

Palmer liked Bill because he didn't look like a criminal and he certainly didn't act like one either. 'Bill was always banging on about peace and love and then he'd hammer anyone who got in his way,' explained one of Palmer's old associates.

John Palmer insisted Psycho Bill was by his side wherever he was staying on the island. But his 'career' came to a premature end when he beat up one of Palmer's Las Americas enemies so badly that the man was rumoured to have died from his injuries.

Palmer's former associate explained: 'Bill had to disappear for a while but he never came back. Last I heard he was living in a shack on a beach in the north of Tenerife where they had the biggest surfing waves.'

Palmer later discovered from a police contact in America that Psycho Bill had been on the run from the FBI because he was a suspected serial killer. Palmer's old associate added: 'JP thought that was fuckin' funny and used to tell everyone he wished Bill had done some serial killing on Tenerife.'

Meanwhile John Palmer encouraged his Lebanese henchman Tel and his equally large kid brother to 'front up' many of his more dubious activities, including collecting protection money from many of the bars and clubs located near Palmer's timeshare resorts.

The two Lebanese brothers were even more hated than Palmer out on the streets of Las Americas. If anyone complained to Palmer about them, he'd pretend he'd talk to the brothers without any intention of doing so. Palmer preferred to leave them pretty much to their own devices.

Even when one of Palmer's most trusted Clumpers told him that Tel had been dealing in cocaine behind his back, Palmer chose to ignore it. He wanted to have a hold over Tel in case anything really big flared up.

John Palmer didn't like his Clumpers stepping out of line, though. When one of them beat up two street prostitutes after refusing to pay them for sex, he was hauled in front of Palmer and told that what he had done was 'out of order'.

This particular Clumper was another one of Tel's recruits, so Palmer wondered if the incident had been deliberately set up to make him look bad.

One of Palmer's associates later recalled: 'JP had already given this lad a final warning after a similar incident, so he decided the fella needed to be taught a lesson because violence to women was something JP would not tolerate.'

John Palmer read the riot act to the man and then slipped out of his office in the Holiday Village complex just as the man was being tipped upside down on a chair. Moments later the was hit over the head with a small leather cosh. Palmer listened stony faced just outside the door as his Clumpers smashed the man with chairs and ashtrays before kicking and punching him while he lay on the ground.

Then Palmer knocked on the door, opened it and said: 'That's enough, lads.'

He'd wanted to make sure the word went round about what happens to anyone who attacked innocent folk, especially women and children. This was John Palmer's very own twisted version of good public relations.

Five minutes later, the man was bundled out of a car in a quiet side street in Las Americas and told to go and get himself a stiff drink because he was a 'very lucky fella'.

CHAPTER FIFTEEN

THE ULTIMATE ENTERTAINERS

LAS AMERICAS, TENERIFE, SUMMER 1989

Most of the British holidaymakers who turned up in John Palmer's 'manor' of south Tenerife were the sort of people who preferred Benidorm to the Greek Islands. Palmer himself adored classic English seaside entertainment like sing-songs, vaudeville, stand-up comics and drag queens. So he began employing light entertainers to give vaudeville-type shows to entertain his time-share resort customers.

When they weren't on stage, Palmer put his troupe to other uses. One stand-up comedian who worked in the Holiday Village resort at the time explained: 'JP employed a bunch of us ranging from drag queens to stand-up comics. I called myself Elvis the Eel and even wore an Elvis wig and cracked jokes about Las Vegas. At first we was all delighted to get regular work as it was rare at our end of the showbiz trail. JP even paid decent wages for an entire season with accommodation thrown in on a sunny holiday island. What could be better?'

The comic continued: 'But some of us were roped in to do JP's heavy work if he was short of Clumpers. We even went round Las Americas doing some debt collecting for JP at one stage. It was part of the deal and was made clear to us from the beginning. If we refused, we'd end up on the next bucket shop flight home.'

On a few occasions, John Palmer thought it would be amusing if his team of entertainers collected his debts in 'full costume'. The same comic explained: 'We must have looked well weird. One guy was dressed up as a clown. Another was in full drag and I was in my Elvis outfit although I sounded more like Tommy Cooper. JP reckoned it was a good way to not be recognized in case there were any problems with the police. But I think he just found it very funny.'

When Tel and his brother failed to show up one evening, Palmer ordered a drag queen called 'Bobbi' to visit all the bars and clubs who paid him weekly protection money. The stand-up comic explained: 'Bobbi had been an armed bank robber in his previous life and he was built like the proverbial brick shithouse, so he knew exactly how to get money out of people.'

When one bar owner told Bobbi to 'fuck off' he produced an iron bar from under his dress and smashed it over the head of the owner before setting light to the barman's beard. The bar paid up immediately.

Palmer 'laughed his head off' when he heard what had happened and congratulated Bobbi because his attack on that owner would ensure that no one else stepped out of line when they heard what had happened.

John Palmer showed immense loyalty to his crew of light entertainers, which was completely out of character. When Elvis the Eel discovered that his own parents had been tricked into buying a timeshare property by Palmer's staff, he demanded a meeting with Palmer. The same man explained: 'I was spitting blood because my mum and dad were only there to see me doing a stand-up at the Holiday Village. Then one of JP's bastard touts had twisted their arm, dragged them into the reception and got them to sign on the dotted line before they knew what had hit them.'

Elvis the Eel continued: 'I was taking a really big risk confronting JP because we all knew what he was capable of. But this was my mum and dad we were talking about. So, I burst into JP's office and started ranting at him about what happened. JP looked me straight in the eye and I thought he was about to pull out a gun on me. He didn't say a word for ages and then he said he'd get the contract cancelled immediately and how sorry he was.

'I was stunned. Then JP asked me to sit down on a sofa next to his desk. A few seconds later, he stood over me and said very quietly, "Don't ever come in here like that again, son. If it had been another day I'd have had you taken out of here on a stretcher."'

John Palmer had evolved into a lawless leader of a marauding group of insurgents determined to take over every profitable business and squeeze money out of every holidaymaker who turned up on the southern half of Tenerife. Palmer was buying up acres of previously unusable wasteland, bribing the local planning department to get permission to build entire resorts and then having those resorts constructed in double-quick time.

Palmer needed conduits to launder the vast amount of money his timeshare empire was raising, so he bought at least three more restaurants in Santa Cruz, and even ran them at a loss deliberately, so they'd soak up his cash in order to be claimed against tax.

But Palmer's most outrageous building project put everything else in the shade. He'd purchased yet more wasteland but decided it was too near to the capital to turn into a viable timeshare complex. So he got planning permission to build the island's first and biggest waterpark.

To John Palmer that waterpark was the ultimate 'in joke'. He liked telling his criminal associates he'd only built it so he could 'wash' all his dirty money. Most of his close associates heard the joke many times but made sure they laughed out loud every single time.

The waterpark itself featured an enormous slide and became very popular with holidaymakers and residents alike. But behind Palmer's back some in authority on the island felt insulted by the fact that Palmer 'the criminal' now owned one of the island's biggest tourist attractions.

Back in Madrid, the waterpark was greeted with incredulity by Judge Garzón. He tried to use it to put pressure on local government officials in Tenerife to help expose Palmer's criminal activities but they seemed terrified of the mere mention of Palmer's name.

In 1989, one of Palmer's most loud-mouthed criminal associates decided to turn over half of the London underworld. Michael Michael – whom John Palmer had originally met through Bill and Ben, those two London crime family brothers involved in the Brink's-Mat deal – became a Scotland Yard police informant. Michael was an accountant who'd been helping run a string of massage parlours with his common-law wife, Lynn. He'd been arrested on suspicion of a £3 million mortgage fraud that seemed to be connected to money laundering.

In exchange for a relatively light eight-month prison sentence, Michael became a registered informant and was even given the pseudonym Andrew Ridgeley, after the singing partner of George Michael, from the 1980s pop duo *Wham!*.

Michael passed information about various London criminals and their activities in the UK and Spain to his police handler. Copies of Michael Michael's contact sheets (forms filed by his police handler) named a bunch of John Palmer's associates as being involved in major drug-smuggling rings. Informant Michael also told police Palmer was laundering large sums of money from his base in Tenerife.

Michael claimed to have laundered huge amounts of cash for Palmer through a currency exchange bureau, especially set up in West London for this purpose. Women were often hired as couriers to fly the cash in from Tenerife with two-week return tickets. But instead of staying, they usually returned the following day.

Michael Michael told police how he'd paid out tens of thousands of pounds in bribes to corrupt police officers on behalf of numerous criminals, including John Palmer, in exchange for information about other criminals and ongoing police investigations. Detectives known to have gambling or drug problems were also named by Michael. Michael claimed that such information was often sold on to the highest bidder within the criminal underworld.

In Madrid, Judge Garzón read an outline of Michael Michael's statement with interest because it dovetailed exactly with what they'd been hearing about Palmer's money laundering activities.

However, there were also still problems when it came to extraditing British criminals back to the UK, even though the treaty between the UK and Spain had supposedly been reimposed and should have meant Spain was no longer a bolthole for fugitives.

But Spanish laws remained complicated and open to abuse;

in theory a foreigner could be expelled if he'd served more than a year's imprisonment in another country or if his presence was an embarrassment to a nation considered friendly. But for the moment, the Spanish still only required foreigners living in their country to have a genuine up-to-date passport in order not to be thrown out, as John Palmer had found to his cost when he took off for Brazil while on the run from those earlier bullion-smelting charges.

John Palmer still definitely had an eye for the ladies, though. He began a relationship with a beautiful German student called Saskia Mundinger, who was working as a sales rep for his time-share operation. Some of Palmer's associates say that Palmer was completely smitten by Saskia. Eventually, she announced she was pregnant and returned to her family in Germany to have the child.

Palmer was so swept up by Saskia that initially he followed her to Germany on his private jet and insisted on attending the birth of the child. He even made his older brother Malcolm godfather to the child. But then his lawyer warned him that he risked being deported to the UK from Germany if any charges were made against him.

So Palmer flew off again, leaving Saskia to bring up the child alone. He eventually agreed to pay her an allowance of £60,000 a year. It was a small price to pay for her silence but Palmer saw little of the child, a boy called Parisch, even after Saskia eventually moved to London.

Saskia later said she pulled away from Palmer when he broke his promises to see his son. She explained: 'When Parisch was six I asked John not to see him as it was breaking his heart when he didn't turn up.'

Back in Tenerife, Christine Ketley was relieved when Palmer returned to the island safely, unaware of the true reason for his most recent 'business trip'.

In Madrid, Judge Garzón was now also looking closely at Tel's activities as Palmer's henchman and concluded that the Lebanese ex-militiaman might prove to be the weak link when it came to nailing Palmer. Garzón's police agents on Tenerife had evidence from other criminals that Tel was secretly developing many of his own criminal enterprises, including money laundering on behalf of foreign criminals now based on the island. Also, Tel had undeniably close connections to terrorists in the Middle East.

Out on the mean streets of Las Americas, Tel and his brother continued knocking down doors and threatening violence and retribution. One British couple who wanted to open a bar in Las Americas were told they needed to visit Tel's office 'for advice'. They found him surrounded by five bodyguards and, said one witness, 'his upper lip was sweating profusely and his eyes were darting everywhere from the amount of cocaine he'd been shoving up his nose all day.'

Tel told the couple he wanted six million pesetas (£24,000) to arrange all the relevant council licences for the bar, plus another 60,000 (£240) pesetas protection money each month. For that, Tel told them, 'You only have to pick up the phone if you need help. If there's trouble in your bar, whatever, we will make it disappear. But if you don't pay . . .'

One of Tel's henchmen on the island later recalled: 'Tel knew everyone. He even started referring to Tenerife as "my island". Tel told me once that nothing could happen on the island without his permission. He was starting to sound more and more like JP.'

It seemed to some that Tel had also grown closer to the island's police than even Palmer had. One source said that around this time Tel paid for a police basketball-team strip as a 'gesture of good will'.

And it wasn't just trigger-happy ex-militiamen who were using John Palmer's name on the streets of Las Americas. When Palmer heard that a barmaid in one of the most popular taverns on the Golden Mile was claiming she'd been Palmer's secret lover for years, he dispatched drag queen 'Clumper' Bobbi to pay her a visit. The woman never mentioned the alleged affair again and refused to speak to a reporter who tried to expose the story a few months later when the rumours reached the British newspapers.

When Judge Garzón discovered that John Palmer was so rich he'd been able to afford his own private jet, he ordered his men working undercover in Tenerife to monitor the Learjet closely and asked his Scotland Yard counterparts to do the same whenever the aircraft was in the UK.

Perhaps not surprisingly, John Palmer's own personal sense of paranoia increased significantly around this time. He not only wore his bullet-proof vest whenever he got on and off his Learjet but he also started using it when he was out and about generally, whether it was in the West Country or Tenerife.

One associate later explained: 'JP said the vest made him feel more secure. One time we arrived in Tenerife on the Learjet and there was a panic on board because the bullet-proof vest had gone missing and he didn't want to leave the aircraft without it.'

Palmer sat on the plane for more than half an hour until one of his Clumpers came back with another vest for him to wear.

John Palmer also used his Learjet plane to spend more time in the West Country in a noble attempt to show estranged wife Marnie that he was a good father. Driving through the Wiltshire countryside in the dead of night to and from Bristol airport became a regular occurrence. Palmer later joked that his Range Rover was so used to the ten-mile journey that it could have driven itself.

He would head down a nearby dual carriageway and then turn right into an underused country lane, which then led to two more small left-hand turns that eventually took him past a golf-club entrance before finally reaching the gate. Palmer's car would stop while either he or one of his Clumpers got out and undid the latch of the gate. Then his vehicle would move slowly and quietly up a muddy track leading straight to the hangar where his Learjet was housed.

Usually, Palmer called ahead so the Lear – registration number N-37Z – would already have been towed out of the hangar and waiting on the tarmac with the steps extended. Palmer would then swing his car right up beside the aircraft before heading up the six steps and inside to take his seat. A Clumper would then jump in the car and park it round the back of the hangar.

One engineer who sometimes worked on Palmer's aircraft later recalled: 'It was usually all done with military precision. I remember one time I arrived at the hangar just as JP was getting into his plane and we stopped and chatted. But I noticed JP seemed anxious to get on the aircraft as quickly as possible so we didn't talk for long. He kept looking over his shoulder as if someone was going to come out of the nearby woods and shoot him.'

John Palmer's timeshare employees were well aware that if any of them discussed their work with outsiders they would most probably receive a visit from Tel and his mob. Palmer wanted to keep a lid on his working practices. He believed the timeshare business had still not peaked and he wanted more 'mugs' to buy into his once-in-a-lifetime concept. He also wanted to make sure none of his staff were ever tempted to talk to the police in either Spain or the UK.

Outside on the streets near to Palmer's eleven resorts, his timeshare hustlers continued to be paid £50 for getting any tourist into a taxi and then through the main doors to the Holiday Village complex where they'd most likely be greeted by motherly Flo Robinson and her two Jack Russell terriers Sid and Nancy.

John Palmer had always prided himself on his ability to judge people and he became deeply troubled by one of the Colombian reps, who'd flown into Tenerife for a meeting to discuss Palmer's cocaine shipment deal with the South Americans.

The man – known as 'The Professor' – had been despatched to the island to try and reduce Palmer's monthly fee for waving through their shipments of cocaine. One of Palmer's oldest associates later explained: 'The Professor was German and JP said he had no doubt the bloke was an old Nazi. He'd admitted settling in South America after the last war. He was over seventy and wore a white suit and fedora and seemed to come from another planet.'

The Professor asked Palmer a lot of pointed questions about his operation and whether he felt that his connection to the Brink's-Mat case and all the missing gold might endanger the safety of the Colombian cocaine shipments.

As usual, Palmer was slow in coming forward and there were some long periods of silence between the two men. Eventually, the Professor asked for a brandy, downed it in one and promptly began talking more like an SS officer than a coke baron.

The same associate later explained: 'JP said this old Nazi then started banging on about how he'd killed people in the past so he kept quiet and just let him rant.'

Then the Professor accused Palmer of trying to steal some of the Colombians' cocaine. This infuriated Palmer who reacted by not only denying it but suggesting maybe it was time to end their 'special agreement'.

The Professor informed Palmer that *no one* had the right to pull out from a deal with the Colombians. Only they would decide if that was to happen.

The meeting with the Professor ended with Palmer realizing that for the moment he had no choice but to continue the Colombian deal and he even accepted a lower monthly 'retainer'. But Palmer decided there and then that he needed to get out of the deal before any more 'evil Nazi bastards' came across the Atlantic for face-to-face chats.

But at least Palmer came away from that meeting with something useful. He'd used his trusty handheld tape recorder and knew that having a record of what had just been said might prove invaluable during any future negotiations with the Colombians.

Guns were undoubtedly a part of daily life in Las Americas. Tel travelled everywhere with a sawn-off shotgun and his brother carried at least one automatic. John Palmer tried to dissuade the Lebanese brothers from carrying firearms in the daytime because he didn't want any shootouts provoking Spanish law enforcement into cracking down on his operations. Palmer had even convinced one of his senior police contacts on the island that he'd keep arms off the streets if he was allowed to get on with his own activities without interruption from the police.

Palmer himself only very occasionally carried a gun and he certainly was not in the habit of pulling it out to make any veiled threats.

However, Palmer, Tel and his brother, plus an assortment of Clumpers and the occasional visitor often made a five-mile trek up into the mountains behind Las Americas to do some target practice. Most of the guns were supplied from arms shipments that Palmer had a share in. Occasionally, some extra entertainment was provided thanks to bigger weapons such as bazookas, short-range rocket launchers said to be able to take out a tank at fifty metres. These weapons came through the same illegal shipping 'lanes' as the Colombians' cocaine.

One time, Palmer and two associates killed three deer with one bazooka rocket and then had to hotfoot it from the mountainside when a local farmer reported them to the police.

On other occasions, Palmer took visiting criminals with him for a day out at a disused quarry which had been turned into a makeshift shooting range. Palmer insisted on using full-scale paper targets shaped like a man, similar to those used on military firing ranges. He even joked to one associate that he bought them from certain individuals with the island's police force when in fact that was absolutely true. Palmer encouraged visitors to take home their paper targets complete with bullet holes to show their friends and relatives.

But, as ever, John Palmer's days out in the mountains had an ulterior motive. He wanted to show his enemies back in the UK that he and his men were tooled up with a variety of weapons at all times and would take on anyone who dared to invade his territory.

Back in Madrid, Judge Garzón received new intelligence from Tenerife that groups of men identified as Palmer's 'security men' had been attacking rival timeshare workers with knives and baseball bats. Sometimes cars were even set on fire and properties smashed up. On one occasion a British rep had been shot during one such vicious turf war between Palmer's Clumpers and a rival timeshare outfit. Palmer's henchmen were also charging rival timeshare companies a fee if they went ahead and opened their businesses on the island.

And leading those 'units' of thugs on behalf of John Palmer were Tel and his brother. They in turn would dial in their two favourite South Americans, the Sharks, who'd drive slowly around the streets of Las Americas in their sinister black limousine reminding everyone who was in charge.

CHAPTER SIXTEEN

HAMMER AND TONGS

MARBELLA, COSTA DEL SOL, SPAIN, EARLY 1990

Sometimes John Palmer used his private jet for the most menial of tasks. Once he blew £10,000 on fuel getting the Learjet to fly from Tenerife to London to drop off some tickets for a big football match because Palmer had promised them to the two London crime family brothers Bill and Ben.

Then, during a brief visit to Spain's Costa del Sol, Palmer signed away total control of his three timeshare resorts on the mainland to a business associate after a gang of old-school London gangsters connected to the Brink's-Mat gang tried to muscle in on Palmer's operation. Palmer didn't mind pulling out of the Costa del Crime because he sensed it was a dangerous environment with hitman shootings on virtually a weekly basis and most villains so drunk and high on cocaine that they'd pick a fight with anyone they could lay their hands on.

While in Marbella, Palmer shared a couple of pints with some old faces, including some of the so-called 'guv'nors' of the Costa del Crime at the time. All of them were on the run from British police for a variety of heavyweight crimes. Palmer explained to them why he'd pulled out of the area. He insisted that the

Costa del Sol timeshare development was not as successful as his Tenerife operation.

He also held a meeting with one of his underworld heroes, Great Train Robber Charlie Wilson, who was looking for partners in a cocaine deal. Wilson introduced Palmer to a 4ft-8in-tall local Spanish godfather called Manuel who 'signed off' on deals that took place on his territory.

Palmer said afterwards he could barely keep a straight face when the 'midget gangster' joined them. Palmer eventually told Wilson he'd love to do business with him and his Spanish 'mate' but his timeshare operation took priority for the foreseeable future. Charlie Wilson wasn't too impressed but he had no idea that Palmer was already well tied in to the Colombians in Tenerife.

John Palmer was relieved to get out of southern Spain. He loathed the commute between Malaga and Tenerife, which was as far from Spain as Malaga was from the UK and he was always happy to arrive back on *his* island.

On Tenerife, John Palmer behaved in public as if he didn't have a care in the world. He bought caseloads of his favourite French wine which was rather conveniently called 'Chateau Palmer' and cost around £200 a bottle. Palmer liked to joke to new associates that the wine had been named after him.

One time he got a caseload delivered to his retro yacht, the *Brave Goose of Essex*, staying on the vessel for two days with a couple of his Clumpers until they'd glugged every last drop. Many noticed that John Palmer's yacht rarely left its berth in the marina and seemed to be more of a showpiece than a proper ocean-going vessel.

For the first time in his adult life, John Palmer had slightly taken his foot off the accelerator. His timeshare empire seemed to be virtually running itself after he and Tel had ironed out a few troublesome characters trying to set up rival firms.

He already had tens of millions of pounds but he couldn't resist the prospect of even more.

'Hello squadron leader, JP here,' said John Palmer in a phone call to his chief pilot from his recently acquired brick-sized mobile phone.

It was clear from the tone of Palmer's voice that he wanted the Battlefield Express fired up.

'What time d'you want to depart?' asked the pilot in his usual cool-as-a-cucumber tally-ho voice.

'Be with you in about an hour. File a trip to Tenerife,' said Palmer, referring to the flight plan, which was supposed to be submitted before any flight could take off.

Within the hour, the Battlefield Express was lifting up off the tarmac at Bristol airport. Palmer and another criminal associate were supping on a glass each of Moët when the pilot got a call via the cabin intercom from his boss.

'Change of plans, wingco. We're heading to Jersey. Can you refile it?'

The pilot sighed and did exactly as he was told. This wasn't the first time Palmer had changed the plane's destination after takeoff – and neither would it be the last. Luckily there were no concrete rules back then about changing flight plans, even after take-off.

Forty-five minutes later the Battlefield Express glided effortlessly down through the low cloud hanging over the Channel Island of Jersey. Five minutes later, they'd touched down and were taxiing towards a hangar reserved for private planes.

Palmer liked going to Jersey because he didn't have to show

his passport to get through customs. The Lear pilot that day had no idea that in the main cabin Palmer and his associate were dividing up at least two dozen brand new credit cards between them.

After Palmer had patiently waited while his pilot filled out all the required landing paperwork, he and his associate walked casually across the tarmac towards the main airport terminal where they rented a small car.

Palmer and his associate then drove round every single cash dispenser machine on the tiny island, withdrawing maximum amounts from each. Three hours later they returned to the Lear with at least £100,000 in cash and all their fake credit cards, which Palmer had bought from a money-lender for £10,000 that very afternoon in Bristol.

One of Palmer's associates explained: 'JP knew he only had about a twelve-hour window to max out those cards before they'd start being flagged up as nicked. It was typical JP.'

Palmer and his associate celebrated in style on board the Lear as it flew down to Tenerife. When one of John Palmer's all-time favourite rock and roll tracks came on the speaker system he later said he was in heaven. As Palmer sang along to the words of 'A Million Miles Away' by Rory Gallagher, he found himself thinking about the good old days back in Birmingham when he was a scallywag without a care in the world.

A joint operation between Jersey and Bristol police was quickly launched when the trail of the fake credit cards was uncovered. But neither force realized who John Palmer was. Two weeks later police traced the pilot of the Learjet through his signature logging in the Lear's arrival in Jersey. A squad of officers raided the pilot's home but found nothing. It only later emerged that the completely innocent airman had been 'fingered' by one of

Palmer's associates in order to create a diversion. The police even later apologized to the pilot about having been fed incorrect information.

But why was Palmer – worth at least £200 million by this stage – even bothering with such a relatively small criminal enterprise as a stolen credit card scam? One of his oldest associates later explained: 'JP liked the "hit". He adored the feeling that comes with getting away with stuff. You can't buy that. It's all down to what we in the trade call The Buzz.'

Back in Tenerife, Palmer's lover Christine Ketley further cemented her relationship with him by getting pregnant. Many noted that it all happened shortly after Palmer had had a child with his young German lover, Saskia. One old Palmer associate explained: "'Christine was good for John because there were far fewer secrets between them than he had with Marnie. I don't know if she knew about the other woman but her pregnancy seemed to suggest she did."'

It must have grated with Ketley that Palmer refused to marry her because he didn't want to hurt the feelings of Marnie and their two daughters. Everyone on the island knew Ketley was 'the one' as far as Palmer was concerned but how many of her lover's secrets did she really know?

John Palmer's Learjet flight crew always remained in the cockpit before, during and after most flights as Palmer and his associates got on and off the aircraft. Besides loading small wooden crates allegedly containing guns, Palmer's cronies sometimes carried longer boxes that looked as if they could contain much larger rifles.

Sometimes, John Palmer slipped on board his Learjet at Bristol airport with just a couple of minutes to spare accompanied by a woman, occasionally even two. One associate explained: 'There would end up being a lot of giggling coming from the main cabin but no one would ever dare ask JP who these women were.' Often the same women would be flown home to the UK the following day on bucket shop flights to save Palmer the cost of his own jet fuel.

It is even claimed that Palmer had a long-running affair with a British TV presenter, which would seem on the face of it to be a very risky exercise for Palmer. One associate explained: 'JP loved the fact this woman appeared on the telly all the time. It made him feel a bit special. She was an upper-class type with a cut-glass accent and JP used to joke about being her bit of rough. Mind you, who's ever heard of a bit of rough worth £300 million?'

Palmer's secret lover also happened to be married, so it was not in her interests to blabber to anyone about the relationship. After the affair eventually fizzled out, Palmer's latest mistress tried to persuade him to agree to an exclusive interview on camera about the timeshare fraud accusations.

One of Palmer's oldest associates later explained: 'JP was appalled by her suggestion. I think he rather loved her and was upset that she'd been using him all along.'

As fears about his own safety grew, John Palmer began taking flights in the middle of the night. He had a VHS video machine installed with a TV screen and watched movies to occupy the increasing amount of time he was spending airborne.

Palmer hated most gangster pictures because they seemed to portray such an exaggerated version of the world he came from. He particularly disliked *The Long Good Friday*, starring Bob Hoskins as a very Palmer-like top-dog criminal, and he struggled with serious dramas generally. Slapstick comedies like the British classic film *The Plank* with Eric Sykes were more up his street. He also liked the James Bond films, especially the ones that starred Sean Connery.

In early 1990, Palmer traded in his Learjet for an upgraded 55 version and delighted his air crew by paying them larger 'fees' in those brown envelopes they got after every flight. One later recalled: 'By this time, JP often slipped the envelopes into our inside jacket pockets even as we were still steering the plane to its hangar. We considered him to be a very wealthy, but legitimate businessman. After all, everyone knew about his timeshare empire.'

The purchase of that second Learjet marked a distinct change in the type of characters whom Palmer invited on board the aircraft. One crew member later recalled: 'One time JP arrived in a stretch limo with these three huge Russians or Eastern Europeans.' It is believed these passengers were packing guns and Palmer wanted to keep them sweet by not forcing them to put their arms in the box, which would then be put in the luggage hold.

During this particular flight, one of the Russians pulled out a Glock automatic and placed it on the tray in front of his seat. None of the other passengers passed comment.

The flight-crew member explained: 'If we'd known about that gun we would have refused to take off because if it had gone off inside the plane we would have crashed. We were flying at 30,000 feet at the time and the Lear would have spun out of control in seconds.'

Around this time, Palmer also purchased a Bell Jet Ranger helicopter to pick him up and drop him off at Battlefield whenever he was visiting Marnie and their daughters. The noisy machine was far from popular with his neighbours. One of them later commented: 'We all knew Mr Palmer was some kind of criminal by this time but he'd kept himself to himself until the helicopter began flying in and out of the area. It sounded and looked like one of those American helicopters from the Vietnam War. A few people round here were a bit upset about the noise until we pointed out what Mr Palmer did for a living and the complaints soon stopped.'

In Tenerife, Palmer's police sources told him that America's Drug Enforcement Agency – the DEA – were about to visit the island which he presumed was linked to the Colombians, whom the DEA had promised to destroy as part of the US's so-called war on drugs.

In fact it wasn't just Palmer or the Colombians they were interested in. Tel's background as a militiaman with connections to terror groups in the Middle East had flagged him up as a person of interest.

Tel had been photographed meeting members of the Hezbollah and other terror-linked individuals back in his home country of the Lebanon.

This was beyond John Palmer's remit. Villains were one thing but international terrorists were a different matter altogether.

CHAPTER SEVENTEEN

FLEXING MUSCLES

LAS AMERICAS, TENERIFE, SPRING 1990

John Palmer was concerned that his powerbase in southern Tenerife might be slipping a bit after those recent skirmishes with rival timeshare operators. So he decided it was time to flex his muscles once more.

One of his oldest associates in Tenerife explained: 'JP got all the main new rival "faces" on the island to come in and meet him in pairs. Then sometimes one of them would be taken away at gunpoint by Tel while his partner was told he'd be killed if they didn't leave the island immediately. When one gang refused to play ball with JP, their man was found floating in the harbour the following day.'

John Palmer hoped the gangsters would return to their bosses and warn them off any plans to move on to Tenerife full-time.

Over the following months, it's said that a handful of bodies washed up on the beaches near the Golden Mile. Many believe to this day that they represented a warning to anyone planning to out-muscle John Palmer that there was only one possible outcome.

At one of his penthouse apartments overlooking Las Americas,

Palmer's lover Christine Ketley was always relieved to see Palmer back in one piece. Ketley begged Palmer to slow down and start enjoying a more simple life with her and their dogs. But his answer was always the same: 'Sorry, love, but I've got a business to run.'

So Palmer continued reaping vast financial rewards from timeshare. He was also quietly expanding his money-laundering business. Most people did not want to declare all their income to the tax man. Alternatively many others had huge amounts of money which were the proceeds of crime that they needed to spread around so as not to alert the authorities. John Palmer provided a carefully organized 'filter' to clean this cash to avoid attracting the attention of the police and tax authorities.

Palmer also recognized it wasn't just villains who needed their money cleaned, either. There were big-time business tycoons all over the world crying out for someone to help them hide their cash.

Palmer knew one 'likely lad' from the Midlands area we'll call 'GB', who was well on his way to becoming a multimillionaire in London thanks to laundering other people's cash. Some of their clients were even well-known celebrities and powerful businessmen. Those 'clients' had even helped GB become a fine, upstanding member of some of London's most exclusive clubs. This had then enabled him to move even further up the social scale where there were many more potential 'clients'.

In early April 1990, John Palmer decided to ship his collection of vintage sports cars over to Tenerife from his Learjet hangar at Bristol airport. One source explained: 'Late one night a bunch of articulated car transporters turned up at the hangar. They took them all off to Bristol Docks where they were put on board a freighter and shipped to Tenerife.'

As ever, Palmer had an ulterior motive for wanting the cars in Tenerife. The same source explained: 'I heard he hid a lot of gold and cash and stuff in those cars and then had them put in sealed containers before they were shipped over.'

So in the dead of night, the cars were taken on a fleet of trucks from the port in Tenerife straight to the underground car park beneath Palmer's main Island Village skyscraper headquarters. Their existence was kept a closely guarded secret for many years because Palmer saw those cars as his get-out-of-jail card in case the authorities ever grabbed all his cash.

Meanwhile, more than a thousand miles further north on the so-called Costa del Crime, a chilling message was about to be sent to John Palmer and the rest of the underworld.

MARBELLA, COSTA DEL SOL, SPAIN, 23 APRIL 1990

In the garden of a large detached villa called Chequers, spring sunshine was beating down on the lawn and the swimming pool as a warm breeze blew gently through the pine woods that backed on to the house. A man of about sixty years of age lit the barbecue and then crouched down to pick some mint from one of his favourite flower beds for a dinner he was preparing for himself and his wife to celebrate their thirty-fifth wedding anniversary.

Half a mile away, a man in a white van had just met his friend who'd been waiting with his yellow mountain bike under the shade of a big eucalyptus tree. The youth with the bike nodded as the van parked up and the driver got out. Without saying a word, the youth with the bike strolled up a small side street dotted with ornate street lamps and houses on one side and a huge empty plot of land opposite. The youth walked past number 7, a white house, then to number 9, then number 11. There was no number 13 on the next house, just the name: 'Chequers'. The owners were superstitious. The front of the property was covered in colourful bougainvillea.

In the back garden of that same house, the elderly man continued preparing the wedding anniversary meal. He didn't hear the doorbell ring. His wife answered it and found a nervous, pale-faced young man standing on the doorstep in a grey tracksuit. The shadow from a baseball cap pulled down over his forehead almost completely hid his eyes.

With a familiar-sounding south London accent, he told the woman he had a message for her husband from a business associate. The woman invited the young man in and encouraged him to leave his bike in the porch.

In the back garden, the woman's husband was expertly slicing up tomatoes and cucumbers for a salad when his wife called out that he had a visitor. As the younger man stepped on to the patio area in front of the pool, the older man nodded in his direction while the couple's Alsatian dog growled menacingly under its breath but didn't move.

A few moments later the wife – now inside the house – heard raised voices but thought little of it. She was used to these sorts of 'discussions'.

In the back garden, the visitor karate-kicked the old man in the testicles. As he doubled over, struggling for breath, another powerful follow-up karate strike broke the older man's nose.

When the Alsatian leapt to his master's aid, it received a vicious kick in the chest, which snapped its front leg and shoulder bone like a twig.

Then the visitor took out a Smith and Wesson 9mm pistol from under his tracksuit top and fired it twice at point-blank range. The first bullet pierced the carotid artery of the old man's neck. The second entered his mouth and exited out of the back of his head.

Back in the kitchen the elderly man's wife heard two loud bangs but thought they'd come from construction work on a nearby building site. Moments later, she rushed into the garden and saw her husband staggering towards the pool, blood spurting from his neck.

The victim tried to stand up as he stared straight at his wife, but could not speak. Then he pointed his finger at something. She thought it was his open mouth. Blood was streaming from it. But he was trying to point to the back wall, which the gunman had just climbed over to escape.

Legendary Great Train Robber Charlie Wilson had just paid the ultimate price for falling out with a bunch of old-school British criminals over a drug deal financed partly by two members of the original Brink's-Mat robbery gang. It seemed the Curse of Brink's-Mat had struck yet again.

John Palmer heard the news about Charlie Wilson in a call to his big white mobile phone a few hours later. He shrugged his shoulders, leaned back in the armchair in his vast office, lit a Cuban cigar and nodded gently to himself.

Palmer believed he was safe as long as he stayed put in Tenerife.

'Let 'em come out here and I'll sort them all out,' he told one associate.

John Palmer had work to do. He'd decided to step up the laundering 'game' because it seemed to have the potential to be more profitable than even the timeshare business. Palmer believed he could dominate the market without ever having to leave Tenerife. He'd get his clients to fly out on his Learjet for meetings. They'd love it.

John Palmer was clearly addicted to money. He didn't care where it came from. The memories of the council shoes with those holes in them clouded his every thought.

Meanwhile London was busily transforming from a gritty, run-down, grimy city into a cosmopolitan centre for the immensely wealthy. A place where money and power ruled. John Palmer's old Midlands crony had worked his way into the secretive money-laundering world of mega-rich tycoons, and was already now on the verge of being richer than even John Palmer. These new London residents dealt only in cash and had brought with them an almost never-ending supply of money, thanks to the plundering of the vast mineral wealth formerly in state control following the break-up of the old Soviet Union a couple of years earlier.

As part of John Palmer's money-laundering 'service', he employed a pair of financial experts in Tenerife. They ran a legitimate business, which provided perfect cover for such activities.

Palmer's couple used code names such as Fiat, Honda, Champagne, Cristal and Caviar to refer to customers in detailed diaries covering all their money-laundering deals. Entries between 1988 and 2000 suggest they laundered up to £50 million, but that was only a small percentage of the money John Palmer would end up 'cleaning'.

Palmer's money-laundering operation had to be planned with military precision. His two financial experts even sometimes participated in street exchanges with couriers while transferring huge sums of cash. Palmer later said he never had any problems with theft from the couple because they knew that if any of his cash went missing it would spell curtains for them.

The couple were soon dealing in quantities of money ranging from £200,000 to £400,000 at any one time. Brown paper bags containing such sums were often labelled with phrases such as 'the big man' in relation to who was due to pick them up.

Special routines were devised just in case they were ever being watched. This involved going to local hotels where a courier would collect a large bag before going to a local supermarket and then buying a holdall and filling it with the cash. On a typical day, the couple would then meet a courier in a street.

But often no transaction would take place until they'd reached somewhere else, just in case they were being watched. The couple juggled mobile phones, which contained special codes for each number.

The couple eventually left the island after Palmer paid them off handsomely because he felt it was sensible to change personnel regularly. Palmer then began running three separate such money-laundering teams simultaneously.

As huge amounts of cash came pouring in, Palmer became even more socially detached from everyone, apart from his closest family members. 'It was as if he lived for money,' said one old Tenerife associate. 'Nothing else and no one else mattered. He liked to touch it, feel it and smell it. It became like his drug.'

At home, Palmer's obsession with money made him into even more of a recluse than he was before he bought his original Learjet. He often liked nothing more than listening to his favourite music lying on his king-size bed while flicking wads of cash through his fingers.

Palmer only ever really ventured out for any amount of time to use his latest Lear 55 as a taxi service between Tenerife and the West Country. He was effectively running two wives at the same time but it seemed to suit Palmer's temperament. He got bored easily and having one family in the UK and another in Tenerife kept him on his toes. Palmer dreaded the moments when he had nothing to do. He wanted to fill every living second, otherwise the dark thoughts and bad memories from his childhood would come flooding back.

Back at Battlefield, Palmer's home near Bath, neighbours and local residents definitely preferred it when Palmer was in Tenerife because there wouldn't be any noisy arrivals and departures by his helicopter from the field behind the coach house.

Palmer – still obsessively wearing his bullet-proof vest whenever he was outside his home – now insisted that Marnie and their two daughters had at least one bodyguard at all times, especially when he was in Tenerife. Marnie – who knew nothing about her husband's criminal activities – had objected at first but Palmer insisted.

Palmer failed to mention that the money-laundering business was filled with even more dangerous characters. They included Russian mafia members renowned for not caring about 'collateral damage' when it came to attacking their enemies.

Back in the UK the fallout from the Brink's-Mat robbery was about to turn deadly once again. More criminals with connections to the heist were being targeted in what police and underworld alike now openly call 'The Curse of Brink's-Mat'.

SHERNHALL ROAD, WALTHAMSTOW, EAST LONDON, FRIDAY 22 DECEMBER 1990, 6.58 P.M.

Terry Gooderham, a 39-year-old businessman, and his girlfriend Maxine Arnold, 32, were at their home preparing for an evening out with Maxine's mother when they got a phone call and popped out dressed casually in tracksuits. Gooderham didn't even bother to take his wallet or watch and Maxine left her handbag behind.

At four the next morning a police patrol spotted Gooderham's F-reg black Mercedes in a secluded car park at Lodge Lane, near Epping Forest – a spot regularly used by courting couples. The lights were on and the glass of the front offside window was broken. Moving closer to investigate, the officers discovered the horribly mutilated bodies of Gooderham and Arnold.

Police using dogs and metal detectors quickly sealed off the area and began a search for the murder weapon and other clues. Friends of Gooderham insisted his death didn't have anything to do with his tangled love life – he had two live-in girlfriends based in separate homes owned by him.

Police revealed they found a small quantity of cocaine in Gooderham's Mercedes, even though a post-mortem on both bodies did not find any traces of the drug. It had clearly been left by the killer to confuse police.

It then emerged that Gooderham owed in excess of £150,000 to the same London crime family that John Palmer had dealt with during and since the Brink's-Mat gold bullion operation. There were also rumours that Gooderham had double-crossed a cocaine baron who also had links to the Brink's-Mat raid.

The 'icing' of Charlie Wilson and the murders of a number of other characters connected to the Brink's-Mat robbery finally started to take their toll on Palmer's nerves and he began moving even more between penthouse apartments and villas on Tenerife. He acquired one secret property above a Chinese restaurant on the outskirts of Las Americas. It could only be reached through the restaurant itself.

One associate explained: 'I was in a meeting with JP in the actual Chinese restaurant one night and he asked me if I fancied a nightcap at his place. Then he got up and told me to follow him. We walked through the stinking kitchen of the restaurant to a small elevator door next to the gents' toilets. He pressed a button and a lift appeared. It couldn't hold more than three people.

'Anyway, we squeezed in it, JP pressed the button and it creaked and struggled up at least ten floors. The he opened the lift door and we walked straight into the most amazing apartment I have ever seen. It had a glass floor with carp swimming in a tank underneath your feet. The view across Las Americas and the Golden Mile was incredible.'

As Palmer showed his guest around the apartment he said: 'This is the perfect place, except for one thing.'

'What's that, JP?' asked his associate.

'I hate the smell of beef chow mein.'

Holidaymakers who'd already bought into John Palmer's time-share ownership deals would turn up on holiday in Tenerife only to be kept waiting for hours in order to get the keys to what was their own property. Then they'd be hit with a £460 maintenance fee before they could even walk into their own villa or apartment.

One holidaymaker – a 73-year-old partially disabled former prisoner-of-war – later said: 'We'd already paid by post and had a receipt. There were heavies all around there and a queue of people like us, all being treated the same. The woman at the reception just smirked and said she was just doing her job. I said, "Yes, just like the Gestapo used to say,"' he reported.

That 'woman at reception' was Palmer's long-standing

employee Flo Robinson, who by this time had been nicknamed by many timeshare owners as 'Rosa Klebb', the name of Goldfinger's notorious henchwoman in the James Bond film of the same name. Flo still kept her two Jack Russell terriers, Sid and Nancy, by her side at all times and a sign above her desk read: *'The more I meet people, the more I love my dogs.'*

Even when disaffected timeshare owners set up their own group called the Timeshare Owners' Association, John Palmer wasn't bothered because, as he told one associate, 'We've got 'em by the balls. They got no choice but to pay.'

Palmer cynically sneered at what he perceived to be the sheer stupidity of his victims. When he'd first started out in the timeshare business all those years earlier, he'd wondered if anyone would fall for it. But by this time he was describing it as being 'as easy as taking candy from a baby'.

Palmer began employing armed guards at his Holiday Village complex, whose job was to prevent complaining victims from entering the headquarters building. Most of these so-called 'security guards' were run by Tel and his brother and some of them were even rumoured to be on-the-run terrorist friends of his from the Middle East.

At one stage, the two brothers appeared in court in Granadilla – the nearest town to the Island Village complex – to answer complaints by Palmer's timeshare owners that they had been intimidated. But they'd only been arrested after assurances they would not be imprisoned, even if found guilty. Palmer encouraged the 'arrests' because he wanted it to look as if he and his 'people' were helping the Tenerife police's crackdown on the timeshare business.

As part of the same 'two-faced' campaign, Palmer also agreed to pretend to care about his 'customers' by appearing in front of a local judge to answer complaints from timeshare owners. Palmer was then informed like a naughty schoolboy by the judge that he had 'a moral obligation' to look after the complex and its residents. Palmer smiled coldly, then nodded at the judge – whom he knew from various charity functions – before going straight back to his headquarters to inspect the accounts, which showed he was still as rich as God.

A couple of times, Palmer faced the full fury of his timeshare victims when he made the mistake of walking out and about in Las Americas. But the angry holidaymakers never got too close to Palmer because his Clumpers would step between them. But Palmer was sufficiently shaken to decide that in future he would only ever arrive and depart at his skyscraper headquarters via the underground car park.

To add to John Palmer's ongoing paranoia, there were rumours that three of his innocent timeshare fraud victims had clubbed together to have him killed. Initially, Palmer laughed off the stories but then he heard from a police contact that a man had been detained near the Holiday Village skyscraper headquarters who was known to be a timeshare victim.

As a result, Palmer decided to go much more 'low key' and began driving around Las Americas in a modest blue Opel Omega, often with his untrustworthy henchman Tel carrying his shotgun under his overcoat and proudly informing anyone who asked about his weapon that he had a licence for it.

And in the middle of all this – on March 24, 1991 – Palmer's lover Christine Ketley gave birth to a son, James. To some people, the happy event might have been a time for reflection but not for John Palmer. He continued working round the clock on his empire.

John Palmer's timeshare resorts were all owned by a web of companies in England, the Isle of Man and Tenerife itself, making them untouchable. In the UK, Battlefield was in Marnie's name, so they couldn't confiscate that either. Palmer believed he had the authorities over a barrel and ordered his financial associates to continue moving huge amounts of cash around the world to further frustrate investigators. In Madrid, Judge Garzón watched in amazement as the UK's legal system completely failed to nail Palmer.

In the middle of all this, John Palmer paid out huge sums to lawyers whenever he felt he'd been unjustly maligned in the UK media. For example, Palmer once forced a tabloid newspaper to print an apology about an article that implied he was the legal owner of certain timeshare resorts. One of Palmer's Spanish lawyers insisted this was not the case and even produced the paperwork to prove it. The newspaper was left with no option but to print an apology, despite knowing that he was indeed the true owner.

Numerous mainly UK-based journalists turned up on Tenerife after hearing the timeshare horror stories. John Palmer had loathed the press ever since the Brink's-Mat robbery. He couldn't understand why they didn't simply mind their own business. He hadn't harmed any of them personally, so why did they have it in for him?

Palmer had arrogantly presumed he could distance himself from his criminal empire by claiming he'd sold the timeshare business and was no longer responsible for it.

But when investigative reporters began digging they found evidence to the contrary. One newspaper, the *Mail on Sunday*, confronted Palmer with irrefutable evidence that he was still the registered owner of the resorts, despite his claims.

Palmer denied it but the newspaper went ahead and published all the details of a Tenerife registration document issued by the island's Tourism Department, which stated:

Mr John Palmer, referred to as a jeweller, British passport number B343169 with domicile in The Coach House, Battlefield, Lansdown, near Bath, is 'the unique administrator' of Holiday Village Management.

John Palmer's main 'line of defence' at the time was that he'd handed control of the timeshare complex to a committee and that he had no direct contact or involvement with the seventeen satellite companies connected to his resorts.

It eventually dawned on John Palmer that the longer he kept spinning the timeshare saga along in the media, the more he'd get away with laundering increasingly large sums of other people's dirty money.

Palmer often invited potential money-laundering 'clients' over for lunch in Tenerife courtesy of his Learjet. As one old associate later explained: 'JP knew how to press all the right buttons. He'd lay on champagne on the plane and by the time these characters turned up in Tenerife they were ripe for a deal.'

Palmer would always outline his money-laundering terms to avoid any later 'confusion'. He took a 50 per cent commission on all deals over £1 million. It sounded outrageous to many, until they considered the alternative which was paying at least 90 per cent to the British taxman.

As word of Palmer's 'services' spread, a wide range of wealthy individuals began turning up on his private jet from London. Palmer was rubbing his hands with glee. He loved the way that all these supposedly rich and famous people were coming cap-in-hand to him.

But John Palmer's fast-growing reputation as someone who could handle the blackest of cash was about to entice one of the most unlikely characters Tenerife has ever welcomed to its shoreline.

CHAPTER EIGHTEEN

WATCHIN' YER BACK

LAS AMERICAS, TENERIFE, 3 NOVEMBER 1991

John Palmer looked irritated within seconds of taking a call on his mobile from a gruff-sounding character, who said he was sailing into a nearby marina and wanted to meet Palmer 'immediately'. When Palmer tried to find out the identity of the caller, another younger voice came on the line and insisted that it would be worth Palmer's while if they met on the caller's yacht, which was rather conveniently about to dock alongside Palmer's vessel, the *Brave Goose of Essex*.

John Palmer was typically suspicious and believed he might be walking into a trap, so he got two of his Clumpers to pop down to the marina and check out the man's yacht. When Palmer heard who owned the vessel, he ordered two of his men to drive him to the marina immediately.

Half an hour later, Palmer sat down at a teak table on the aft deck of a pristine motor yacht called the *Lady Ghislaine* and smiled charmingly as he was asked if he could launder dirty money belonging to a larger-than-life character called Robert Maxwell, an ex-MP and recent owner of the Mirror Group of newspapers in London. Maxwell had been one of the world's most powerful press barons, some said second only to Rupert Murdoch, until he decided to start stealing money from his own company's pension fund.

But the Robert Maxwell now sitting opposite criminal John Palmer was a much more dishevelled figure than the one he'd seen photos of in the newspapers. Palmer later mocked the fact that the obese former press baron had a badge on his shirt that said 'Captain Bob' on it.

Robert Maxwell told Palmer he had £10 million in cash that he needed to turn into dollars as quickly as possible. He admitted it was the only money in the world he had access to. Palmer took a deep breath, smiled and asked the one-time Labour politician, 'Have you got the money here?'

Maxwell hesitated and looked across at one of his assistants. 'Why do you ask?'

'Well, it doesn't mean much if you've still gotta travel half-way round the world to get it, does it?'

Maxwell's face darkened.

'Don't talk to me in that tone, young man.'

Palmer already hated Maxwell's guts and they hadn't even started discussing terms.

'Forget it, mate,' replied Palmer. 'You either want to get shot of your cash or you don't. I'm not here to win a popularity contest.'

'D'you know who I am?' boomed Maxwell.

'Yeah, some dodgepot who's stolen a load of pension money from his own company.'

Maxwell's face contorted and he slammed his fist on the table.

'How dare you talk to me like that!'

Palmer stood up and said nothing. He nodded to his two Clumpers and all three calmly walked to the gangplank at the rear of the yacht without once looking back at Maxwell. It was the last time anyone other than Maxwell's crew ever saw him alive.

Two days later, on 5 November 1991, John Palmer smiled when he heard that Maxwell's bloated, naked, twenty-stone body had been recovered from the Atlantic Ocean. According to the crew on his yacht, Maxwell had decided to urinate over the side of the vessel at 4.25 a.m. that morning and then promptly fell into the sea and drowned.

The official ruling at a Madrid inquest held a month later was death by a heart attack combined with accidental drowning, although three pathologists had been unable to agree on the exact cause of his death. Maxwell had been found to have been suffering from serious heart and lung conditions. Murder was ruled out by the Spanish judge but some still believed it might have been suicide.

Palmer later told one associate: 'Maxwell was a fat, arrogant bastard and I'm not surprised he died but I bet it wasn't a natural death. Characters like him usually upset so many people one of them always takes a pop at them in the end.'

He could so easily have been talking about himself.

John Palmer prided himself on rarely losing his temper with people in authority, especially the police. During his adult life, he was hauled into police stations on at least half a dozen occasions but usually he'd end up alerting his lawyer and walking out within a matter of hours. It was all part of the job. He didn't even hold it against the police. They also had a job to do, he'd reason.

Palmer was now feeling trapped on Tenerife. He wanted to see his family back in the UK but he feared arrest and incarceration there because he knew he was being lined up for a further prosecution. So he took a huge gamble when his lawyer in London informed him that the police intended to arrest him for a mortgage fraud when he next stepped foot in the UK. Palmer's legal adviser got an assurance from detectives that Palmer wouldn't get a custodial prison sentence for such a relatively minor offence.

So Palmer boarded his Learjet – number G-JITN – at its usual spot outside the fire station at Tenerife South-Reina Sofia airport and was not seen again on the island for months. Palmer wanted to surprise the police and the underworld by showing them he had nothing to hide. It was an artful, purely tactical move but it made complete sense.

Back at Battlefield with Marnie and their daughters, Palmer felt safe in the UK for the first time in years. In many ways he preferred to be in respectable, rural Wiltshire and away from the greasy spoon cafés and tinpot bars of Las Americas.

It had been a mighty relief to see his two daughters and rekindle his relationship with Marnie. She could have told him not to come but she knew how important it was to make her husband feel wanted despite all their past problems.

When the police came knocking at Battlefield with an arrest warrant, Palmer took it in his stride because he knew he wasn't going to get thrown in jail.

Throughout this period, Palmer occasionally phoned Christine Ketley back in Tenerife to make sure everything was going okay on the timeshare front. Many were impressed by Christine Ketley's ability to cope. She was a stable character unflustered by most things. Her parents had provided a loving family home for her as a child in a modest 1930s pebble-dashed house in

Brentwood, Essex. Her father had once been a clerk with the local gas board, a world as far removed from crime as it is possible to get.

Having returned voluntarily to the UK, John Palmer eventually received an eighteen-month suspended sentence for his part in a mortgage fraud linked to his British timeshare victims. It was a drop-in-the-ocean charge and Palmer presumed it was all the police could come up with, so he was now in the clear and the case even slipped through the courts without much media coverage. Palmer's old friend Garth Chappell – who'd earlier been found guilty of involvement in the Brink's-Mat theft – was also convicted on the same mortgage fraud case. Palmer, who'd admitted obtaining nearly £65,000 by deception, was ordered to pay £13,052 compensation and £5,000 costs.

However, fresh rumours of a deal between Palmer and the police soon began circulating in the underworld and, inevitably, reached the eyes and ears of Brink's-Mat robbers Mickey McAvoy and Brian Robinson. They saw it as yet more evidence that John Palmer was a double-dealing bastard. One of their associates later said: 'Palmer must have done a deal with the cops, otherwise he wouldn't have gone back to England to face the music in the first place.'

There were rumours inside the underworld that McAvoy and Robinson were expecting to be given their share of the gold when they were released from prison after serving their sentences. Palmer and others must have been nervously counting down the days to the pair's projected release date in 2000 by this stage.

McAvoy and Robinson were extra-careful to keep a clean sheet inside Long Lartin prison, near Evesham in Worcestershire, as they patiently bided their time. Even when other inmates at the prison attempted a mass breakout, the two Brink's-Mat 'king-pins' played no role in the trouble and didn't even leave their cells. As one of their oldest associates later explained: 'Serving time was just part of the job for those boys. They accepted their "bird" like true professionals but at the end of the day they expected to walk out to their share of the gold and Gawd help anyone who got in their way.'

Just after the mortgage fraud case, John Palmer insisted to a Bristol newspaper reporter through his London solicitor that he'd not been involved with his Tenerife timeshare operation for six years and nor had he any links with the management company behind it. But no one really believed him, least of all those two Brink's-Mat robbers expecting a lot of money to be waiting for them when they got out of prison.

Palmer spent the majority of the following twelve months in the UK because he was determined to convince the authorities that he'd walked away from his Tenerife activities, including the timeshare business, and that was why he'd come back to face the mortgage fraud charges in the first place. It was a clever move because it threw a lot of his enemies off the scent.

Palmer's decision must have upset Christine Ketley, not least because she'd only recently given birth to the couple's baby son. Palmer occasionally jetted in and out of Tenerife but it was never for longer than a few days at a time.

Then in early 1993, John Palmer got a very rude awakening. One of his lawyers contacted him to say that the Brink's-Mat company were seeking another asset-freezing injunction which would allow Palmer's finances to be fully scrutinized. On his lawyer's advice Palmer immediately headed back to Tenerife, warning Marnie that he might not return to the UK for a very long time. Days later the asset-freezing injuction was granted in the High Court of London and Palmer's finances began to be examined in minute detail for the first time. It later emerged that much of the information was provided from Madrid by Judge Garzón, who was still hoping that he and the British authorities could eventually 'pincer' John Palmer once and for all.

In February 1993, Palmer was informed by his lawyer in London that he was subject to an asset-freezing Mareva Injunction granted to the Brink's-Mat company in the High Court of Justice, enabling investigators to track Palmer's substantial financial resources. Palmer eventually made a one-off payment of £360,000 to Lloyd's the insurers as a result of this civil action, although he continued to plead his innocence of involvement in the 1987 robbery. And everyone in law enforcement across Europe and the UK knew that that payment was nothing more than a very small drop in the ocean for John Palmer.

But not long after this, Palmer was legally obliged to make another, much larger payment of £3 million to the same loss adjusters on the basis that they would stop pursuing him. It was still chickenfeed to Palmer, who by this time was conservatively believed to be worth between £350m and £400m.

However, in Spain, Judge Garzón had no intention of letting Palmer off the hook. He had fresh evidence linking him to more criminal activities, including alleged deals with foreign mobsters. The Spanish also outlined violent timeshare-related incidents blamed on Palmer's associates.

For the first time in years, John Palmer wasn't sure which way to turn. He sensed that Judge Garzón was out to get him and wondered what he could do to stop him in his tracks.

*

Back in the 1970s when John Palmer had first begun operating as a professional criminal, the underworld was a solidly based sub-society with its own economic structures, class system and laws. But by the 1990s, the rules had changed and the younger villains didn't think twice about threatening everyone, not just other criminals. By this time, the economy, judicial system and peace on the streets were all at risk from individuals whose power was increasing in inverse proportion to the police's ability to put them behind bars.

Now virtually every criminal had their own firepower. A minor industry had even sprung up to accompany the demands of increasingly gun-conscious gangsters in both Spain and the UK. The high number of contract killings clearly implied that professional criminals were prepared to commit the ultimate crime to achieve ascendancy in the underworld.

In December 1993, the death of the world's most notorious cocaine baron, Pablo Escobar, in a shootout with security forces in Medellin, Colombia, reminded John Palmer that his deal with the Colombians was even more risky than when he first agreed it all those years earlier.

He also realized that Escobar's death would spark even closer scrutiny of his own activities on Tenerife by British, American and Spanish authorities.

John Palmer remained locked into that 'shipping agreement' he had with the Colombians, despite his earlier clashes with that old Nazi, the Professor. Palmer knew he risked his own life and that of many others if he simply told the Colombians where to put their cocaine. The Professor had made it crystal clear that anyone who tried to walk away from such deals would be dead meat.

The DEA's own Organized Crime Drug Enforcement Task

Force in fact stepped up their probe into a number of European-based druglords with alleged connections to the Colombian cartels. The Americans hoped they'd be able to gather sufficient evidence to round up people like John Palmer and many others and get them in front of a Grand Jury in Florida. The DEA had already persuaded Palmer's arch-pursuer Judge Garzón in Madrid and the British police to help them nail Palmer. The DEA wanted to establish evidence to prove dozens of charges against Palmer and others on their main hit-list, including conspiracy and money laundering, as well as drug dealing.

Up until now, John Palmer had had it pretty much all his own way. Most of the old-school UK professional criminals had avoided Tenerife thanks to Palmer's fearsome reputation. But when problems did flare up, he found himself with few people to actually turn to. Palmer confided quite a lot in mistress Christine Ketley on a personal level but his criminal activities away from the timeshare business were always off limits between them. He didn't want Ketley to know anything about that 'side' of things because then that would make her vulnerable to pressure from authorities if he was ever arrested again.

Palmer's problems on this level were fuelled by his distrust of most men and that often prevented him for opening up and talking about the killings and crimes which he'd been connected with over the years.

Occasionally, Palmer was seen out in Las Americas with a couple of associates in one of the local bars or clubs despite his recent problems with angry timeshare victims. But this was usually only because he was trying to nail down a deal. One old associate explained: 'JP still didn't trust people enough to make proper friends with anyone. He'd spent more than thirty years working as a criminal and he couldn't just turn into a friendly character overnight. Sometimes he'd call up and ask if I could get a card game together and he'd come over and play. But it was hard to get anyone to join the game because JP was not someone you wanted to hang out with. And when it came to making conversation, he didn't really know where to start.'

Another of Palmer's oldest associates said: 'JP once told me he thought he had some kind of mental problem because he could never sit still like other people. He always wanted to be doing something and that usually involved making money.'

Meanwhile Tel continued carrying his licensed shotgun around at all times, but he'd been making secretive inroads into other 'businesses' not connected to his employer. Palmer still ignored the rumours because he knew Tel was more than capable of using that gun or informing on him to the police. But when Palmer began keeping Tel at arm's length, the Lebanese former Hezbollah soldier of fortune soon worked out what was happening.

Unknown to Palmer, Tel had set up an illegal arms route between the island and his home country of Lebanon. This enabled him to once again get close to his old friends inside the terror group Hezbollah. They wanted arms on a huge scale and Tel was determined to oblige. He even stopped charging high prices to Hezbollah because he felt an affinity with them and hoped that one day he could rejoin them full-time in the Middle East, despite all those earlier problems between them.

Every now and again, a Hezbollah representative flew into Tenerife to negotiate with Tel for more arms. Tel would proudly take his visitor on a tour of the bars and brothels of Las Americas, safe in the knowledge that no one would ever dare charge him or his friends and associates for sex with a prostitute, let alone a drink.

*

In the summer of 1994, John Palmer's Brink's-Mat gold associate Kenneth Noye was released from prison after serving his sentence for VAT fraud and handling the bullion. Noye was hated by the police and hero-worshipped by villains in equal measure, and Palmer knew the police still felt they had some unfinished business with Noye after he'd been acquitted of murdering their undercover officer John Fordham in the garden of Noye's home during the Brink's-Mat investigation.

Naturally, Noye and just about every other criminal connected to the Brink's-Mat gold had been closely following John Palmer's 'career' in Tenerife. Many were extremely jealous of Palmer's success in the timeshare game. After all, he'd managed to turn a supposedly straight business – timeshare – into something more profitable than any traditional criminal activity.

On his release from prison, Kenneth Noye completely steered clear of Tenerife, despite Palmer issuing a half-hearted invitation to him to come and unwind on the island after his long prison sentence. Like Palmer, Noye was a workaholic and threw himself back into a variety of criminal enterprises when he got back in the 'real world'.

Noye travelled to the Mediterranean island enclave of Northern Cyprus – under Turkish rule – with a plan to invest a lot of his cash into a timeshare development in partnership with Brink's-Mat gold handler Brian Reader. Noye believed it could earn him a fortune, just like it had for John Palmer in Tenerife.

Three million tourists – mainly from the UK – visited the Greek-governed southern half of Cyprus every year but only 30,000 came to the north and Noye believed an explosion of tourism was inevitable. But Noye and Reader ended up losing at least half a million pounds on their timeshare scheme. Palmer later rubbed salt into Noye's wounds by telling him that

Northern Cyprus was always going to be a dead-duck because it just didn't have enough visitors and no direct flights from the UK.

Noye didn't like feeling inferior to anyone, least of all John Palmer.

CHAPTER NINETEEN

THE BIG CHEESE

Despite all his recent close shaves, John Palmer remained a relatively happy man. Well, as happy as you can be with at least half a dozen people wanting you dead. Palmer had made a shrewd move by recognizing that Tenerife was a far safer place to operate from than the bullet-riddled Costa del Sol. But now the tide seemed to be turning.

Kenneth Noye's release from prison had once again turned the media spotlight back on Palmer because reporters were obsessed with the Brink's-Mat gold, much of which was still missing. John Palmer knew only too well from his experiences during the gold smelting operation that all publicity was bad publicity, so he'd done everything in his power to avoid journalists for years.

Palmer particularly disliked an investigative journalist called Roger Cook, whose ITV crime documentary series *The Cook Report* had become a big ratings hit.

Cook and his team of former tabloid reporters turned TV researchers had set out to bring John Palmer to justice. They soon discovered that it wasn't just timeshare which was feeding enormous amounts of cash into the very rich bank of John Palmer. A source told Cook that by this time Palmer was making a lot of his income from money laundering.

Cook and his team recruited the services of a couple of faded South East Asian criminals to help set a trap for Palmer. The two men were wired up with microphones and a mini-camera and then lured Palmer into a meeting at one of Palmer's favourite swish hotels, the Ritz in London, to discuss some 'money matters'.

Cook's undercover crooks, posing as heroin traffickers, secretly recorded Palmer offering to launder up to £60 million a year. Palmer would later be seen by millions of TV viewers on film demanding a 25 per cent commission, saying: 'I'm not cheap, but I'm good.'

Palmer also offered to sell the same investigators arms from the Russian mafia and asked if he could supply a foreign hitman to do a job in Britain. Palmer – the streetwise villain who prided himself on his basic instincts – had been stitched up like the proverbial kipper.

When confronted by Roger Cook outside the Ritz shortly after the meeting, Palmer jumped into a taxi. But Cook's camera crew caught up with Palmer when the cab stopped at a nearby red light. Cook ripped open the taxi door and started asking Palmer even more questions about his criminal activities. Palmer refused to say anything and eventually his taxi moved off and later that same day he flew off in his jet to Tenerife. He believed he'd be safer on the island while he waited for all the media heat to die down.

A few weeks later, Palmer's private jet touched down at Bristol airport after an uneventful four-hour flight from Tenerife. As the aircraft speedily taxied towards its hangar in the far corner of the airfield, John Palmer donned his trusty bullet-proof vest and peered out of the porthole. A crowd of about twenty people were swarming around the exact spot where the plane was about to stop.

Palmer anxiously studied the faces in the crowd, wondering who they all were. They didn't look like the police. Palmer wondered if it was some kind of pre-planned diversion by a crafty enemy, who'd then cut Palmer down the moment he emerged from his aircraft.

Just then Palmer's eyes zoomed in on the sizeable figure of TV investigator Roger Cook. Next to him were two men with cameras on their shoulders. Two bright camera lights illuminated the spot where the plane was about to stop.

Palmer smashed his fist down on the tray in front of him. That 'nosey bastard Cook' had just invaded every inch of *his* space.

Palmer buzzed the cockpit breathlessly and asked if there was anywhere else they could taxi to but the answer was no. Palmer's deal with Bristol airport was that he had to disembark from the aircraft in exactly the same spot every time he arrived or departed.

Palmer swallowed hard, tensed his fists, then unclenched them in the hope it would help him stay calm while those TV cameras focused on him.

After a difficult ten minutes ducking and diving questions from Cook and a pack of other reporters, Palmer got in his Range Rover and headed back towards Battlefield. He was infuriated by the TV reporter and starting to want revenge for all the unnecessary aggravation that Cook was causing him.

A few days later, Roger Cook informed his audience of ten million in an episode entitled 'The Laundry Man': 'Palmer had turned crime into cash thanks to the largest timeshare fraud in history.'

THE MANSION: Palmer's luxury home Battlefield, near Bath, where he smelted down much of the gold stolen during the Brink's-Mat heist. FROM THE AUTHOR'S COLLECTION

HUSBAND: John Palmer and wife Marnie outside Battlefield after his name was first linked to the Brink's-Mat gold bullion. FROM THE AUTHOR'S COLLECTION

ISLAND VILLAGE: (*left*) Palmer's headquarters in Tenerife when he was earning hundreds of millions from his timeshare empire. FROM THE AUTHOR'S COLLECTION

LUXURY YACHT: (*above*) Palmer's vessel *Brave Goose of Essex* was allegedly used to torture his enemies and as a hideaway by the multi-millionaire gangster. FROM THE AUTHOR'S COLLECTION

ULTIMATE STASH: (*left*) One of Palmer's many classic sports cars, worth at least ten million pounds, which he kept hidden in the basement of his timeshare headquarters. FROM THE AUTHOR'S COLLECTION

SECRET ENTRANCE: Palmer used this nondescript gate on the edge of Bristol Airport to fly in and out of the UK on his private jet. FROM THE AUTHOR'S COLLECTION

PRIVATE AIRCRAFT: Palmer's Lear Jet – nicknamed *The Battlefield Express* after his luxury home near Bath – was used 'like a taxi service' by Palmer.

FROM THE AUTHOR'S COLLECTION

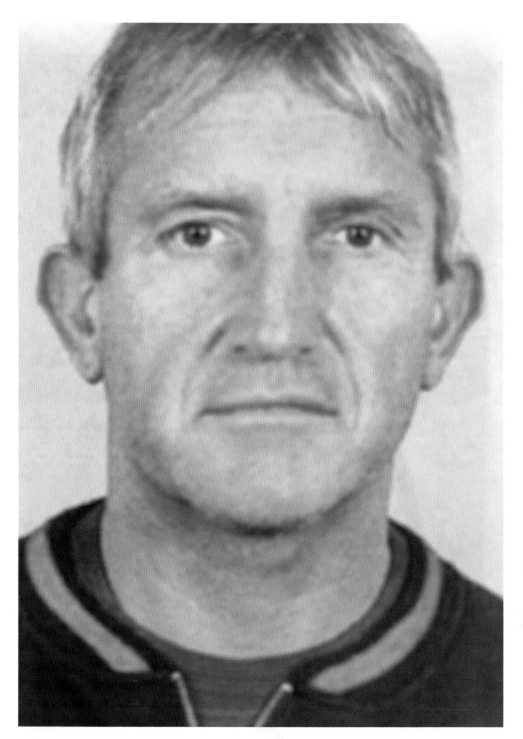

ACCOMPLICE: Palmer teamed up with notorious Kent criminal Kenneth Noye to handle tens of millions of pounds worth of gold bullion stolen during the Brink's-Mat heist. © REX

BRINK'S-MAT HEIST: The world's biggest gold bullion raid on a warehouse near Heathrow Airport in 1983 helped turn Palmer into Britain's Gangster Number One.
© REX/MALCOLM CLARKE

HATTON GARDEN JOB: The world famous raid on the vault in the heart of London in April, 2015, may well have sealed Palmer's death. © REX/MET

PROUD FATHER: (*left*) Palmer with son James at his graduation ceremony at the University of Birmingham where James got an economics degree. © REX/SHUTTERSTOCK

IN THE SHADOW OF DEATH: (*below*) Palmer in the garden of his Essex home just hours before his execution. © REX/ SHUTTERSTOCK

WATCHING HIS PREY: (*above*) It was through this fence bordering Sandpit Cottage that Palmer's killer watched his every move before striking. FROM THE AUTHOR'S COLLECTION

ESCAPE ROUTE: (*left*) This isolated woodland pathway – used mainly by horse riders – was used by Palmer's killer after the shooting. FROM THE AUTHOR'S COLLECTION

THE ACCUSED: Palmer attending his own timeshare fraud trial at the Old Bailey. © REX/ALEX SLAWTHER

Cook informed his viewers that Palmer was using myriad legitimate companies to mix his dirty money with clean cash, and
promised he'd be keeping a close eye on Palmer and intended
to make more programmes about him.

It was the reference in the programme to Christine Ketley, his
long-term mistress back in Tenerife, that infuriated Palmer more
than anything else. The money laundering stuff was 'work' but
Cook had veered into personal territory and in Palmer's mind
that was unforgivable.

Back in Tenerife, evil Lebanese mercenary Tel and his kid
brother continued lurking in the shadows of Las Americas.
Palmer knew the pair were up to no good and decided it was
time to 'iron out' a few of the 'ongoing problems'.

LAS AMERICAS, TENERIFE, SEPTEMBER 1994

The purring Mercedes pulled up at the kerb in a deserted tree-
lined avenue and the driver – Tel's younger brother – got out to
inspect his front tyre because he was sure he had a puncture. As
he was leaning down and looking at the wheel, a high-powered
motorcycle approached. Tel's brother looked up just as the pil-
lion rider took aim and squeezed the trigger while at the same
time yelling out 'It's me!'

Tel's brother threw himself to the ground, crawled into his
car and tried to drive off, but was impeded by the hand brake,
which he couldn't release. Meanwhile the motorcyclist doubled
back and this time pointed the pistol into the car's interior
and fired two more shots, neither of which found their mark.
Tel's brother later told police that although his attackers wore
helmets, he'd recognized one of them as being a 34-year-old

German male who often worked as one of John Palmer's notorious Clumpers.

A few days later, Tel and his brother began looking around for investors in a new timeshare business. They would include Tel's friends in Hezbollah, who were looking for a big return for their money. By this time, Tel was consuming vast quantities of cocaine, which was leading to a lot of erratic decisions. Both brothers knew perfectly well that once Palmer found out they'd helped set up their own timeshare operation, a war was inevitable. But Tel and his brother didn't seem to care. They reckoned they could handle anything Palmer threw at them.

Tel was soon openly boasting in the bars of Las Americas that he was also now running a money-laundering operation that was far more successful than Palmer's. He claimed he was washing more than £500 million on behalf of a bunch of Eastern European gangsters, as well as criminals from Britain, Russia and South America. Most in the Tenerife underworld at the time took his claims with a pinch of salt, or rather cocaine.

However Tel was, without doubt, supplying weapons and money to the Amal and Hezbollah militias in Lebanon. He was even later linked by security services in two countries to the theft of 1,300 French passports that eventually ended up in the hands of Al Qaeda.

John Palmer then heard that Tel had befriended a wealthy Russian oligarch who'd settled on the island and agreed to bankroll Tel's new timeshare company after Tel had guaranteed that he could ruin Palmer's timeshare operation. Tel also had ambitions to take over all Palmer's so-called ancillary businesses, such as the protection rackets, and of course he'd already set up a rival money-laundering outfit.

*

It dawned on John Palmer that his once beloved Tenerife had the potential to become his mink-lined coffin if he wasn't careful. Palmer's timeshare and money-laundering businesses were still booming. But he now knew others were circling just like those Birmingham criminals who'd taken over his jewellery business all those years ago.

In a bid to inject some fresh enthusiasm into his timeshare staff, Palmer recruited a dozen tough-talking sales managers from Florida through a couple of mobster contacts from Miami Beach. But the Americans were not impressed by Las Americas and soon headed back to the US. Palmer didn't care because he'd had to pay them all high salaries. But at least their presence in his resorts had acted as 'a kick up the arse' for the rest of his staff, who'd been getting a bit complacent.

Just like any business, recruitment was the key to John Palmer's success. He spent thousands every month placing adverts in Spain and the UK for junior timeshare staff promising them free accommodation and apparently generous bonuses.

Most of the lower-level staff members were under the age of 25. But the majority worked in a ruthless sales environment with small basic salaries topped up by bonuses linked to almost impossible sales targets. As a result, most of Palmer's staff lived virtually on the breadline. Many held down at least two outside jobs and some even ended up working as prostitutes and bar staff to top up their salaries. Palmer knew all about what they were up to. But he didn't care because he liked his staff lean and hungry as it would make them even more desperate when it came to selling his timeshare dream to all those holidaymakers still turning up in Tenerife.

*

By the spring of 1995, cocaine use had become so blatant on Tenerife that most people using the drug didn't even bother hiding it and Tenerife's long-standing nickname, the White Island, was known to everyone.

When one wisecracking crook offered John Palmer a snort in a restaurant, he slammed his knife and fork down, stood up and spat in the man's face.

'You takin' the mickey,' screamed Palmer, as two of his Clumpers stood over the man. 'I don't have cokeheads running my businesses and I never will. Get outta here now before my boys teach you a lesson.'

Palmer's aggressive attitude towards drug takers undoubtedly had a detrimental effect on his social life. One of his oldest associates later explained: 'When it got round that he'd rip the head off anyone who did coke in front of him, the number of his so-called friends shrunk to virtually nothing.'

Palmer's blood would boil over whenever he caught sight of three or four hefty 'faces' disappearing to the lavatory with running noses. He told one friend: 'It's insulting. Do they think I don't know what they're up to?'

Palmer told an associate that one of the most impressive things about the Colombians was that none of their top men ever took cocaine because they considered drugs to be their product, but anyone who actually took the stuff was a fool.

John Palmer sometimes talked about how he wished Spain was still in the grip of its late Fascist dictator General Franco. In those far-off days, the police and army had absolute authority and the bad pennies never even had time to turn into deadly criminals. Palmer liked the notion of a country where most criminals were squashed underfoot like ripe tomatoes while the cunning Mister Bigs like himself could thrive, thanks to whole-sale bribery and corruption of some individuals.

But the new Spain had a point to prove to the rest of Europe. It was no longer a backward enclave run by a bloodthirsty dictator. Foreign criminal 'vermin' like John Palmer were giving the country a bad name. So back in Madrid, Judge Garzón was urged by senior politicians to make an example of British criminals like John Palmer. Spain needed to stand up to such contemptible characters.

CHAPTER TWENTY

SPREADING THE WORD

LAS AMERICAS, TENERIFE, SUMMER 1995

Dawn streaked the Atlantic with crimson and the cicadas were already singing as Palmer's tatty Vauxhall with Spanish plates nosed its way through the back streets of Las Americas. Palmer was on his way home to Christine Ketley, their dogs and four-year-old son James. By this time, Palmer never went to 'business meetings' on Tenerife without either himself or his Clumpers being armed and, as usual, he always wore his bullet-proof vest. To make sure those present knew he was 'packing', Palmer would greet 'associates' with a tight hug that enabled them to feel the cold steel of the gun pressing into them. Usually it had the desired effect.

At the time, Palmer owned at least two handguns including a Glock .38 automatic, which he'd been given by the Colombians more than ten years earlier. Palmer knew that certain 'parties' were now circling his kingdom and just like a despot he'd decided he would see them all off.

John Palmer had long since embraced his own twisted version of new technology with a succession of large white or grey brick-shaped mobile phones, which he took everywhere with him. The reception wasn't always great but he liked the way he could brief his men on the phone rather than in person or in a rain-sodden, isolated layby.

John Palmer had always hated sit-down meetings, thanks to his illiteracy. But he remained obsessed with keeping a record of everything that was said to avoid any later 'problems' and continued to use his handheld tape recorder at any opportunity.

Palmer told one associate: 'With this thing [the phone] I can get hold of anyone at a moment's notice. That means more deals, which means more money. Can't be bad, can it?'

Palmer loved pulling out his huge mobile phone with its black rubber aerial from his tatty brown leather briefcase and then watching the expression on everyone's faces. One old associate recalled: 'It was a right monster and he'd slap it down wherever he was meeting people and just wait for them to say something. Most people were still on message pagers at the time but of course they were no good for JP because he couldn't read or write properly.'

Palmer often proudly gave his associates a demonstration of his mobile phone and occasionally he'd even encourage them to call their wives to test it out. He loved the fact that so few of them knew how to use a mobile and how clumsy, suspicious and unsure they were about it.

Meanwhile Palmer continued to use his favourite gadget of all – his latest multimillion-pound Learjet – to try and persuade more money-laundering customers to put their business his way.

However the lure of his luxurious aircraft didn't always do its job. One criminal who flew to the island for a lunch meeting with Palmer arrived back at the airport in Tenerife to be told that Palmer's jet was out of action and he'd have to fly back to the UK on another aircraft which was half the size of the Lear and had only one engine.

As one of Palmer's associates later explained: 'The guy was outraged and never did any business with JP again after that. The plane JP always offered as a replacement when the Lear was out of action was a flimsy prop job, which didn't exactly exude confidence for such a long journey.'

Another of Palmer's 'business associates' got so angry about being offered an inferior plane back to the UK that he pulled a gun on Palmer's aircraft mechanic and insisted he fire up the Lear to fly him back. When Palmer – at his Holiday Village headquarters in Las Americas – heard what had happened, he drove at high speed out to the airport to calm the situation down. Then he ended up spending £5,000 on getting his 'client' a regular first-class flight via Madrid on Spain's Iberia airline. One associate later explained: 'JP was always a tight bastard and I think he often made his guests fly back to the UK on that smaller rust-bucket prop job because it saved him at least two grand in fuel charges.'

At the Island Village timeshare headquarters in Las Americas, one cocky young salesman asked Palmer outright if he'd really handled the Brink's-Mat gold. Palmer smiled and insisted: 'I'm a jeweller and jewellers never ask where the gold comes from or else we'd never be able to deal in it'. The salesman who talked to Palmer later recalled that he 'had a twinkle in his eye' as he answered the question.

The same salesman recalled that a few days later he stumbled on at least thirty armed security guards searching the Island Village main reception area. They were turning over desks and shouting at people, including some of Palmer's staff in the reception area. When the young salesman tried to find out what had happened he was told to shut up by manageress Flo Robinson. He then asked to see Palmer, and Flo informed him that Palmer was not available. When the young salesman pushed for a fuller explanation, Flo admitted that Palmer had fallen out with a business partner who'd tried to sell his waterpark behind Palmer's back while he'd been on a trip to the UK.

The young salesman later explained: 'Apparently JP was in some dispute with this bloke so he'd just gone ahead and put it up for auction.'

Palmer had been so outraged he'd sent his Clumpers over to teach the businessman a lesson and this had resulted 'in a lot of broken bones'. The attack, which had just happened at the Island Village headquarters, was payback time by Palmer's rival. 'It was getting really nasty,' the timeshare salesman later said.

Around this time, loud bangs could often be heard in the distant streets of Las Americas. 'It could have been cars backfiring or it might have been gunfire,' the salesman later recalled.

This was a world created by John Palmer and now he needed to work out how to hold on to it.

John Palmer continued dispatching his Clumpers on to the streets of Las Americas to 'spread the word' that he was by no means dead and buried. Often fuelled by cocaine and steroids, Palmer's henchmen laid into anyone linked to rival timeshare companies, especially the one being fronted by Tel.

And on the side, Palmer's Clumpers began charging every person they encountered 1,000 pesetas (£7) personal protection money if they wanted to avoid being beaten up.

At one well-known bar in Las Americas, the weightlifter doorman threw one of Palmer's timeshare reps down the stairs during an altercation. The bar was regularly used by Tel's boys, so Palmer's Clumpers returned that same night and put a bar stool through the same doorman's eye.

'It was fuckin' mental out there,' said Palmer's timeshare salesman.

As a result of such clashes, Tel flew in a fresh 'unit' of Hezbollah fighters to work for him in exchange for free accommodation, high wages and a non-stop supply of women, alcohol and drugs. Tel even encouraged the Arab fighters to wear red and white *keffiyehs* (head cloths) whenever they wandered the streets of Las Americas. He wanted Palmer to hear all about them.

And Palmer was certainly worried by such developments. He didn't know how to deal with professional soldiers. He was used to washed-up old villains having the occasional shoot-out or punch-up but this was on a different scale altogether.

Eventually John Palmer sent three of his Clumpers to visit Tel with an urgent message. Palmer suggested a complete truce on the island, but Tel didn't believe a word of it. He'd spent many years watching Palmer raking in the cash and he knew that Palmer would never offer to back down because it would be seen as a sign of weakness.

Infuriated and insulted by the message from Palmer, Tel ordered his men to follow Palmer's three Clumpers after they left his office. They were later ambushed down a dark side street near Palmer's timeshare headquarters in the centre of Las Americas.

Tel followed up that attack with a message to Palmer politely suggesting that there could be peace between them if Palmer handed his money-laundering operation over to Tel and his Russian associates.

Palmer was outraged: 'That "greasy Arab bastard" is out of

order,' Palmer told one associate in his Tenerife office. 'Tell him to get lost.'

Tel smashed his fist into a door when he heard Palmer's response. Then he picked up a phone and called his Russian backer, who immediately pledged to pour even more money into their new timeshare operation, so they could undercut the deals Palmer was offering his customers.

Shortly after this, Tel flew to London and met up with the two London crime family brothers Bill and Ben, whom he'd earlier met while working for Palmer. Tel knew the brothers didn't like Palmer and he appealed to them to help him destroy Palmer once and for all. But they trusted Tel even less than Palmer and refused to cooperate. Instead they sat back and watched what was happening in Tenerife. The brothers fancied moving their operations to the island at some stage but they wanted John Palmer and people like Tel out of the way first.

Las Americas – once considered the perfect child-friendly resort – began featuring regular shootouts between gangsters, sometimes in broad daylight. Stabbings became virtually a daily occurrence on the streets near Palmer's Island Village timeshare skyscraper headquarters. High above in his penthouse apartment, John Palmer wearily looked down at all the chaos and wondered how best to deal with it. At one stage, he even flew in a dozen old-school 'Clumpers' as new recruits from the UK and sent them on to the streets of Las Americas in pairs as part of a 'private security squad'. As one former timeshare salesman later explained: 'The United Nations they was not!'

Palmer ordered his new Clumpers to 'see off' any of Tel's Hezbollah gangsters. But it was a lot easier said than done.

Three of Palmer's men were soon disfigured by a couple of burly Muslim ex-paratroopers from Georgia who'd joined the Hezbollah cause in the Middle East. The local Guardia Civil (paramilitary police) were in complete disarray. They'd sat back and encouraged Palmer to sort things out but now they were being leaned on by their bosses in Madrid, who themselves were being pressurized by Judge Garzón. Certain individual Tenerife police officers told Palmer to get his remaining Clumpers off the streets immediately. Palmer then arrogantly demanded that the police target Tel and his men. But it soon became clear that Tenerife police were more terrified of the Hezbollah terror crew than Palmer.

One evening, six men armed with baseball bats attacked Tel and his brother. They were pummelled so badly that both had to be carried away on stretchers by local paramedics. The incident only came to light after Tel's timeshare salesmen complained to the Guardia Civil about what had happened.

Spanish authorities later said the six attackers were working as security guards for John Palmer. They were arrested by police and Palmer noticed that the police attitude was hardening. His own police contacts on the island were saying that law enforcement chiefs in Madrid were pressing for more arrests and action against the timeshare sharks and other criminals who were plaguing southern Tenerife.

Two days later, Palmer's six 'security guards' were charged with attempted murder, threats and intimidation connected to the attack on Tel and his brother. It was becoming clear to Palmer that his once tame police officers on the island were no longer on his side.

The six arrests were surprisingly big news in Spain and the UK so they heaped further pressure on John Palmer. The suspects were charged and held for forty-eight hours before being released and ordered to report to police every two weeks.

But law-abiding citizens in Las Americas were predicting yet more bloodshed out on the streets. It seemed like a neverending cycle of fear and terror.

CHAPTER TWENTY-ONE

THE HOLE

LAS AMERICAS, TENERIFE, SEPTEMBER 1995

John Palmer was now waiting for World War Three to break out on his doorstep.

It was during this ominous impasse that a couple of youths on a motorbike watched John Palmer get out of his car to press the button that opened the gate to the underground car park below his Island Village timeshare skyscraper.

Moments later three shots rang out. Palmer didn't receive a scratch thanks to his trusty bullet-proof vest and the shooter's poor marksmanship. Palmer brushed off the incident, even telling one associate it was 'all in a day's work'.

Had John Palmer really made so many enemies that he didn't even know who to point his finger at any more? Many months later he learned that a joint Spanish/UK police unit had watched the attempt on his life take place in Las Americas and done nothing about it.

Palmer claimed the shooting was encouraged by the police after they told one of his enemies where he would be at a specific time and then sat back and waited for him to be targeted.

A Scotland Yard police source later admitted: 'It's true the police were watching Palmer but when the shooting failed they decided not to reveal themselves.'

In fact, it now seems likely that John Palmer set up the 'hit' himself because he wanted to test whether the police were on his tail. He presumed they'd have to reveal themselves if someone was taking a shot at him.

Unknown to John Palmer, police investigators in Italy and France were also busy assembling evidence linking Tel to terrorism. Tel's own assets in Lebanon – said to be worth at least £10 million – were frozen. Tel even hired a team of lawyers to fight that decision and eventually won the right to prevent the asset-freezing order from being enacted. But all this went on without the knowledge of John Palmer because it was never mentioned in the media.

Back in Madrid, Palmer's *numero uno* enemy Judge Garzón considered the violence and chaos in Tenerife to be the perfect excuse to further expand his investigation into all of John Palmer's alleged criminal activities on Tenerife, from timeshare to terrorism.

On the war-torn streets of Las Americas, John Palmer's army was seriously depleted.

Desperate for some more trustworthy staff after his experiences with Tel, Palmer even flew over some associates from the Midlands and appointed them as senior timeshare executives. They were delighted to get a chance to live in the sun and earn a decent crust. After all, Palmer's criminal activities had always been the stuff of legends back in Birmingham. Within weeks, one of Palmer's associates was carrying a Crvena Zastava 99mm automatic at all times because the streets of Las Americas were far from safe. Palmer's new Clumpers were reportedly in possession of silenced Uzi submachine guns and hundreds of rounds of ammunition. Magazines with cartridges for the Crvena were even later discovered at one of Palmer's penthouse apartments.

John Palmer still liked to think he had people's respect when it came to his territory in southern Tenerife. When three drunken Welsh holidaymakers challenged him to a fight in one of his favourite bars in Las Americas the whole place went quiet. Unusually, Palmer did not have any Clumpers with him at the time and he wasn't armed. But when the bar staff tried to 'guide' the Welshmen off the premises, they began kicking up a fuss.

Palmer then got so pissed off that he slapped one of them round the face. This man's two friends then came steaming towards Palmer. Moments later a hefty-looking Newcastle night-club bouncer called Danny stepped between them and saved Palmer from getting a beating. Palmer was so impressed he hired Danny on the spot.

At six foot six inches, Danny certainly had an imposing presence. However, he was in the habit of buffing up his biceps with copious amounts of baby oil. In fact, Danny's arms and chest were so shiny that Palmer immediately gave him the nickname Diesel 'because he runs on oil'.

Diesel clearly lacked the intelligence of Tel, whom Palmer had once begrudgingly described as 'slippery as a snake but far more lethal'. Diesel seemed to spend most of his time looking in the mirror while smearing his muscles with yet more lashings of baby oil. He also upset a lot of people with his tactless remarks. Many soon concluded that Diesel was so off his face on steroids he'd fall over if anyone so much as blew in his face.

Then Diesel's heavy intake of drugs led to him narrowly avoiding shooting innocent bystanders in Las Americas during an exchange of gunfire with Tel's men. When Palmer heard it, he read Diesel the riot act. Diesel then stomped off in a sulk and was never heard of again.

Palmer recruited as 'senior henchmen' a Glasgow-born hard-man called Scotty Miller. Palmer had first met Miller when he delivered the carp that Palmer kept in the underfloor fish tank of his secret apartment above the Chinese restaurant in Las Americas. Miller had even at one stage worked at a well-known Las Americas travel agency called The Green Lagoon.

Scotty Miller prided himself on his ability to fight but he also considered himself a serious artist and used to paint with oils for at least three hours a week. Most of Scotty's pictures were of views from the balcony of his flat overlooking Las Americas and he even had a couple of exhibitions in local art galleries, as well as being written about in the local Tenerife English-language newspaper. Palmer liked the fact that Scotty wasn't a 'flashy bastard'.

Palmer often joked with Scotty Miller about his broad Scottish accent. Palmer claimed no one ever understood a word Scotty was saying and Palmer himself constantly asked him: 'What are you on about, Scotty?'

One day, Palmer sat Scotty down and told him all about the problems with Tel and his associates. Palmer described it as a 'war' and warned Scotty Miller that 'more people are gonna get hurt'.

Scotty Miller shrugged his shoulders and took it all in his stride.

With Miller and Palmer's newly 'imported' Midlands associates now by his side at all times, John Palmer began trying to stamp his authority on southern Tenerife once again.

He wanted to ensure that some 'big statements' about his

intentions reached his rivals on the island, including Tel and his Hezbollah fighter unit. Palmer believed he needed to get the 'fear factor' back, which meant people wouldn't dare cross him.

So Palmer ordered Miller and his brother to hang about round the corner from a local bar where he knew a number of Tel's henchmen drank late into the night. The Millers then swooped on one of Tel's men as he drunkenly stumbled up a nearby dark alleyway. The pair brought their 'catch' to the marina where John Palmer's under-used yacht the *Brave Goose of Essex* was moored.

The semi-conscious victim was dragged up the gangplank on to the aft deck of the yacht, where he was greeted by Palmer sitting at a table supping a glass of his favourite £200-a-bottle Chateau Palmer red wine.

Then he turned to the two Miller brothers and said: 'Right, boys.'

Palmer usually avoided direct involvement in violence but he'd been very angered by the recent clashes in Las Americas and wanted this to serve as a lesson to anyone who dared to challenge his authority.

Half an hour later, Tel's henchman was flung into a row of prickly bushes on the side of the dusty main road to Santa Cruz. He was minus four toe nails and his left ear was hanging by a thread of skin from the side of his face. When a passing police car stopped to help him, the man insisted he'd fallen over trying to walk home after a drunken night out.

CHAPTER TWENTY-TWO

LONG-TERM CONTRACT

A few weeks later, John Palmer defied his own suspicious nature and broke cover to return to the UK. He wanted to see his daughters and have a break from all the tensions on the island. But all Palmer's paranoia was to prove well founded a few hours after his Learjet landed at Bristol airport. One of his lawyers called his mobile to say that a couple of detectives from Snow Hill Police Station, on the edge of the City of London, had been in touch to request an interview with Palmer, which they insisted was *not* connected to any alleged crime he might have committed.

The two officers refused to disclose to Palmer's lawyer the exact nature of what they wished to discuss but insisted it was 'a matter of life and death'. Palmer huffed at the dramatic nature of the message. He certainly didn't fancy going to Snow Hill Police Station under any circumstances. But Palmer's lawyer recommended they attend the police station as it did sound important.

Palmer suspected it was all a trick to get him into the police station and then clamp some handcuffs on him. His lawyer assured Palmer he would be with him at all times, so that would not happen on his 'watch'. Later that same day Palmer and his lawyer walked into Snow Hill Police Station.

The detectives seemed cordial at first, almost impressed to be meeting Palmer and his 'brief', which further infuriated Palmer. His lawyer insisted they should not use an interview room since the detectives had promised this was not connected to any alleged crime committed by Palmer.

So a few minutes later, Palmer, his lawyer and the two detectives settled in a quiet corner of a local pub and the police finally laid their cards on the table. They said they'd received a tip from a 'very credible source' that a criminal known to Palmer was planning to have him killed by a hitman.

Palmer did not respond at first because he was always guarded about showing his emotions, especially to police officers. For at least a minute no one uttered another word.

Then Palmer took a big deep breath and smashed his fist down on the table, almost knocking over all their pints of beer.

He was outraged that this man he thought was a friend should be trying to kill him. He was also even more irritated that the police knew about it because that made him powerless to seek revenge.

A colleague of the two detectives later said they were astonished by Palmer's reaction. 'He wasn't upset, just angry that anyone should dare to try and kill him and of course he couldn't hit back at them because the police would instantly know it was him.'

As one of Palmer's oldest associates explained: 'JP had no control of the situation and he hated that. He'd been effectively neutralized by those two coppers and he couldn't do a thing about it.'

Palmer later claimed the police deliberately told other criminals about the hitman who'd been hired to kill him in the hope it would put Palmer in further danger. The police themselves strongly denied this and later pointed out to Palmer's lawyer that they were simply doing their job and trying to protect the life of John Palmer, even though he was a renowned criminal. They also didn't want people out on the streets of London taking pot shots at each other and risking collateral damage.

Detectives at Snow Hill even offered Palmer a deal; if he talked to them about 'certain things' then they'd ensure his safety by mounting a round-the-clock guard on him. Palmer sneered at such a suggestion because the last thing he wanted was a bunch of policemen shadowing his every move. So John Palmer took his chances back in the real world.

But as a result of that police action, British, American and Spanish law enforcement agencies now knew there was a price on John Palmer's head, further undeniable proof of his criminal activities.

Palmer began travelling everywhere with three armed bodyguards. And he became obsessed with getting his own back on the man who'd hired an assassin to kill him. But then it dawned on him that there was a way to solve this problem without anyone even getting hurt.

Palmer got one of his associates to track down the criminal who wanted him dead and a proposition was put to the man. How about they agreed a fee for the hitman to be paid so he *wouldn't* carry out the contract? Palmer's associates pointed out the going rate for a killing of a criminal of the magnitude of John Palmer was most probably between £100,000 and £150,000. Palmer offered the man who wanted him dead £1 million in cash to call off the contract. He could then pay off the hitman and personally make at least £800,000 in the process

Two weeks later, the contract was cancelled. Palmer knew there was a big risk the killing would still go ahead. But he decided that if there was any suggestion the £1 million had been paid on false pretences then he'd be the one doing the killing.

Once back in Tenerife, Palmer assembled all his senior Clumpers and timeshare staff, ordering them to tone down the violence and retribution that was still occurring in his name on the island. His staff were surprised by his change of attitude but agreed to cut it all out.

Palmer even encouraged his latest 'senior henchman' Scotty Miller to get himself a 'straight' day job because he had an inkling that the police were watching him very closely and wanted to make sure everything was 'whiter than white'. So Miller took a job as an estate agent in Las Americas while still providing Palmer with muscle whenever he required it.

John Palmer kicked back for a bit and tried to reassess his position on the island. He didn't want to cut and run because he'd spent more than twenty years building up this empire, but he had to come up with a way to get rid of all the evil characters gathering on his doorstep.

Las Americas had turned into a seedy, crime-riddled version of Palmer's much-loathed Costa del Sol with small-time hustlers on virtually every street corner. An epidemic of petty offences was sweeping through the area; muggings had become commonplace. Burglary was so rife that anyone in a detached property was advised to keep dogs *and* a decent burglar alarm with direct connections to the local police station. 'It's getting bad out here.

The police need to sort out all this crime,' Palmer told one old associate, without a hint of irony in his voice.

Palmer feared that the resort would soon stop attracting holidaymakers and that could spell curtains for his timeshare business. He never once conceded that the dropping visitor numbers were undoubtedly connected to the adverse publicity he'd been attracting for years, thanks to his multimillion-pound timeshare scam and his marauding gangs of Clumpers, who were targeting anyone who upset him.

Palmer still owned so many businesses in southern Tenerife that – he admitted to one associate – if he died suddenly at least 50 per cent of those businesses would never be traced.

As part of this network, Palmer even secretly purchased one of the most popular brothels in Las Americas. He'd always said he'd never be involved in the sex business. But with Tel and his clan causing chaos, Palmer realized he needed to know what was happening out on the streets of his labyrinthine fiefdom. Palmer rarely used prostitutes himself but appreciated that they often had their ear to the ground when it came to what was happening.

Palmer hired a public-school educated one-time cocaine dealer called Phil to run the brothel. Phil amused Palmer by using the premises as a rehearsal hall for his heavy rock band, which played in local bars at weekends. Palmer often turned up un-announced at the club with a group of associates, public officials or even certain individual Tenerife police officers. He'd then encourage them to sleep with the prostitutes, who stood around the main bar area dressed in skimpy see-through dresses and chunky platform shoes.

One night, Palmer strolled in with one policeman and two other men just as Phil was performing The Who's 'Behind

Blue Eyes' with three band members. Half a dozen prostitutes were standing at the bar clapping along to the music as Phil ended the song with a Pete Townshend-style leap in the air before jokingly attempting to smash his guitar over the top of a standing amp.

Palmer joined in the applause and then requested Phil's rendition of his favourite Roxy Music track 'Love is the Drug'. Once again, the prostitutes politely applauded as Phil and his band played. Palmer was so pleased he gave each of the prostitutes £200 'tips'.

Phil's attitude towards the brothel was summed up later by one of his associates, who said: 'Phil made sure that place had a different atmosphere from anywhere else I'd ever been. He called it "The Happiest Whore House in Tenerife" and maybe he had a point.'

In 1996 the *Sunday Times* newspaper's highly respected Rich List was published and John Palmer found himself alongside the Queen as joint 165th richest person in Britain with an alleged fortune of £300 million.

When Palmer first heard about it, he thought it was a trick by Scotland Yard to try to expose him. But when a copy of the *Sunday Times* article was faxed over to his office in Tenerife, Palmer immediately got one of his associates to read it out loud and realized it was genuine.

Palmer was so chuffed he immediately held an impromptu party on the ground floor of his Island Village headquarters to celebrate what he saw as his finest achievement.

Halfway through the gathering, Palmer tapped his champagne glass with a fork and asked for his audience to be quiet for a moment.

'Well, well, well. Who'd have believed it?' said Palmer. 'As rich as Her Majesty the Queen.'

Then Palmer paused as he milked the moment.

'Not bad for a kid who can't read and write, eh?'

The audience cheered.

'All the drinks are on me!'

After that, John Palmer did something he hadn't done for years; he hit the seedy nightspots of Las Americas with a vengeance. Although just to be on the safe side, he made sure his meatiest Clumpers went ahead of him that night to check none of Tel's terrorist mates were around. And, naturally, he kept his favourite bullet-proof vest on at all times.

John Palmer's generosity that night seemed to mark a big change in his attitude towards spending money.

A few weeks later, during a brief stay at the exclusive Ritz Hotel in Paris, Palmer was about to start lunch with an associate when he asked the waiter to go through the entire wine list. Eventually, he ordered a very rare red called Petrus, which the waiter said was €490 (£350) a bottle. Palmer nodded his approval. He was so pleased with himself that he even insisted the waiter help him taste it.

Then Palmer ordered a second bottle. But this time Palmer's companion at the table glanced at the wine list and noticed that it was actually €4,900 (£3,500) a bottle. The waiter had either misread the price or deliberately deceived Palmer.

For a few moments, Palmer sat back and said nothing.

Then he laughed and said: 'What the hell. Let's have another one anyway.'

One old associate later recalled: 'JP loved telling this story against himself because he'd been the idiot who couldn't read or write properly and it had cost him thousands of pounds. He didn't even care about the waiter having conned him.'

In fact, Palmer was so tickled by what had happened that he carried a copy of the restaurant bill round with him and showed it to his associates at every opportunity. The same associate later explained: 'I reckon JP wanted to show people he wasn't the tight-fisted bastard many villains said he was and this was his way of telling everyone.'

Back in Tenerife, Palmer discovered that employing those associates from the Midlands in his timeshare business maybe hadn't been such a good idea after all. One of them fled the island in 1996 following a fire-bomb attack on his luxury villa. He'd fallen out with Palmer when he went to work for Tel and his Russian backer's rival timeshare resort.

The same former executive was eventually traced to Morocco, from where he was extradited to France on fraud charges connected to Palmer's timeshare empire. He ended up being jailed for four years and four months. Shortly after this, French prosecutors began assembling a substantial fraud case against John Palmer for ripping off hundreds of French holidaymakers in Tenerife.

John Palmer believed his former executive might have 'negotiated' his way out of a longer sentence by telling the French about Palmer's criminal activities. Palmer even dispatched two of his Clumpers to France to 'have a friendly chat' with the man in prison.

But those problems with one troublesome ex-employee would fade into insignificance compared to what was about to happen.

CHAPTER TWENTY-THREE

KILLER ON THE ROAD

M25/M20 INTERSECTION, SWANLEY, KENT,
19 MAY 1996, 1.15 P.M.

John Palmer's close associate Kenneth Noye, with a bloodied nose and swollen eyes, swerved to avoid two other cars at high speed. Noye, whose short temper had already led to the death of a policeman in the garden of his house, had just knifed an innocent motorist called Stephen Cameron to death during a road-rage attack.

As he sped through the Kent countryside, Noye made a flurry of frantic phone calls to try and rally his associates in order to hatch an escape plan. Among those he phoned was John Palmer. Without mentioning what had just happened, Noye told Palmer he needed to leave the country immediately and asked Palmer to lend him some transport.

Less than an hour later, Noye's Land Rover Discovery – still containing the knife he'd used to kill road-rage victim Cameron – was in a three-car convoy turning into a scrapyard. Minutes later the vehicle was crushed into a compressed box of jagged steel.

Not long after this, Noye was the only passenger in Palmer's

Bell Jet Ranger helicopter as it took off from a field near Bristol and headed to a golf course in Caen, in Normandy, France. From Normandy, Kenneth Noye is alleged to have then flown from an airfield in Palmer's Learjet to Madrid in Spain.

John Palmer later said he had no idea Noye had been involved in the road-rage killing in Kent, which was leading the TV news by that evening but without any mention of Kenneth Noye's name.

After landing at a dusty airstrip south of Madrid, Kenneth Noye was picked up by a limousine and driven south towards Seville. He was travelling under a false passport in the name of Alan Green.

Noye knew that the moment police worked out he was the man involved in the road-rage attack, he'd once again become Britain's Public Enemy Number One. But until they made that connection, Noye was determined to ensure he put as many miles as possible between himself and the police.

It wasn't until more than a week later that John Palmer heard on his car radio that police were linking Kenneth Noye to the killing. One old associate later recalled: 'JP went ballistic. He couldn't understand why Noye hadn't told him in the first place. He felt Noye had used and abused his trust and he knew that this killing was going to have a ripple effect on a lot of his criminal enterprises, as well as the timeshare game.'

Palmer later insisted that if he'd known Noye had committed the road-rage killing he wouldn't have helped him. Palmer later confronted Noye about it and accused Noye of 'taking the Mickey'. Noye pleaded innocence and insisted he'd been set up by the police in revenge for the killing of the undercover policeman in the garden of his home. But Palmer already knew from his own police contacts that Noye was as guilty as sin.

Palmer felt betrayed. He'd loyally tried to help his old associate but now he was determined to turn his back on Noye before the police and UK security services came down on him like a ton of bricks.

The worldwide publicity surrounding Kenneth Noye had spurred on Judge Garzón in Madrid. New up-to-date intelligence from the Spanish National Police and the paramilitary Guardia Civil provided more evidence that Palmer and his associates were still involved with swindles, protection rackets, extortion, death threats and violent attacks, as well as revealing the full extent of John Palmer's money-laundering business.

Despite being exposed by Roger Cook on nationwide television, John Palmer continued expanding his money-laundering racket and the money was still clearly rolling in. He even swapped his Learjet for a £7 million silver, black and white Gulfstream jet. This aircraft had more seats and a much longer range of 7,000 miles, which meant Palmer could easily fly across the Atlantic in one hop.

But some of Palmer's closest associates saw the purchase of the new Gulfstream as a wreckless, clumsy move. They couldn't understand why Palmer was boasting about how rich he was. But John Palmer, as ever, had his reasons; he wanted to be capable of flying at a moment's notice anywhere in the world that didn't have an extradition treaty with the UK or Spain, and he refused to hide his wealth because he considered his income from timeshare to be legitimate.

In the London underworld, rumours about the now notorious fugitive Kenneth Noye were ten a penny. Some were suggesting Noye had been killed by other criminals intent on getting rid of him because of the trouble he'd caused in the past.

But Kenneth Noye was far from dead and buried. He'd settled in an isolated area of south-west Spain a long distance from the cocaine nights and psycho-villains of the Costa del Crime. Noye even bought himself a mansion overlooking the sea under an assumed name. He'd also cleverly immersed himself in local Spanish life, meeting a beautiful Moroccan woman and becoming 'stepdad' to her son.

Back in Madrid, the obsessive Judge Garzón had come across disturbing evidence of terrorism, fraud and other crimes connected to Tel, his brother and their cronies.

The Tel dossier soon contained details of companies he owned that were registered in Gibraltar, Senegal, Tenerife, the Turks and Caicos Islands, Lebanon and Belize. It also disclosed how package-trip holidaymakers had been sold worthless 'club cards' by Tel and his timeshare staff on Tenerife.

Garzón concluded that Tel seemed to have serious ambitions to run an even more powerful criminal empire than his former boss John Palmer.

The judge also had the missing Kenneth Noye in his sights. He believed that once Noye was tracked down, he might prove to be very helpful when it came to exposing Palmer's empire.

By this time – late 1996 – John Palmer had met a couple of wealthy Russians on Tenerife and knew Tel had a Russian backer but little more. The island wasn't exactly swamped with them, or so he thought.

However, in the recently liberated Russian Federation, new billionaires were being churned out at the rate of virtually one a day. They seemed to be shadowy characters with unpronounceable names, who were often close associates of Russia's new breed of power-hungry, supposedly democratic politicians. The downfall of communism had actually been followed by blatant corruption on an industrial scale. As a result, Russia was in financial free-fall and many of those same oligarchs needed a good place to stash their illicit cash, or at least launder it.

John Palmer only truly woke up to the Russians on Tenerife when one of his timeshare employees was seriously injured in a hit-and-run incident. Palmer discovered that the Russian mafia were behind the attack and had connections to the oligarch who was rumoured to have financed Tel's timeshare operation set up in direct competition to Palmer's business.

Palmer feared he'd soon be boxed in by the Russians. They'd already started taking over bars and buying apartments and hotels, especially in and around Las Americas. Law-abiding Russian citizens had also earmarked the island as an ideal sunshine holiday destination. They liked the cheap food and booze and equally cheap entertainment.

Teams of burly ex-servicemen from the Caucasus were being spotted out on the streets either selling timeshare or women. Some were trigger-happy characters with nowhere else to go, while others were sharp-eyed, lower league criminals who'd been run out of their own neighbourhoods back in Moscow and St Petersburg by richer, more powerful criminals, who were thriving under new Russian president Boris Yeltsin.

John Palmer's pride had taken a huge knock. For the first time in his adult life, he felt as if he had been well and truly snookered. The Russians were doing exactly what he'd done twenty-odd years earlier but with a lot more firepower.

So Palmer decided it was time for a 'different' approach. Early one evening he put on his bullet-proof vest and strolled into a

Las Americas bar he knew to be owned and frequented by Russians. 'The place went quiet, like something out of a spaghetti western,' one of Palmer's oldest associates later said. 'JP had walked right into the lion's den. It was a brave move.'

Palmer sat down with a man he'd been told was an enforcer for Tel's billionaire Russian oligarch, who was nicknamed 'Misha Faberge', and owned the biggest house on the island. Palmer's sources had told him Misha had been one of Boris Yeltsin's 'personal bag carriers' and he'd been rewarded for his loyalty with the mining rights to some of the world's richest deposits of iron ore.

Palmer sat down and put a proposal to the oligarch's henchman.

Less than an hour later, John Palmer was being frisked by two bodyguards on duty outside Misha the oligarch's fortress home in the mountains overlooking the capital Santa Cruz. Misha turned out to be an aggressive, stocky, bald man in his early sixties with narrow eyes and a sweaty brow.

John Palmer then thrashed out a deal with Misha to sell him a 50 per cent share of his timeshare business on Tenerife. Palmer even revealed how to launder money through the timeshare business. He also agreed to help the oligarch set up similar timeshare 'branches' back in Russian Black Sea holiday resorts, as well as the business districts of Moscow and the newly rechristened St Petersburg.

But most important of all, Palmer told Misha that Tel had to leave the island if the deal was to go through. Palmer knew it was a gamble to make such a demand and was very relieved when the Russian shook on it. Misha said he owned an apartment in Switzerland where Tel could go.

Palmer rounded off his meeting with his new Russian business partner by singing the praises of his long-range Gulfstream Jet, which could fly nonstop to St Petersburg from Tenerife in four hours. Palmer also took up an offer of a new bodyguard from the Russian oligarch. His name was Igor and he turned out to be ex-KGB. Palmer agreed to take him on to humour Misha but was convinced from the outset that the bodyguard was only there to spy on Palmer.

But did Palmer know anything about Misha's 'colourful background'?

Misha was actually a senior member of Russia's most feared mafia group, the Tambovskaia, based in St Petersburg. They controlled the port, the entry and exit of goods, collected their commissions, a percentage of the oil and gas market, and were worth billions of dollars, according to those who knew about such things.

Before the fall of communism, Misha had twice been jailed for smuggling stolen art worth tens of millions of dollars. Shortly after his release from prison in 1990, he became a deputy in the Duma – the Russian congress. Later, after arriving in Tenerife, Misha was accused of ordering the murder of a Russian government deputy called Galina Starovoytova, renowned in the West for defending human rights and denouncing corruption in the new Russia. Misha and an associate were interviewed by police but released without charge. There were strong rumours that Misha's close friend, the soon-to-be Russian president Vladimir Putin, had personally ordered the killing and that Misha was one of his select band of 'killers'.

Misha's vast wealth and power plus his undeniable connections to Putin put him on a much higher level that neither Tel or John Palmer. On Tenerife, Misha drove a Porsche Cayenne and a BMW 645 but rarely ventured out of his large mountainside hacienda. However, secret FBI intelligence files later outlined how Misha was still making millions from his favourite pastime: trafficking in stolen works of art. His nickname 'Misha Faberge' even referred to the quality of the reproductions and fakes he frequently dealt in.

Back in Madrid, Judge Garzón knew all about Misha, his mafia connections and his friendship with one of Russian's most powerful politicians, Vladimir Putin. What Garzón didn't know at that time was that, besides his huge villa in Tenerife, Misha also owned an isolated farmhouse west of Marbella on the edge of the Costa del Sol. He called the property El Presidente in honour of his close friend Putin and often spent holidays with his family there.

Judge Garzón and his investigators were warned to be extremely careful because it was deemed likely that Misha's associates would try and take out anyone who threatened to expose his links to Putin.

Back at one of John Palmer's opulent penthouse apartments later that same evening, Christine Ketley was stunned by the speed with which Palmer had signed away half of his timeshare empire, the business they'd built up together. He explained to her that he had little choice in the matter. Palmer later said it was better than losing 100 per cent of it in a gun battle.

One former associate later recalled: 'A lot of us told JP we thought he was making a big mistake. But he reckoned it was fine. He even told me he liked the way this fella Misha did business because it was clean and fast without any dramas, which was in many ways exactly how JP operated.'

Palmer believed his deal with Misha meant he'd be able to continue running his other criminal activities on the island without any outside interference. But not for the first time in his life, John Palmer had completely underestimated the 'opposition'.

One of Palmer's oldest associates on Tenerife explained: 'That Russian weren't going to stop at half his timeshare business. He wanted it all.'

However, John Palmer did have another trick up his sleeve. He was still locked into that cocaine shipping deal with the Colombians and he saw Misha as a perfect exit strategy.

Palmer offered to hand over the Colombian deal to his new oligarch associate. At first the Russian was highly suspicious. But after Palmer had explained it all in detail, the two men shook hands on it and Palmer left the meeting a very relieved man. Palmer had been trying to wriggle out of the Colombian deal for years.

Palmer promised to set up a meeting between Misha and the Colombians to rubber-stamp the deal. But when Palmer informed the Colombians about Misha later that same day, they were furious because they didn't trust Misha as far as they could throw him.

The oligarch was equally annoyed when he heard from Palmer that the Colombians had called the deal off. But then Misha insisted on a meeting with them anyway because he realized that newly rich Russia could be the world's next big cocaine destination. When the Colombians heard via Palmer about this potential new marketplace for their produce, they softened their attitude towards the oligarch. After all, Tenerife was perfectly located as a transport hub between South America and Russia.

John Palmer was mightily relieved because his head would have been on the block if the deal had fallen through.

Soon Palmer's Gulfstream was flying between Tenerife and

St Petersburg more than the UK. Misha and his 'people' even had plans to set up new timeshare operations in a host of Mediterranean locations, as well as inside Russia itself. It was clear to Palmer that Misha was using timeshare as a filter for money laundering.

A few days after their deal, Misha introduced Palmer to another mega-wealthy Russian 'businessman' with close links to Vladimir Putin. His name was Boris Berezovsky and he was said to be the man who set up all Putin's moneyspinning deals after the fall of communism. The two men got on well and Berezovsky invited Palmer to visit him in St Petersburg to discuss some new 'business opportunities'.

He even offered John Palmer free use of his own sales offices in St Petersburg. Berezovsky and Misha wanted Palmer to help train Russian reps to use the sort of heavy-handed tactics that had been so successful for his Tenerife timeshare teams down the years.

A couple of weeks later, John Palmer called up his Gulfstream flight crew and put them on standby, packed a bag and headed to the airport in southern Tenerife for a flight to St Petersburg to meet Berezovsky.

A few hours later, just south of St Petersburg, Palmer's Gulfstream banked steeply as it prepared to begin its descent to the city's Pulkov airport. Up front in the cockpit, Palmer's pilot received a message from Russian air traffic controllers telling him that his plane did not have permission to land. The pilot was surprised because all the correct flight-plan paperwork had been submitted and then accepted during an earlier stop-off in Germany where Palmer had visited his lovechild by the German student he'd met in Tenerife. When the pilot questioned the air traffic controller's order, he was told there had been no mistake and he was ordered to turn the plane around and head to Finland to refuel for the return journey.

In the main cabin, John Palmer had no idea what was happening until he peered out of the porthole next to his seat and noticed a Russian MiG fighter jet hovering alongside one of the wingtips. Then he looked across the gangway and noticed another identical jet alongside them close to the other wingtip.

It was only at that moment the pilot came on the speaker system to inform Palmer they'd been refused permission to land. The jet fighters were there to escort them out of Russian air space. The Gulfstream only just made it to an airport in Helsinki, Finland, on its reserve fuel tank.

Palmer was gobsmacked. He'd dealt with the police, DEA agents, even politicians in his time but he'd never come against the full strength of a nation's air force. He'd heard rumours that Berezovsky and Misha were very tight with Vladimir Putin, but was astounded when Misha called him later that day to say that Putin had decided he didn't want Palmer in St Petersburg on that day because a group of US senators were visiting the city at the same time.

Palmer wondered how much longer any of his businesses in Tenerife were going to survive.

Not surprisingly, Misha, Berezovsky and their Russian 'staff' soon turned John Palmer's Gulfstream into their personalized chauffeur service. One of Palmer's oldest associates later recalled: 'Those Gulfstream flights to and from Russia were pretty wild. Often there'd be a couple of Russian ex-forces tough-guy types on board with hookers.' Occasionally the pilot had to insist couples return to their seats because they were making the plane unstable by having sex in the toilet.

John Palmer was trapped in deals he didn't believe in with

a bunch of Russian mobsters who didn't really care if he lived or died. Sometimes his Gulfstream air crew would suddenly be sent to Russia, where Palmer's so-called associates were picked up and brought either to Bristol or Biggin Hill in Kent or back to Tenerife. A few hours later, the same passengers would be flown back to wherever they'd come from in the first place.

Palmer told one associate at the time that the Russians were the most ruthless, cold-blooded villains he'd ever come across. They thought nothing of gunning down an entire family if one member of that family dared to cross them or owned something they wanted.

And Tenerife-based oligarch Misha and his St Petersburg mobsters continued to hold the biggest trump-card of all. They had the upwardly mobile and extremely ambitious Vladimir Putin on their side.

John Palmer was now nothing more than a pawn in a huge worldwide power game.

CHAPTER TWENTY-FOUR

TIGHTENING THE NET

LAS AMERICAS, TENERIFE, SPRING 1997

An influx of dozens of Italian Mafia members caught the police and John Palmer off guard when they began turning up in Tenerife. The mobsters initially used a real-estate business as cover while they set up a drug trafficking ring, purchased brothels and even started smuggling girls in from the Balkan states, as well as providing a safe haven for dozens of Italian criminals on the run.

The Cosa Nostra wing of the Sicilian Mafia were reported to be using a well-known Las Americas hotel as their operational base. John Palmer ignored this news because he had enough on his plate with the Russians. Not long after this, the Italian mafia were also rumoured to have infiltrated key sectors of Tenerife's economy, including tourism and construction.

Palmer assured his 'friends' in the Tenerife police that he and his new Russian partners would 'sort out' the Italian mafia boys in exchange for them once again turning a blind to eye to all their criminal activities.

But this uneasy peace on the streets of Las Americas was short-lived. New gangs of Eastern European criminals were starting to take over much of the island's so-called low-level criminal activity. There were also a couple of Liverpool and Irish gangs lowering the tone of the place even further. One of Palmer's oldest associates later explained: 'It was a fuckin' tinderbox and JP was caught right in the middle of it.'

When John Palmer heard from a Tenerife police source that Judge Garzón was about to send police units from Madrid to the island to tail him, he hosted a meeting with local tourist officials and tried to urge them to turn back any new law enforcement units arriving from the mainland. Palmer pointed out that too many police on the streets would put off visitors to the island.

With Misha's team of Russians running most day-to-day aspects of his timeshare empire, Palmer tried to work his way into becoming a more influential, almost upstanding, member of the community. He became the go-to person for so-called 'domestic problems' and he was seen as the only linkman to the Russians, who terrified most of the island's population.

Palmer even made clear his disgust when a 'White Slave Trade' network in Tenerife was exposed by a Madrid daily newspaper. It was centred on the illegal trafficking of women from mainly Eastern European countries. The women were provided with return tickets from their home countries by members of an organized crime group linked to the Italian Mafia.

However, as soon as the women arrived, their return tickets were taken from them and they were forced, under threat both to themselves and to their families back home, to work as prostitutes. The three men behind this turned out to be a 27-year-old Croatian, a 25-year-old Bulgarian and a 43-year-old

Italian, who'd rented local properties and turned them into brothels.

Palmer was so upset by this 'invasion' that a crew of his Clumpers went to see the three white trade operators and the sex trafficking route was immediately closed down. But John Palmer knew other small-time hoods from Eastern Europe and beyond would soon replace them on the island; indeed, it was pointed out that this sex trade would have effectively hit the profits of Palmer's rock'n'roll brothel run by ace guitarist Phil.

Residents living in homes close to John Palmer's main Island Village timeshare complex even complained to Palmer about Eastern European drug dealers hanging around on nearby streets, preventing children from being out at night for fears over their safety.

So Palmer organized for some of his Clumpers to go out and 'sort things out' after the police claimed they were too under-staffed to take any action. The very next evening, the street drug dealers had gun barrels pointed up their nostrils and fled the area immediately. Palmer was hailed as a 'good man' by the locals. But what pleased Palmer the most was that the residents said they'd prefer to come to him rather than the police when they had any problems in the future.

The Italian Mafia 'problem' then came to another head when police acting on a tip-off provided anonymously by one of Palmer's henchmen arrested a man and promptly unmasked his double identity as a renowned Mafia boss and estate agent. He turned out to be a 'financial adviser' to the bloodthirsty Calabrian branch of the Italian Mafia.

In Madrid, Judge Garzón had a big breakthrough when a couple of Tenerife policemen who were in close contact with Palmer were caught blatantly 'adjusting' crime figure data from the Las Americas area. Spain's Ministry of Law and Order immediately ordered inspections at every police station on the island. Spanish investigators led by Judge Garzón took part in the raids and found more evidence of John Palmer's still-ongoing criminal activities on the island. Spanish police also had in their possession taped conversations between leading members of Misha's Russian crime syndicate on the island, in which they discussed the fact that Tenerife had certain police officers and judges who could be bought.

But it was money laundering rather than timeshare and crooked cops that was obsessing Judge Garzón by this time. He recommended greater liaison between the police and Spain's ministry of economy and taxation, in order to keep watch on investments made by foreign individuals or companies, many of whom did not pay either income or business tax, despite their field of operations being centred in Tenerife.

Palmer knew full well he needed to bring forward an exit plan because his days on Tenerife were numbered. He didn't necessarily want to return to the UK, either. He still had tens of millions of pounds that urgently needed laundering, so he bought himself a chateau in Normandy for the bargain price of £200,000. It needed at least ten times that amount to restore it to its former glory.

Chateau Poupeliere was located in Sainte-Honorine-la-Chardonne, in the Orne Department of Normandy, and stood on fifty hectares of land. It had its own church, swimming pool, full-sized golf course plus tennis courts and a 'village' consisting of twenty-three houses. It was also just a thirty-minute hop to Kent on Palmer's Bell Jet Ranger helicopter and three and a half hours from Tenerife. France felt like a much classier proposition than the Canary Islands. Palmer already had a taste for expensive red wine and cigars. Now he would have the chateau and its vast wine cellar to match it all, even if he was resigned to wearing a bullet-proof vest for the rest of his life.

With Tenerife melting down, John Palmer began moving between his various residences on the island even more than before. By this time, he owned at least half a dozen luxury apartments as well as three villas, which he sometimes liked to use as boltholes when he wanted to disappear for a while. Palmer admitted to one old associate at this time that he didn't like the way his life was evolving but he was stuck with various financial commitments in Tenerife. This included paying out £50,000 a month to keep his businesses afloat and pay long-standing bribes to specific local government officials and certain individual police officers. Palmer began to look more nervous and drawn out at this time. Some recalled him being hesitant and almost bumbling in his appearance. And Christine Ketley seemed to be spending a lot of time back in Essex.

Palmer was often seen out dining alone wearing odd socks and dirty-looking unironed shirts. Even Palmer's trademark lightweight double-breasted suits were looking a bit tatty around the edges. And his beloved crocodile shoes had definitely seen better days.

John Palmer was down a cul-de-sac with nowhere to turn. He knew his cold-blooded Russian partner Misha wouldn't pay a penny for his remaining 50 per cent share of the timeshare business. They'd just kill him and take it for themselves. Palmer needed to disperse his other businesses as quickly as possible to avoid arrest and also make himself look far less wealthy than he really was.

The two Brink's-Mat robbers Mickey McAvoy and Brian Robinson were due out of prison at any moment and Palmer didn't want to end up being the next victim of the so-called Curse of Brink's-Mat.

But John Palmer's obsession with money meant he still couldn't bring himself to cut all his losses and just quit Tenerife.

Over in the sparsely populated south-west corner of Spain, on the Atlantic coast just below the ancient city of Cadiz, John Palmer's Brink's-Mat gold bullion co-handler Kenneth Noye had reinvented himself thanks to a new identity and a clever disguise, which he hoped would prevent anyone from working out he was Britain's Most Wanted Man.

Noye had even used some of his Brink's-Mat cash to buy a £200,000 yacht, which he immediately rented out to local hashish gangs to use for drug smuggling from Morocco.

Noye seemed to have access to a never-ending slush fund, even though when he had been released from prison he was supposed to have been penniless. Noye then invested half a million pounds in a meticulously organized hashish-smuggling operation set up by another notorious criminal based in Gibraltar – just a two-hour drive from Noye's Spanish hideaway on the windy Atlantic coast.

Villains like Palmer and Noye could never stop scheming and planning their next jobs. By now it was in their blood.

CHAPTER TWENTY-FIVE

TUMBLING CARDS

BIGGIN HILL AIRFIELD, KENT, APRIL 1997

John Palmer was worried. The mental strain caused by dealing with Misha and his Russian friends was starting to make him doubt his own sanity – he needed a break from wartorn Tenerife. So one day in April 1997 he flew back to the UK with lover Christine Ketley on his Gulfstream jet.

Palmer later said he should have known better and not allowed his emotions to rule his head.

As his jet came to a halt at Biggin Hill airfield in Kent, a unit of Flying Squad detectives surrounded the aircraft. Palmer and Ketley were immediately arrested on charges of conspiracy to defraud involving 17,000 European families who'd bought into their timeshare 'dream', the majority of whom were German and British. The couple were taken off the Gulfstream separately and Ketley was accompanied by a woman police officer to a south London detention centre.

Two hours later, John Palmer was shown into a cell at Holborn Police Station. He'd already been told he would not be going anywhere until his first court appearance the following day. Palmer later told one associate he actually felt safer in police custody that evening than being in Tenerife. Palmer even got his solicitor to pop over the road to an Italian restaurant and get him a T-bone steak and a good bottle of red wine.

Following his meal, Palmer settled down for a nap. He later said he was surprised he felt so relaxed that evening in his cell. It was as if a huge weight had been lifted from his shoulders and now he could start planning the next stage of his life.

He'd known for a long time that Judge Garzón and Scotland Yard had been gathering evidence against him and he'd actually been surprised it had taken nearly eight years to finally charge him.

The following day, John Palmer and Christine Ketley appeared at a bail hearing in court. Much to the shock and disgust of many police officers present, the couple immediately secured bail and were free to travel back to Tenerife once a week to attend to Palmer's various businesses. Palmer was said to have provided a personal cash surety of £1 million in order to secure the couple's freedom. The money was paid into the court on the spot and Palmer then paid £200,000 cash for an apartment just round the corner from the Old Bailey, where his eventual trial would be held.

The main bail condition for Palmer's release while he awaited trial was that he returned to London every Friday to sign in at a police station in the City of London.

Palmer liked to be back in his office in the Island Village complex by lunchtime every Monday. And some who encountered him during this period say that Palmer was a noticeably calmer character after his arrest for conspiracy to defraud. Palmer even urged his lawyers to slow down the court process while he tried to cover his tracks, especially back in Tenerife. He didn't want the trial going ahead too quickly because he needed time to hide a lot of incriminating evidence.

Palmer was informed by police via his lawyer that if he insisted on pleading not guilty then it would probably take at least eighteen months before a trial could be heard because of the complicated nature of the frauds he was accused of committing. That delay was music to John Palmer's ears.

In late 1997, John Palmer was implicated in something which he feared could seriously affect his chances of getting off those fraud charges. Police alleged that he and others connected to the Brink's-Mat job had financed an audacious plot to spring one of Palmer's criminal associates from top-security Whitemoor Prison, in Cambridgeshire. The escape plan involved smuggling in quantities of Semtex explosive, then blasting a hole in the prison wall before flying the villain to freedom by helicopter. And detectives alleged that Palmer's Bell Jet Ranger was going to be used.

Palmer immediately insisted the accusations were laughable. But he couldn't deny he knew the man involved, who was also a close associate of Kenneth Noye. He'd been serving eighteen years in prison for his part as leader of a multimillion-pound drug-smuggling operation. The escape bid was allegedly a 'thank you' to the inmate for being a loyal and trusted associate. In other words, he hadn't 'grassed' them up. In the end, the escape plan was foiled just days before it was due to be carried out.

So while awaiting trial on the fraud charges, Palmer continued flying back and forth between the UK and Tenerife. He used Biggin Hill airfield in Kent because it was much closer to the City of London apartment he'd purchased than flying in via Bristol.

Each week, Palmer would host intense meetings with law-yers at the flat, trying to prepare an airtight defence against the charges. It was a slow process thanks to the thousands of pages of depositions from so-called timeshare victims, as well as the mountain of paperwork connected to the complicated financial details behind Palmer's timeshare empire. Prosecutors alleged this would prove both Palmer and Ketley had broken the law on a massive scale.

Meanwhile, back on the streets of Las Americas, John Palmer's Russian so-called partners led by the mysterious oligarch Misha were charging around like crazed Cossacks on horseback swiping their sabres in all directions. As one of Palmer's oldest associ-ates later recalled: 'Those bastards took no prisoners. They just stamped hard on anyone who didn't do what they said. A lot of the residents here were terrified and kept calling JP's mobile to complain but he didn't want to get involved.'

The Russians were said to be hitting back at anyone who complained about Palmer's old timeshare operation even more violently than Palmer ever had. One particular incident summed it up: a gay couple from Eastern Europe fell for all the usual timeshare patter and then went back to head office in Las Amer-icas to sign on the dotted line. But then they demanded a refund after realizing they'd been conned. Two Russian ex-paratroopers then appeared from a back office just like Tel had done for years.

A source who worked briefly for the Russians takes up the story: 'This couple weren't just manhandled out of the office. They were taken round to an alley behind the building and beaten black and blue, then one of the Russians pulled out an automatic and shot both of them in the foot and left them there. Incredibly they both survived. The Russians called them faggots and implied that they deserved everything they got. I was so sickened I quit the next day.'

*

Over in south-west Spain, it took a supposedly genuine mistake by a criminal associate of Kenneth Noye to finally bring Britain's so-called Public Enemy Number One to justice. The police had joined forces with MI5 to electronically monitor the mobile phones of many of Noye's associates, including John Palmer. One of those associates took a call from a phone that was traced to the Barbate area of Spain, near Cadiz. The police swooped on Noye as he enjoyed a candle-lit dinner with his Moroccan lover in a local restaurant. The fiancée of Noye's road-rage victim Stephen Cameron was on hand to confirm that Noye was indeed the man she saw knife to death the love of her life.

The publicity from Kenneth Noye's arrest further irritated Palmer, not to mention other criminals directly involved in the Brink's-Mat job. It turned the spotlight back on them at a time when incarcerated robbers McAvoy and Robinson remained in their cells counting down the months to their release from prison.

While Noye was in Madrid's Valdemoro Prison awaiting extradition back to the UK on road-rage murder charges, Judge Garzón went to see him. Noye threw Garzón a few 'titbits' about Palmer in the hope it might help drag out the extradition process. Noye was desperate not to be sent back to the UK to face trial because he knew he'd end up getting a life sentence.

His artful plan didn't succeed but it certainly wasn't the last time he'd try and do a deal with the powers that be.

CHAPTER TWENTY-SIX

IN THE DEAD OF NIGHT

LAS AMERICAS, TENERIFE, SUMMER 1999

John Palmer was almost forty-nine years old and felt at a cross-roads in his life. His home in paradise had turned nasty and he missed his real home back in the Wiltshire countryside, as well as wife Marnie and their daughters.

Meanwhile, British tabloids projected 'Gangster Wars on the Costa del Crime' every time there was an incident in southern Spain. Such sensationalism irritated Palmer so much that his Clumpers stopped reading the newspapers to him every morning.

John Palmer had an inbuilt hatred of all journalists fuelled by his encounters with Roger Cook. Palmer even ordered his Clumpers to track down a local Tenerife-based freelance photographer, who snapped Palmer with a long lens after he'd landed in Tenerife in his Gulfstream jet. This particular photographer was eventually 'persuaded' by Palmer's associates to hand over the offending roll of film.

By the late 1990s the UK's police and customs services were working together inside the National Criminal Intelligence Service and one of their main targets was John Palmer. In the autumn of 1999, still unsure if they could achieve a successful prosecution of Palmer in his coming fraud trial, NCIS joined forces with Spanish police under Judge Garzón in Madrid to form a new unit devoted entirely to monitoring John Palmer and his crime empire. With help from UK intelligence services and the RAF, a worldwide surveillance operation codenamed Alpine was launched.

The main spine of Operation Alpine was based around the blueprint of a plan given to the security services by the same DEA unit who'd earlier come across Palmer during his dealings with the Colombians. The DEA had used similar techniques to monitor and then pinpoint the position of Pablo Escobar in the days and weeks leading up to his death at the hands of security forces in Medellin in 1993.

Telecommunications was the key to monitoring John Palmer and his associates. Unable to penetrate his organization with a spy, UK and Spanish police had to get inside his organization from a distance, later describing it as 'ears on target'. Sometimes this would involve specific wire taps. On other occasions it could be shadowing relevant targets and, at certain crucial moments, it even meant using RAF Beechcraft twin-engined planes specially converted into £30-million spy planes which were crammed with state-of-the-art electronic eavesdropping and direction-finding equipment.

The wingspans of the planes were six inches longer than standard models because of the antennae built into them. Five more antennae could be lowered from the belly of the aircraft once the plane was in flight. Aboard the planes, operators worked at computers set up for listening once the aircraft had reached an altitude of between 20,000 and 25,000 feet. Not even cloud cover could prevent surveillance.

Inside the plane, the two operators with headphones could monitor four locations simultaneously. The Beechcraft was even capable of transmitting real-time streaming video footage of a target to fixed or vehicle-mounted ground receivers.

The key to this type of high-level surveillance was that the target left the battery in his mobile phone. The operators could turn it on remotely if and when required without triggering the phone itself. This would enable them to get a fix on Palmer at all times of the day and night. It didn't matter how many mobile phones he threw away as long as he had one.

Surveillance specialists stationed at RAF Spadeadam in Cumbria worked in conjunction with the RAF's 14 Squadron based at Waddington in Lincolnshire, from where the Beechcraft aeroplanes were despatched on their spy-in-the-sky activities. They'd fly so high above Palmer that he would never even know he was being 'watched' and the Beechcraft planes were given complete freedom of UK and Spanish airspace while monitoring Palmer and his associates.

Palmer's obsession with 'cleaning' rooms of listening devices was pointless much of the time as high-tech surveillance was being activated from aeroplanes and ground vehicles instead. Customs officials also focused on Palmer's numerous money transactions as well. They turned up bank accounts everywhere from Gibraltar to the Cayman Islands and it was clear it mainly came from timeshare and money-laundering operations.

Palmer later told an associate that the Colombians had earlier warned him that the same DEA squad who hunted down Escobar might be on his tail, but Palmer didn't believe he was a big enough fish to warrant around-the-clock surveillance.

Across the street from his main base in Las Americas, members of a special squad under the command of Judge Garzón, sitting in unmarked cars, discreetly watched and photographed everyone coming in and out of Palmer's Island Village timeshare head-quarters.

One of UK Customs' most senior drugs investigators during the 1980s and 1990s later explained: 'We were working hard on Palmer at that time and he was masterminding huge money transactions all over the world. We could see what was happening with Palmer but until we had some concrete evidence it was difficult to even contemplate an arrest. You can't nick someone for guilt by association.'

The shadow of prison now lay ominously over John Palmer. He felt the noose was tightening around his neck and he recognized the need to pull the ultimate rabbit out of a hat if he was going to remain a free man. So he invited members of his legal defence team to fly over to Tenerife in his private jet to see how his business operated because he recognized that unless they understood his timeshare 'world' than he had no chance of being acquitted.

As a result, three of Britain's most highly respected legal brains found themselves on board Palmer's Gulfstream jet taking off from bumpy Biggin Hill airfield. Palmer had always told his lawyers he had nothing to hide and that he was determined to do everything within his power to avoid prosecution. Palmer's earlier Brink's-Mat trial had been less easy to control but these latest charges against him were, he believed, impossible to prove as long as his defence team understood the complicated nature of the allegations.

On board Palmer's plane that day, his defence team were offered champagne and snacks served by an attractive young air hostess specifically hired by Palmer for this flight. As Palmer sat back in his special lucky seat number three, he calmly and politely informed his lawyers that all the scams and high-pressure tactics used by his reps were nothing more than overzealous salesmen trying to do their job properly.

Two limousines with blacked-out windows were waiting at Tenerife South-Reina Sofia airport to whisk everyone to the Island Village resort in Las Americas. Passports had even been shown to customs officials at both Biggin Hill and Tenerife because Palmer wanted to prove to his visitors that he was a normal, law-abiding citizen.

Palmer even persuaded Misha and his men to agree not to be around when the lawyers turned up. According to one of Palmer's associates who met the lawyers while they were there: 'JP put on the charm and made sure they knew they could have anything they wanted during the trip. But I remember they all looked a bit bemused because they were most definitely out of their comfort zone.'

The three-man legal team ended up spending a total of three days on the island, during which they were shown what Palmer claimed was 'every aspect' of his timeshare business.

Wherever they went, doors opened for Palmer and his entourage. He rarely had to pay for anything but was careful to produce wads of brand new peseta notes just in case he actually needed them. It looked to the legal team as if John Palmer owned half of Tenerife, although no one said anything to his face about it.

One evening, Palmer took the lawyers out to an upmarket burger restaurant he'd acquired a few years previously on the outskirts of Santa Cruz. As the lawyers chomped on their burgers, Palmer toasted them all with a bottle of his latest favourite red wine, Vega Sicilia, which cost at least £200 a bottle.

One of his associates later recalled: 'They all looked a bit thrown because where they came from burgers and fine wine didn't really mix, but JP didn't care.'

After dinner, the three lawyers were taken to the nearby bowling alley owned by Palmer. When one of the team managed to knock down all the pins with one ball, bad loser Palmer looked stony-faced and announced he was off for an early night.

The only time the legal team saw any sign of Palmer's temper was on the final night of the trip, when he took his visitors to another restaurant he owned, also on the outskirts of Santa Cruz, for an early meal at 6.30 p.m. It was completely empty, which wasn't so surprising because the Spanish never ate in the evening before 9 or 10 p.m.

Palmer ordered steak for his main course but when it arrived he complained that it was overcooked. The others kept quiet as Palmer watched the waiter walk away from them, then he threw his napkin on the table and marched off towards the swing doors to the kitchen.

Soon raised voices were heard and what sounded like the thump of a fist on a table. Palmer eventually reappeared a bit red in the face. Sitting down back at the table, he put on a cheesy smile and filled everyone else's glasses with more wine.

One of Palmer's oldest associates later explained: 'JP wanted to impress those lawyers but he was furious with himself for behaving that way because he liked to always have his temper in check in front of outsiders.'

But that trip to Tenerife by his legal team proved very costly for John Palmer. After they'd left, he told associates he was worried that they didn't really 'get' his timeshare business. One associate later explained: 'JP wasn't happy about them. He reckoned if they didn't understand his timeshare business then he had no chance of winning because the entire case hinged on the business side of things.'

A few days later, John Palmer got a call from Giovanni Di Stefano, a lawyer who'd worked on one of his earlier cases where he had contested money-confiscation orders. He told Palmer he had some strong views on how Palmer might be able to wriggle out of those fraud charges.

Palmer was so impressed by Di Stefano's brazen approach that he agreed to meet him after he'd sought out the opinions of a few associates who'd used Di Stefano's services in the past.

Di Stefano's career had skyrocketed since they'd last met, thanks to a list of high-profile clients ranging from his Brink's-Mat gold associate Kenneth Noye to Robert Mugabe. Many of these so-called 'clients' were nothing more than people Di Stefano had offered his services to. But the publicity attached to these characters helped keep Di Stefano's name in the spot-light. As a result, other genuine but less famous clients were virtually queuing up to pay him handsomely for his services.

One of those who knew Di Stefano at the time described him as: 'A bald-headed weasel who never looked you in the eye and constantly had a sweaty upper lip.' Many believe that John Palmer knew about Di Stefano's own dodgy background but used it to guarantee he'd never blabber about Palmer's criminal activities.

Di Stefano was extremely dismissive of Palmer's legal team and encouraged him to break the so-called 'golden rule' of the legal defence by presenting his own case at his coming trial at the Old Bailey. 'You can do a better job than any of them,' said Di Stefano.

At first Palmer was reluctant to turn his back on the lawyers who'd so skilfully got him off those earlier Brink's-Mat charges.

One of Palmer's oldest associates later explained: 'Di Stefano was unlike any lawyer JP had ever met before. He was sly and streetwise and seemed to understand everything about JP's time-share business, which is more than can be said for his so-called "serious" lawyers.'

Eventually Palmer used an excuse that his original lawyers were overcharging him, which of course they were not.

However, they did continue to handle Christine Ketley's defence, which would hopefully establish beyond doubt that she had not been directly involved with any of the timeshare allegations facing Palmer. He didn't want to 'taint' her chances of an acquittal by appearing to be too close to her during their trial.

John Palmer later claimed he'd never really felt comfortable with the 'posh characters' he came across in the legal profession. And in Giovanni Di Stefano he reckoned he'd found a combination of Jack the Lad and Perry Mason. Di Stefano also seemed incredibly upbeat about Palmer's chance of an acquittal.

'In those early days, Di Stefano was like a breath of fresh air,' recalled Palmer's associate. 'He didn't talk in riddles like most lawyers and he never disagreed with anything JP said.'

Palmer also ignored cautious warnings from his own former lawyers, who dismissed Di Stefano as being 'about as relevant to the law as a milkman'.

Palmer decided they were all jealous and irritated by his decision to dispense with their services. He later said: 'They [the original legal team] were friends, I'm disappointed [to lose them]. I'd spent three hundred thousand pounds on lawyers and they weren't putting a case together.'

John Palmer's recently acquired apartment close to the Old Bailey became the nerve centre for Palmer's new defence team, led by Giovanni di Stefano. Most of the apartment was filled with ten-foot-high stacks of boxes containing thousands of pages of details and statements connected to the fraud charges. Di Stefano had at least eight assistants poring over every page looking for facts that might save Palmer when it came to the actual case.

Typically, John Palmer turned his legal defence into a full-time job. He travelled in and out of London at least twenty times over the coming months. He'd also decided to defend himself at all the pre-trial hearings, as well as the eventual court case itself. Palmer saw it in simple financial terms. He later said: 'This case was gonna cost me fifty or 60 million if I lost. They never expected that I would defend myself. It's a rubbish, rubbish, rubbish case and I was determined to win it.'

Having fired his original legal team, Palmer then unofficially hired the services of his favourite QC John Mathew as a consultant to 'train' him up for the oncoming trial. Mathew had defended Palmer with such skill during his earlier Brink's-Mat gold-smelting trial that he had been acquitted of all charges. Mathew was considered to be one of the finest defence QCs in the country, having also represented Kenneth Noye when he was acquitted of murdering a policeman in the grounds of his home.

John Mathew was paid a 'generous hourly rate' by Palmer to coach him during regular meetings at Palmer's flat in St Paul's. But it was to prove a struggle because Palmer's inability to read or write properly meant he had to memorize everything. One associate explained: 'Sure, JP had a photographic memory but this was stretching it a bit too far. John Mathew was patient, though, and worked out a "system" which would ensure that JP could cope.'

Meanwhile 'lawyer' Di Stefano's mind constantly worked overtime, trying to calculate what was to his advantage, rather than Palmer's. And in the middle of all this, Di Stefano continued to be regularly featured in the tabloid newspapers thanks to his long list of so-called celebrity clients. 'Di Stefano was a showman and JP's coming trial was being heralded as a big event, so he saw it as the perfect stage for his talents,' one of Palmer's associates later explained.

In many ways, Palmer looked on Di Stefano as a court jester. He found the Italian entertaining and he didn't even bat an eyelid when Di Stefano said he was having a few 'problems' at home and asked to stay at Palmer's apartment. One of Palmer's oldest associates explained: 'Di Stefano seemed to be living out of a suitcase but this all greatly amused JP. Palmer believed that Di Stefano was "good camouflage" because his antics took the heat off Palmer in the run-up to the Old Bailey trial.'

Palmer was particularly amused by a televised press conference given by Di Stefano about another one of his 'celebrity' clients before Palmer's case had even commenced. One source explained: 'We was watching him live on the telly when JP suddenly starts jumping up and down laughing his head off and screaming: "Cheeky bastard's got one of my suits on. No wonder he wanted to kip at my flat. He's got more front than Woolworths."'

Di Stefano had indeed raided John Palmer's wardrobe and 'borrowed' one of his beloved £1,000 Armani suits. Palmer never even reprimanded Di Stefano about his suits and when one of Palmer's associates told him that Di Stefano had been entertaining a few friends at the apartment, he laughed and said, 'Cheeky bastard!'

But besides the jokes and light-hearted banter, Giovanni Di

Stefano's publicity-seeking activities flagged him up to many others in the London legal profession. He claimed to have trained as a lawyer in Italy but no one seemed able to trace any evidence of this. As one of Palmer's associates later commented: 'Di Stefano dismissed them all as being jealous of him because he had such high-profile clients and JP accepted what he said without any argument.'

But had John Palmer had the wool pulled over his eyes?

CHAPTER TWENTY-SEVEN

THE DEVIL'S DISCIPLE

CITY OF LONDON, DECEMBER 1999

As the months passed by, John Palmer's London apartment began to overflow with cardboard boxes, each one containing fresh allegations of timeshare fraud. 'Dodgy brief' Di Stefano even complained to Palmer that he couldn't reach the bathroom at night without moving dozens of boxes first. One visitor to the office later told me: 'There were hundreds of boxes piled high everywhere. It was quite overwhelming when you walked in but JP didn't seem at all bothered by the sheer number of them. He just smiled at his legal team and said, "Well, lads. Looks like we've got a bit of work on our hands."'

Meanwhile, Palmer's £7 million black, silver and white Gulfstream jet sat alongside his £1 million Bell Jet Ranger inside the hangar in the far corner of Bristol airport, a constant reminder to detectives of Palmer's ill-gotten gains. Police were surprised Palmer hadn't tried to sell off his aircraft in case he lost the coming fraud trial and then faced a multimillion-pound confiscation order. But Palmer had changed his mind about his approach to the trial. He felt it would have been an admission of guilt if he started trying to hide his wealth. He intended using these very points to prove his innocence to the jury.

Besides learning from his favourite QC John Mathew how to defend himself at his coming Old Bailey trial, John Palmer also operated fully 'in plain sight' during the months leading up to his trial in the hope it might help convince the jury he had nothing to hide.

Giovanni Di Stefano further pointed out to Palmer that anything published before his coming trial could be labelled *sub judice*, which might lead to an acquittal on the basis that the jury had read this publicity, making it prejudicial to his trial.

Di Stefano suggested Palmer should get his autobiography published. A number of publishers were approached with the project. But when they didn't bite, Palmer ordered a couple of assistants to 'put the feelers out' about hiring someone to ghost-write his life story and then get it self-published before the trial started. Once it was released the judge would – in theory – have no choice but to throw out the case.

A number of well-known non-fiction writers were contacted and asked if they'd be interested in ghost-writing Palmer's story. I was one of those approached.

I immediately turned it down on the basis that Palmer would probably prove to be a very tricky person to interview. I also had an inkling of his main motivation for such a project.

Di Stefano even admitted it might be too obvious as to why Palmer had had his autobiography published and the idea was abandoned.

Di Stefano then suggested they needed a genuine journalistic project to stand any chance of affecting the status of his coming trial.

Palmer was keen for one last throw of the dice, though.

He'd heard from his friends inside Scotland Yard that the evidence against him was far more concrete than he had originally thought, thanks in part to detailed 24/7 law-enforcement surveillance logs and the depositions of thousands of victims of his timeshare fraud.

So, in late 1999, a female freelance journalist was offered an exclusive interview with John Palmer. Within days, she'd travelled to Tenerife to meet Palmer.

Palmer proudly showed the journalist around his marble-floored office on the first floor of his Island Village headquarters, which featured a marble fountain, an aquarium of tropical fish and a huge talking clock hanging above Palmer's desk which announced the time every fifteen minutes. Palmer insisted he needed it because he liked to constantly know what time it was and couldn't read.

When the journalist pulled out a mini tape recorder for the interview, Palmer fidgeted awkwardly with an elastic band before lowering the sound of his voice to a virtual whisper and saying: 'I don't want this taped. It's just a briefing. You just take notes.'

Then Palmer produced one of his own small handheld tape recorders and stood it up on the table between them before flicking a side switch to 'ON'.

'We'll use mine instead,' he said, grinning.

Usually at moments like this, John Palmer would stand up and walk away. But this time he could do nothing because he was the one who'd insisted on the interview in the first place.

Palmer began by immediately informing the journalist that he'd only agreed to the interview because the police were out to frame him. Palmer then denied any involvement with the Brink's-Mat gold and insisted he was not friendly with Kenneth Noye. He also said he was completely innocent of the £20-million timeshare fraud charges he was about to face at the Old Bailey.

'Why should I worry?' Palmer told the journalist. 'I won't be sent down. I'll take as long as it takes to prove that I'm totally innocent. There's not one thing I'm worried about. Only a guilty person is worried.'

Palmer continued: 'I don't have anything to do with the timeshare sales, really.'

Palmer's interview with the journalist lasted more than an hour, during which he repeated over and over again that he was innocent. As usual he did not utter a single swear word throughout the interview.

He also insisted he'd been retired for years and had been taking helicopter pilot lessons during the period when most of the so-called fraud offences had been allegedly committed.

When the journalist showed Palmer a batch of newspaper cuttings outlining his illicit timeshare 'activities', Palmer brushed them off by saying that of course there had been 'a few complaints' over the years but nothing serious.

'How many complaints?' asked the reporter.

'I don't know. I can't tell you. You get complaints for all sorts of things. We didn't have that many complaints in the fifteen years, did we,' he said, turning to his Spanish lawyer, who was monitoring the interview. 'Maybe a hundred or so? Not a big deal.'

The lawyer nodded hesitantly.

'What about the reports of people being frogmarched to the bank?' asked the reporter, referring to the intimidatory tactics used by Palmer's timeshare staff.

'Bring me one,' snapped back Palmer, momentarily losing his cool.

'Rubbish,' he went on, trying to be dismissive. 'Maybe there was one client who got drunk and got into a fight with a security guard. You know Spain, do you think anyone can march anyone to a bank without them complaining to the police? I don't walk around threatening anyone. I'm no angel, but I'm no gangster. I've become a silly gangster legend.'

'Why?' asked the reporter.

'I don't know why.' Palmer took a deep breath to stop himself sounding irritated. 'They blame me for everything.'

Then came another mention of Kenneth Noye. Palmer glanced tensely across at his lawyer, who this time avoided his gaze.

'Kenneth bloody Noye! A drink or two at a boxing match. I've met him once or twice. I never knew him. I don't want to know him.'

Referring to the road-rage killing and Noye's subsequent escape, he went on: 'If I'd been harbouring him, why didn't they come and get him? Would you hide out in Tenerife? I don't know Kenneth Noye.'

A long awkward silence followed.

'The real story,' said Palmer, finally, 'is the total police corruption and using millions of pounds of public funds – for what? Chartered accountants say I've lost ten million.'

'You must have quite a fortune then?' asked the reporter.

'I don't know how much money I've got. I'm not that kind of guy.'

'The *Sunday Times* says you're one of the richest people in Britain,' added the reporter, almost proudly.

'Yeah, well, you ask them how they calculated it,' responded Palmer flatly.

'But you must have some idea,' insisted the journalist.

'Of course I'm wealthy. I've made a very successful business. I've worked very hard.'

'Do your accusers think that because you've made such a fortune it must be dodgy?' asked the reporter, trying to sound more empathetic towards Palmer.

'They do, they do.'

Just then the reporter slowly panned her eyes around the office. Palmer followed her eye-line closely.

'Don't look round my office. I don't like people to look round my office,' he said in a flat, detached tone.

Palmer's lawyer sighed because he was sounding threatening.

'Why not?' asked the reporter.

'I like them to concentrate.'

With that, Palmer got up to go to the toilet.

'Don't let her look round,' he said loudly to his lawyer as if the reporter wasn't even in the room with them.

When Palmer returned a few minutes later, the journalist asked Palmer how many timeshare complexes he owned.

'Quite a few – ten or eleven, not all timeshare, some hotels. I'm more into leisure activities now, bowling alleys, restaurants . . . timeshare is a damn hard business.'

Just then the reporter spotted a copy of *Classic Car* magazine on the desk in front of her.

'You like classic cars?' she asked.

'Yes, I collect them.'

'How many have you got?'

'Lots, don't ask.'

'Where do you live?'

'I sometimes stay on the boat.'

'The boat?' asked the reporter.

'Yes, I've got a little boat. Don't ask me about the boat. Sometimes I stay with my lawyer. Mostly I'm in Village Heights up the hill. I've got an apartment there.'

'Do you miss England?' asked the reporter.

'I miss England. I don't want to go into my personal life. I want you to help me bring this police corruption to task. I'm going to win. Then I'm going to sue every police officer that was involved.'

Palmer was exhausted and promised himself he would never again agree to an interview. He later told an associate he felt as if he had been humiliated by the journalist.

Just before departing, she asked Palmer for the tape of the interview, so she could transcribe it for her intended article. Palmer refused her request, despite his promise at the beginning of the interview.

'Well, I didn't say I wouldn't give it to you tomorrow,' he said. 'You've done my head in. I'll be more fresher tomorrow. We'll have a little snack together.'

Within seconds of the reporter leaving his office, Palmer picked up a heavy glass ashtray and threw it in the direction of his lawyer, who ducked just in time.

'What was that all about? I was supposed to be feedin' her stuff and nothin' else.'

The following morning, the same journalist was this time shown into a side room, away from Palmer's main office.

'I've been having a think,' he began. 'You don't want the real story – you just want all this stuff about how many cars I've got, what a gangster I am.'

The woman journalist paused and then said very quietly: 'Did the word "gangster" ever pass my lips?'

'Oh, I don't mean you personally . . .'

'Can I tape this?' she asked hopefully.

'No.'

The room went silent.

Then Palmer went back to his favourite subject.

'The police have a vendetta against me. I shall enjoy tearing them apart bit by bit.'

The woman journalist rose to leave.

'I think that's about as far as we can go, John.'

Palmer gritted his teeth and offered the woman a half-hearted handshake and a sidelong glance.

'You're a very nice person, but I tell you something,' he said. 'You never once look me in the eye.'

As someone who read the resulting article later commented: 'Palmer thought he was in a police interrogation suite and could deny everything and he'd come out smelling of roses. It just doesn't work like that in the real world.'

John Palmer and Christine Ketley's fraud trial went through two false starts during which trial dates were agreed and then postponed at the last minute after requests for more time to dig up extra prosecution and defence evidence.

By this time, John Palmer knew almost certainly that the police had him under electronic surveillance, which could mean they had a lot of irrefutable evidence to use against him. At one stage, Palmer considered offering to make a deal with the police and prosecutors. But then it was pointed out to him that any suggestion of such an agreement would put him under a death sentence as it would be the perfect excuse for his enemies to have him killed.

And then there was John Palmer's DIY legal work. He stumbled over words and of course couldn't read anything, so everything had to come out of his head rather than from a piece of paper.

Palmer was starting to wonder why he'd decided to defend himself.

CHAPTER TWENTY-EIGHT

BULLET-PROOF LOVE

LONG LARTIN PRISON, WORCESTERSHIRE, FEBRUARY 2000

After serving almost twenty years in prison Brink's-Mat gang ringleader 'Mad' Mickey McAvoy was released in the early weeks of the new Millennium. Fellow robber Brian Robinson was let out a few months later. Their release soon sparked a new round of underworld rumours because of *that* missing bullion. If the gold didn't come to them, then many believed the pair would go looking for it themselves.

McAvoy and Robinson's 'home manor' was on the borders between south-east London and Kent, where many of the Brink's-Mat gang came from, including Kenneth Noye, now back in prison awaiting his road-rage murder trial.

In the middle of this same area of Kent was the airfield at Biggin Hill where John Palmer's Gulfstream still often landed and took off, much to the chagrin of the police and the underworld. Many saw his use of the Biggin Hill airstrip as a deliberate show of defiance from Palmer.

Not long after McAvoy's release from prison, detectives searching for the missing Brink's-Mat gold were tipped off about a 'burial site' on the south coast of England. Officers using hi-tech imaging equipment swooped on a timber yard behind a builders' merchants in Hastings, East Sussex. After initially conducting virtually a fingertip search, a pneumatic drill was used to dig deeper in the covered yard. A Scotland Yard spokeswoman told reporters at the scene: 'This search is based on information we have received following a lengthy inquiry, which has lasted many months. I cannot say exactly what we are looking for.'

But nothing was ever found and many suspected that the original 'tip' was given to Brink's-Mat detectives simply to divert them from other more 'relevant' areas of their inquiries. Cat-and-mouse games had been played out ever since the robbery and they showed no signs of ceasing.

John Palmer was still out on bail at the time, awaiting his trial on the timeshare fraud charges, but once again he became an easy target for the rumour-mongers. Some in the underworld were convinced Palmer had helped detectives try to find the missing gold in return for some kind of deal. Officers insisted there had been no deal. Meanwhile Palmer claimed the police had 'created' the hidden Brink's-Mat treasure story to ensure that the jury in Palmer's coming trial would know about his criminal background and therefore find him guilty.

Then, in the middle of Palmer's frenetic preparation for his coming trial, he got some good news. Just around the corner from his London apartment at the Old Bailey, in May 2000, Kenneth Noye was jailed for life for the murder of innocent van passenger Stephen Cameron on the M25 motorway intersection in 1996. The judge didn't set a tariff but most believed Noye would not be freed until 'he was a very old man.'

Many men might have been broken by such a sentence at the

age of 54 but not Kenneth Noye. Soon after being sent down, Noye began making moves to appeal against his sentence *and* conviction. He claimed he was innocent. He claimed his sentence was out of proportion with the crime he had allegedly committed and he even insisted that his prison conditions broke all the European Union rules for long-serving inmates.

There were rumours in the underworld that Noye was considering telling the police everything about his criminal activities in a bid to try and guarantee his eventual release from prison. Noye was not going to just lie down and disappear. He was convinced he'd one day be freed from prison and he was going to focus on that ambition come what may.

Meanwhile, John Palmer's arch-enemy Tel was keeping himself very busy. He'd set up a new arms supply route between Russia and the Middle East, which was helping 'feed' a number of Middle East terror groups.

Tel himself was by this time rarely seen in Tenerife. He was still based at Misha's luxury apartment in Switzerland from where he controlled all his various criminal enterprises. By this time, Tel had a rabid cocaine habit.

Tel even commissioned a journalist to turn his life story into a book just like Palmer had tried a year earlier. But unlike Palmer, Tel allowed the journalist to tape interviews for the book, which he believed would help his ambition to one day run for political office in Lebanon. In a series of interviews, Tel even claimed he'd helped hide Kenneth Noye after he'd committed the road-rage murder in Kent back in 1996.

Tel told his would-be biographer: 'Kenny Noye, he liked me a lot. He was very quiet, he came to see me, he is just a man for business.' Tel also claimed during the taped interview that

Noye had told him how, in 1986, he'd got away with killing the police officer who was watching his house.

Tel also alleged Noye had proudly recounted to him how he'd persuaded the Old Bailey jury at the Fordham trial that he was acting in self-defence. Tel also claimed he had knowledge that Noye was behind the fatal shooting of a witness to the road-rage murder Noye committed.

When Noye got wind of what Tel was saying, he let Palmer know he was outraged. He believed that Palmer had encouraged Tel to say all this but he had no idea the two had actually fallen out. Palmer recognized that Tel was playing a dangerous game by trying to create aggravation between him and Noye.

Tel had also wanted these 'secrets' to be published to send a message to both Palmer *and* Noye that he could finish them off at any time he wanted.

CHAPTER TWENTY-NINE
PLAYING THE GAME

MILLENNIUM DOME, GREENWICH, SOUTH LONDON, 7 NOVEMBER 2000, 9 A.M.

A speedboat glided up to the Queen Elizabeth jetty on the Thames and cut its two engines to avoid drawing attention. On the other side of the river, four men posing as builders unloaded a JCB, preparing, it seemed, for work on a nearby building site. They revved up the digger noisily so that the sixty-odd visitors already touring the Millennium Dome took little notice of the 'construction workers'.

At 9.30 a.m., the gang, armed with a nail-gun, a hammer, smoke bombs and, bizarrely, a Catherine-wheel firework made their audacious and extraordinary move. They believed no one would dare get in their way.

Their digger clattered at full pelt into the wire perimeter fence, crushing it in front of startled security guards. The vehicle then charged towards the Dome's Money Zone. In the mayhem, four masked men slipped inside the perimeter. Two of them moved through the narrow door of the diamond vault and headed for what they thought was the Millennium Star, a diamond so distinctive it could never be sold on the open market. The other two raiders stayed outside. Police surrounding the building immediately moved in and arrested the 'outside team', knowing that the two 'vault men' would be none the wiser.

Inside the vault, both men were about to start breaking the glass case surrounding the £200-million diamond cluster. They were, in fact, looking at a replica: all the gems had been replaced with crystal copies the day before, following a police request.

And now they were inside that vault, the robbers had effectively imprisoned themselves within the four-foot-thick concrete walls. Without a lookout standing guard, they began viciously smashing the reinforced glass cases with hammers, sledge-hammers and electric nail-guns.

The gang had planned to be in their 55mph speedboat speeding across the Thames to a rendezvous with Russian gangsters at the Mayflower pub in Rotherhithe within three minutes of grabbing the diamonds. Instead, two minutes into the raid, they were ambushed by 200 armed police, who threw distraction devices into the vault and then entered and overpowered the pair and ordered the robbers to drop their weapons and come out. None of the four men put up any resistance.

The Millennium Dome gang were told minutes later that they had been foiled thanks to a police informant. But what has never before been revealed is that John Palmer had unwittingly led the police to the robbery team through communications he had with the gang in the build-up to their robbery. Those conversations were recorded by aerial surveillance specialists in Beechcraft aeroplanes, which had become part of the Palmer monitoring team ever since the launch of Operation Alpine in 1999.

The Dome 'bust' was one of the Flying Squad's finest moments. At the robbers' eventual trial, the judge made a special point of commending the way the police handled the operation and detectives continued to claim they had an informant who'd tipped them off in order not to reveal the surveillance operation on Palmer.

The 'Dome Raiders' – as they became known in the tabloids – later received long prison sentences. John Palmer knew that fingers were pointing at him when it came to the Dome robbery. He was confused and cut all his links with anyone with whom he'd had contact during the period before the raid. In the underworld, there were rumours that John Palmer was so close to the police that they'd encouraged him to 'offer' to finance big heists and had even provided the cash he was using to lure in prospective robbers, such as the Dome Raiders.

Palmer's double-dealing habits seemed to be catching up with him. He was bewildered by what was happening all around him and realized he was in grave danger of losing control of his criminal career. Inside prisons across the UK, Palmer's name was considered contemptible. Professional criminals talked about making sure he was never able to 'grass them up' ever again.

Paranoid John Palmer became increasingly convinced that his journalistic nemesis, TV crime sleuth Roger Cook, was feeding the police with a lot of background information to be used during his approaching fraud trial. Believing that Cook was out to 'get' him, Palmer hired the services of two retired police detectives as 'assistants' to try and find out what Cook was leaking to Scotland Yard.

One of Palmer's oldest associates later explained: 'JP was so pissed off with Cook and as his troubles started to mount up, he became convinced Cook was behind a lot of it. I kept telling him that was bollocks because reporters don't even get on with the cozzers but JP wouldn't let it go.'

One evening Palmer was demolishing a bottle of his latest favourite red wine while watching TV when Roger Cook's unmistakably large features appeared on the screen for one of his regular exposés of the underworld.

'Seeing him there on the telly drove JP nuts,' recalled one of his associates. 'He reckoned Cook had caused a lot of his problems with that earlier exposé. He fuckin' hated his guts.'

Halfway through the programme – which was about British crooks on the Costa del Sol – Palmer threw his wine glass at the TV screen, then switched it off and began brooding.

A few minutes later, Palmer phoned a man who then put him in touch with another man who then gave him a mobile number for a professional hitman. Within twenty-four hours, Palmer had agreed a £20,000 fee to kill the TV reporter. Palmer later told one associate he hated Roger Cook more than any of his underworld enemies.

'What have I ever done to him?' Palmer complained to his associate. 'He should have just minded his own business but he didn't, did he?'

Luckily for Roger Cook, the 'criminal' John Palmer had commissioned to kill one of the country's most famous journalists turned out to be a police informant himself. He told police all about the Palmer 'job' after being arrested for an armed robbery a few days later.

Roger Cook was immediately visited by two detectives at his West Country home. They informed him that Palmer had hired a hitman to kill him and – trying to lighten the mood – the officer told Cook he thought £20,000 was 'a bit cheap'.

That evening armed police were stationed outside Cook's front door.

John Palmer's associates later said they believed that Palmer 'only wanted to scare Roger Cook'. One of them explained: 'JP wanted to see Cook shittin' himself because Cook had been projecting himself on TV as this great investigator who would bring all the bad guys to justice.'

To his credit, Roger Cook refused steadfastly to panic and stayed put in his house and tried his hardest to ignore the threat.

He'd proved to be one of the few people who was not afraid of John Palmer.

John Palmer was growing increasingly worried about his forthcoming trial. His apartment in St Paul's should have been a refuge from the pressures that were mounting on him, but having wide-boy lawyer Di Stefano often staying there meant Palmer couldn't get any time to himself. Sometimes Palmer wanted to shut himself away with a good bottle of wine and enjoy some downtime all on his own. Christine Ketley was spending much of her time with her family in Essex.

Palmer's bullet-proof vest was never far away and he became more paranoid than ever about his personal safety. He even used a car with a driver to pick him up and take him to his favourite restaurant just fifty yards from his apartment next to St Paul's Cathedral.

One of the few evenings that Palmer got to himself occurred on 11 September 2001. He watched the news reports of the terror attacks in the United States and immediately recognized that his future and that of his two aircraft still parked inside his hangar at Bristol airport had taken a definite turn for the worse.

By the time the second New York tower came crashing down, Palmer must have known that all the free movement he'd enjoyed across borders in his private jet would in all probability be coming to an end.

Palmer told one associate later that it was only when he watched the worldwide aftermath of the attacks as coalition troops invaded Iraq and Afghanistan that he fully appreciated just how deadly Middle Eastern characters like Tel really were. After all, it was Al Qaeda terrorists who'd brought the world to its knees and Tel had often sung their praises and had been been accused of providing fake passports to the notorious terror group. Before 9/11 it had all gone over Palmer's head. Now he was beginning to appreciate just how lucky he was to have got out alive after his war with Tel on Tenerife.

Just days after 9/11, Palmer – with one eye on the future and another on his own survival – made contact with British security service MI5 and said he had some very important information to pass on about a Hezbollah terror cell he believed was based in Tenerife.

That information was passed straight over to Spanish intelligence officers connected to Judge Garzón. A few days later, officers swept into Las Americas with the express intention of bringing Tel and his brother to justice. But they and their band of Hezbollah fighters had long since disappeared from the island. Tel was secretly living in Misha's plush apartment in Switzerland and all the others had dispersed around the world.

John Palmer clearly wanted Tel to know that he wasn't the only one capable of destruction.

CHAPTER THIRTY

IN THE DOCK

OLD BAILEY CRIMINAL COURT, LONDON, OCTOBER 2001

In October 2001 John Palmer and Christine Ketley were finally called to the Old Bailey to answer the timeshare fraud charges. As Palmer and lawyer Giovanni Di Stefano approached the main court building on the first day of the trial, Di Stefano stopped briefly to talk to the waiting press-pack. He said: 'We as lawyers can never predict outcome but we anticipate and sincerely hope that justice will not only be done but be seen to be done regardless of whether he is John Palmer, John Smith or anyone.'

Palmer's court appearance must have felt a bit like déjà vu. He'd been here before for those gold-bullion-handling charges and the show of force by the police inside and outside the court must have felt like he'd travelled back in time. Armed officers guarded the front and rear of the building. A police helicopter hovered overhead. As one of Palmer's oldest associates later said: 'They put on a bigger show of force that day than they would have for the bleedin' Queen. It was so over the top. He was being treated like an evil mass murderer.'

Next to Palmer in the dock, Christine Ketley seemed calm and collected. One member of the media in the court that day later commented: 'Ketley didn't bat an eyelid. It was as if she was standing in a queue at Tesco's waiting to pay for her weekly shopping.'

The court heard how Palmer initially invested £5 million in 450 timeshare villas, which eventually earned him £72 million. Prosecuting counsel, David Farrer QC, told the Old Bailey that Palmer was 'the largest shark in the timeshare water' and accused him of callously exploiting his clients. Farrar referred to Palmer running 'the largest timeshare fraud on record' and alleged that Palmer had swindled 20,000 people out of tens of millions of pounds over an eight-year period.

It was claimed that Palmer controlled his empire from behind a labyrinth of companies and expanded his activities with the help of a small army of thugs. The Old Bailey jury also heard how Palmer's staff made even more money for him by targeting existing timeshare owners and persuading them to buy again. Palmer's company promised to sell their customer's old timeshare properties and make them a vast profit. Instead victims ended up with a new timeshare they could not afford, and an old one they could not sell at prices promised by Palmer.

'I've been portrayed as a gangster,' Palmer told the jury as he opened his own defence. 'I am not a gangster or ever have been a gangster.'

Palmer told the jury he'd been 'persecuted' because of his alleged links to the Brink's-Mat robbery. When prosecutors mentioned how his fortune was estimated at £300 million and he shared a spot on the *Sunday Times* Rich List with the Queen, Palmer tried to brush it off but couldn't help sounding smug about his alleged wealth. He even bragged to the jury that he had plenty of money and did not need to make more through a 'Mickey Mouse con', which was what he described the timeshare fraud allegations. But Palmer's courtroom boasts about being super-rich sounded cold and distant.

Under cross-examination by the prosecution and later Palmer, police officers alleged Palmer was connected to the Russian mafia and led a criminal gang involved in fraud, money laundering, drug trafficking, bribery, possessing firearms, and falsifying passports and credit cards.

In a hushed courtroom, Scotland Yard detective Roy Ramm referred to Palmer's appearance on the *Cook Report* TV programme and turned towards Palmer himself and said: 'Our view is that you were a serious organized criminal trapped by his own words into admitting laundering money.'

Ramm described Palmer to the court as 'a strange man', who was well aware of the number of enemies he had accrued over the years. 'He was quite an arrogant man, which led him to dismissing his barrister,' said Ramm. At least four times during Palmer's questioning of Scotland Yard detective Ramm, he described Palmer as 'a serious organized criminal'.

John Palmer soon began sensing that the case was not going his way. Defending himself had been extremely stressful on top of facing a barrage of cross-questioning from the prosecution team. Palmer's constant insistence he was innocent combined with questioning witnesses as his own defender took a huge toll on him. He struggled to concentrate as his mind wandered back to past highs and lows while prosecutors made him sound like the Devil Incarnate.

Sometimes Palmer's mind drifted to Kenneth Noye and how his road-rage killing of Stephen Cameron had probably played the single most significant role in driving forward Palmer's prosecution. The police had been made to look stupid once too often and this was their way of getting their own back.

When Palmer had to switch 'hats' from being the defence lawyer to answering questions in the dock, he tried to do so with calmness and clarity. But he came unstuck when the prosecuting counsel asked Palmer to read a letter out loud that had been written by one of his alleged timeshare victims.

Palmer didn't respond and stood in complete silence for a few moments. He was asked by the judge if he was okay. Palmer nodded, gulped in a mouthful of air and tried to start reading the letter.

'Take your time, Mr Palmer,' said the prosecutor, knowing full well that Palmer was unable to properly read or write.

Palmer stuttered, took a sip of water from a glass, then stopped and stared straight at the prosecuting counsel. He felt they were laughing at him for deciding to run his own defence. And that sense of humiliation was eating away at John Palmer.

Another two-minute gap of silence followed as no one uttered a word in the courtroom.

Then Palmer slammed his fist down on the podium in front of the entire courtroom and threw the letter down.

It was a glimpse into the real John Palmer. For once he was not in control and worse still, he'd been humiliated for something that wasn't really his own fault. It was his bad education which meant he couldn't read or write. It had nothing to do with his career in crime and that hurt him badly. He wasn't used to being made to look like a fool.

In the middle of the trial, there was more bad news for Palmer when the so-called Curse of Brink's-Mat once again reared its ugly head.

The latest victim was 63-year-old alleged Brink's-Mat robber Brian Perry. He was shot by a masked hitman in the chest and back as he got out of his car in Bermondsey, south-east London. Perry was found lying in a pool of his own blood after local residents heard gunshots. The assassin's dark-coloured car – with false number plates – sped off towards the Old Kent Road and was later found abandoned nearby. Whoever commissioned the hit was sending out a very obvious 'message': if the missing gold or the millions of pounds in cash made from smelting all that gold was not forthcoming then there would be hell to pay.

Perry had earlier served a nine-year prison sentence for his role in laundering profits from the Brink's-Mat raid. At the time of his murder, it was strongly rumoured that Perry knew where at least £10 million worth of the gold from the heist remained hidden. He was also suspected of secretly helping the police with their inquiries.

Back at the Old Bailey, John Palmer tried to put aside all his feelings about Perry's murder as the trial turned into one of the longest fraud hearings in British legal history. It even took the jury twenty-one days to reach a verdict.

By the time the foreman of the jury finally stood up in front of Judge Gerald Gordon and said 'Guilty' it almost felt like an anticlimax for the hushed courtroom after such a long and arduous case.

This time there were no kisses to the jury. No smiles on the faces of his friends and family in the public gallery. But when the judge sentenced Palmer to eight years in prison, it didn't seem that bad on the basis that he could get out after serving half of that with any luck.

Palmer was also ordered to pay £33 million in cash and assets to the state and ordered to hand over £2.7 million in compensation to his victims.

As one lawyer later commented: 'Juries do not like listening to people bragging about how rich they are. It breeds resentment.'

Alongside him, Christine Ketley received a two-year suspended sentence after Judge Gerald Gordon said he accepted that in her dual role as mother and lover, it was difficult to divorce herself from what was happening. 'You were in a sense caught by your situation,' he said. As she left court with her family and friends, Ketley breathed the words: 'What a relief.'

Behind the scenes, John Palmer had actually agreed a secret deal with prosecutors in exchange for Ketley receiving a non-custodial sentence. She later said she'd been deeply touched by how Palmer had taken most of the blame over the fraud allegations. But once again allegations that Palmer had informed on other criminals to police spread like wildfire through the London underworld.

Meanwhile the police had at last had their day: Detective Constable Herbie Fryer, from the Metropolitan Police's Serious and Organized Crime Group, told reporters outside the Old Bailey: 'Palmer and his gang deliberately conned thousands of British holidaymakers into parting with their hard-earned cash. They offered dream holiday homes at dream prices – and thousands of people fell for it. The victims' vulnerability was undoubtedly increased by being on holiday far from home, and was exploited by misleading sales talk, alcohol and other tricks. Many of them were elderly or retired couples who lost their life savings thanks to the salesmen's trickery.'

Also, outside the Old Bailey, Giovanni Di Stefano informed the media that John Palmer intended to pay the £2.7 million compensation order but would appeal against the £33 million payment, the highest ever such award, which the court had earlier agreed Palmer could pay in instalments.

Di Stefano, lapping up all the press attention, repeated the same old Brink's-Mat gold excuse by adding: 'Brink's-Mat will always be with him. I'm sad to say that his acquittal has led to a persecution rather than a prosecution.'

Many, including detectives, were actually surprised the eight-year sentence was not longer. Palmer believed he would be out in four years if he kept his nose clean. Elsewhere in the UK prison system, Kenneth Noye considered Palmer's sentence to be like a drop in the ocean compared to the 'life means life' tariff he was facing.

Palmer had broken a golden rule of the underworld; he'd believed he was more astute than his own lawyers and that he would get off the charges without their input. He'd taken the advice of a lawyer whose own professional background was now being thoroughly investigated. Palmer told one associate many years later: 'I screwed that one up. I allowed Di Stefano to run things when I should have known better.'

John Palmer hated feeling any regret about anything he'd done in the past. He looked on it as a sign of weakness. But even he later conceded that if he'd retained the legendary A-Team of lawyers who'd helped him get that acquittal on the earlier bullion-handling charges, then the outcome of this trial might have been very different. That A-Team consisted of solicitor Henry Milner, John Mathew QC and junior barrister Ronald Thwaites. These same three lawyers had successfully defended Kenneth Noye for the killing of policeman John Fordham during the Brink's-Mat investigation, as well as getting several other suspected Brink's-Mat robbers and handlers off.

In Madrid, Spanish law-enforcement agents led by Judge Garzón were approached by a British businessman who claimed he was owed £200,000 by Tel. The informant gave Garzón a dossier containing details of Tel's companies and terrorist connections and claimed the Lebanese ex-militiaman had tried to have him framed for murder when he asked Tel to pay back the debt.

Within days, Tel was arrested in Switzerland where he was living in one of Misha's apartments. He was charged by Swiss authorities with weapons trafficking from the former Soviet republics to various terrorist groups in the Middle East, including Hezbollah. When they raided his home, police also found several envelopes packed with money of different currencies. Besides Tel, others arrested included three Britons, six Lebanese, two French and six Spaniards. Two of the Spaniards were a policeman and a Guardian Civil officer.

John Palmer knew he could so easily have been caught up in the terror racket, which would have resulted in a prison sentence four times longer than the one he got. Was it possible Palmer had traded off Tel in exchange for a guarantee that he would not serve more than half his sentence for timeshare fraud?

Tel was said to be closely linked to not only the outlawed Hezbollah movement in Lebanon, but also the Syrian-backed Amal movement. He and his gang were eventually charged with raising more than £7.5 million for those terror groups through forging credit cards and organizing fraudulent timeshare deals.

Police did not specifically say how much of the money raised by Tel and his gang went to the Middle East.

And at the same time as the Swiss raid, Spanish police swooped on four property companies in Tenerife, including one with a giveaway name called Libano Sur (South Lebanon) as well as an upmarket restaurant in Santa Cruz.

During raids on the other suspects besides Tel, police took away five vans filled with documentation and evidence that would be sent for analysis to the National Court in Madrid, under the juristriction of Judge Garzón. He ordered the freezing of several bank accounts in Spain connected to Tel and his 'friends'. But police did eventually say there was no known connection between Tel's men and those accused of involvement in the terrorist attacks on the World Trade Center and Pentagon on September 11, 2001.

It was clear Tel's arrest was based on a lot of wire-tap evidence. During one phone call, Tel had been heard by authorities discussing a delivery of 'chairs' with Amal terror leader Nabih Berry. Later it was claimed this was a reference to arms.

Tel was expected to face trial within a year. But then something happened which shook John Palmer to his core while he was locked up in prison. Tel was suddenly granted bail and released despite the serious nature of the charges against him.

'How the hell did he get out on bail?' Palmer asked one visitor in prison. 'That bastard's stitched me up. I know it.'

Palmer was convinced that Tel must have started 'singing' to the authorities and in exchange for his co-operation, he was now a free man.

A combination of paranoia and old-fashioned fear was turning John Palmer into a much twitchier character that he'd previously been. Things were happening outside prison that were beyond his control and he didn't like it one bit.

CHAPTER THIRTY-ONE

HELLMARSH

BELMARSH HIGH SECURITY PRISON, SOUTH-EAST LONDON, WINTER 2001/2002

After sentencing at the Old Bailey, John Palmer had been taken straight to Belmarsh Prison, recently constructed and renowned as the most secure jail in Britain. It was very different from Brixton, the only other London jail Palmer had ever served cell time in. Belmarsh had been specially built in 1991 to house inmates considered a security risk. It was the first new prison to be built in London since 1885. Palmer considered Belmarsh to be a ridiculous overreaction against him by the police. They wanted him to look dangerous while he portrayed himself as nothing more than a hard-working businessman.

The atmosphere inside Belmarsh was so flat and dead, that many inmates christened it 'Hellmarsh'. Palmer found himself sharing prison landings with terrorists, murderers and even serial killers. But he considered himself above such riff-raff and tended to talk only to a small handful of old-school professional criminals in there with him. Palmer was concerned about the police planting a spy 'prisoner' alongside him to try and gather more evidence against him. He knew Spanish investigators led by Judge Garzón were still looking at prosecuting him.

Inside Belmarsh, visitors faced a vast array of security procedures that included two air-lock doors followed by a thorough search, which involved removing belts, watches and emptying pockets. Then came an X-ray machine, a metal-detector test and a full pat-down. Visitors were then taken through solid doors and gates just to reach the jail's visiting area.

Palmer's Wing Three cell was just six feet wide by ten feet long. A small, wire-mesh-covered window provided a view of nothing more than a grey wall. Palmer's cell contained a small TV on a plastic desk in a corner and a metal toilet in the opposite corner.

Each morning, breakfast for Palmer consisted of cereal, milk, a teabag, sugar and jam, which he'd collect the night before. He was allowed a kettle in his cell, despite the fact that adding sugar to hot water could easily scar his least favourite warder if they had a fallout.

At 8 a.m., inmates were allowed out of their cells for legal visits, education workshops and employment. Typically, John Palmer went out of his way to get on well with the prison staff. He knew they held the strings to everything inside. Bad behaviour could result in power being turned off in a cell, as well as the water supply being cut off.

Palmer was permitted just one hour a day in the exercise yard, where he'd walk around in a circle chatting with a carefully selected group of three 'guards': other prisoners he paid for protection. A request by Palmer to be allowed to wear his bullet-proof vest in prison was declined. Occasionally, other inmates would gather round Palmer in the hope he might open up about his underworld adventures. But mostly he kept to himself because he didn't want anything he said to be used against him later as evidence.

In the outside world, some of Palmer's enemies came out of the woodwork now he was under lock and key. They ranged from embittered mistresses to underworld rivals. This infuriated Palmer because none of them had ever had the bottle to confront him when he was out and about.

Less than a month after the case ended, Appeal Court judges blocked an attempt to take Palmer's £33 million and Palmer was told he didn't have to pay out another penny. Once again, it appeared that John Palmer had won the day. In his mind, keeping that money was far more important than a few years banged up in prison.

Shortly after Palmer's conviction, police heard rumours circulating that he'd fallen out with Kenneth Noye after lending him his private jet following the road-rage killing of motorist Stephen Cameron on the M25. As a result, both men were kept in separate prisons 'for their own safety'. Palmer remained in Belmarsh while Kenneth Noye was under round-the-clock guard in top security Whitemoor prison in Cambridgeshire, where both men had once tried to help another man escape during that earlier prison-break plot.

Palmer told the police the rumours about his fallout with Noye were rubbish and most likely cooked up by spiteful villains and certain individual police officers. He knew such stories could be very damaging to him and his few remaining criminal enterprises.

Every now and again in Belmarsh, John Palmer came across one of Noye's underworld associates in a prison corridor or the canteen. Usually there would be a quick glance, then a nod and a sly smile. Nothing more.

*

In Tenerife, Billy Robinson – Palmer's onetime favourite henchman – was attacked and badly beaten by a gang of men in Las
Americas. Robinson made no formal complaint to the police
about the incident but Palmer heard rumours that Billy was now
working full-time for a new group of Russians, who'd opened
yet another timeshare operation through which to launder all
their black money.

John Palmer had his trusted henchman Scotty Miller over
in Las Americas, running what remained of his empire. But
his most important priority at this time was an obsession with
being transferred to a 'lighter' prison than Belmarsh.

Palmer still employed Billy's wife Flo to man the fading reception area at Palmer's once impressive Island Village headquarters
in Las Americas, which was being run by Russians working for
Misha, the Russian oligarch.

Palmer had become quite wary of the Robinsons in recent
years after discovering they came from the same part of north
London as the two crime family brothers Bill and Ben, who'd
known Palmer since his Brink's-Mat days. Palmer had his suspicions that the Robinsons might be 'too close' to the crime
family.

After sixteen years on the island, the Robinsons were now
driving expensive cars, wearing designer clothes and seemed to
own at least two villas. Their grown-up son Liam ran a travel
agency and the couple also regularly flew to London where
many of their family members lived.

'But there was a feeling at this time that Flo and Billy were
pushing their luck,' one of their timeshare colleagues later
revealed. 'They were trying to keep everyone happy while sneak-
ing round doing business behind people's backs.'

Whatever the truth of the matter, Flo and Billy Robinson's

two Jack Russell terriers Sid and Nancy had become almost as famous as their owners in Las Americas. The two handbag-sized dogs were renowned for jumping into the pool at the Robinsons' villa while chasing dragonflies.

John Palmer heard about the Robinsons' swimming pool parties and wondered if the couple had been shooting their mouths off about his activities. One of Palmer's oldest associates later said: 'JP had always looked on Billy and Flo as a couple of entertainers, a bit like those Elvis impersonators, drag queens and stand-up comics he'd employed back in the old days. But now he was left wondering in his jail cell what they were really up to.'

Meanwhile, the so-called Curse of Brink's-Mat continued on its path of death and destruction. Following alleged robber Brian Perry's death, two of his oldest associates were murdered near the busy Kent ports of Chatham and Rochester. Jon Bristow, 39, and Ray Chapman, 44, had both separately purchased expensive boats shortly before they were killed. In the south-east London underworld, it was claimed that the two men had been 'bigging it up' with wads of Brink's-Mat cash they said Perry had given them for 'services rendered'.

In prison, John Palmer had no doubts that the Brink's-Mat robbery was going to be the death of a lot more people yet.

There was a new theory doing the rounds that the killings were being carried out by other villains trying to make sure Palmer's associate Kenneth Noye never got released from jail. They wanted to make it look as if the murders had been 'commissioned' by Noye. As one south London underworld source explained: 'Think about it . . . it does make sense . . . It would explain why these executions were being carried out in such a public manner. Noye was the perfect fall guy.'

CHAPTER THIRTY-TWO

BANGED UP

LONG LARTIN PRISON, WORCESTERSHIRE, SPRING 2002

After months of pressing prison authorities to allow him to be transferred to what he considered a 'less rigid' jail, John Palmer finally got his wish and was transferred to Long Lartin Prison, where Brink's-Mat robbers 'Mad' Mickey McAvoy and Brian Robinson had once resided. Many of the inmates at Long Lartin came from old-school professional criminal 'stock', which suited Palmer after the serial killers and terrorists in Belmarsh, although he knew to tread carefully when it came to any of McAvoy's friends still inside.

In fact, Palmer had nothing to do with the transfer. Prison authorities had been secretly approached by British and Spanish security services who needed Palmer in a 'softer' prison so they could more easily monitor him.

One former detective later explained: 'Palmer thought that now he'd been found guilty and sentenced he was off the hook. But the investigations into him racked up a notch after his trial. There was a determination to pursue him on all fronts.'

As a result, electronic listening devices were planted in Palmer's cell and visiting area as well as a house in Essex where Christine Ketley was now living. Within days of Palmer's transfer to Long Lartin, he was recorded giving orders to an associate to make a money transfer of £60,000 into Ketley's British bank account. It was the first of many such transactions that Palmer sanctioned from inside prison, which were recorded by the authorities.

Long Lartin Prison might have been categorized as a maximum-security establishment but it was a much smaller and less restrictive place than Belmarsh. Palmer thrived in the more laid-back atmosphere. He was assured by the governor that if he kept out of trouble he'd be released after serving no more than half of his eight-year sentence.

Palmer even signed up for an adult literacy class held twice a week in the prison library. He seemed to have finally decided to try to improve his reading and writing skills. But police monitors soon concluded that Palmer only joined the classes because it enabled him to have more free time to run all his outside businesses.

Police had been told the surveillance operation on Palmer would be a very lengthy process because Spanish and British prosecutors wanted irrefutable evidence that would guarantee them airtight cases against Palmer.

Inside Long Lartin, John Palmer had his ear constantly to the ground and noticed the underworld was going through yet another seismic change. Drug prices were tumbling and the so-called art of robbery was making yet another comeback. Familiar targets included Heathrow airport, the location for the Brink's-Mat robbery more than twenty years earlier. It remained a transport hub for tens of millions of pounds' worth of goods each day.

In 2002 and 2004, two robberies at Heathrow – or 'Thiefrow', as it had become known in the wake of the Brink's-Mat heist – flagged up a new breed of robbers. Unaware his every move and word was being monitored, Palmer put the word out from his prison cell that he was up for financing some 'big jobs' on the basis that he'd get a generous return on his investment.

Two of Palmer's oldest associates claim Palmer invested from inside prison at least £100,000 cash into the development stages of two robberies carried out in 2002 and 2003.

But thanks to those listening devices inside Palmer's cell, the UK's National Criminal Intelligence Service (NCIS) were once again informed about the robberies before they'd taken place just as they had been for the foiled Millennium Dome job. Ironically, Palmer would later be accused of 'grassing up' those robbers, which greatly contributed to the hatred felt towards him by so many underworld figures.

There was a presumption in the underworld that Palmer had deliberately stitched up the two robbery gangs in order to ingratiate himself with the police. But of course neither Palmer nor his criminal enemies realized he was once again unwittingly feeding all this information to the police, thanks to sophisticated surveillance devices recording his every move.

Soon many inmates began to avoid Palmer because they'd all heard the same rumours that he was a 'grass', although no one had the courage to tell him to his face.

Palmer was then informed by one old associate there was rumour that a new contract had been put out on him. Palmer shrugged his shoulders at the news. He was sick of being targeted and was starting not to care any more.

Palmer promised Christine Ketley that they would live in their newly acquired house in Essex once he got out of prison. Palmer had lost interest in his chateau in Normandy. He eventually got his accountants to sell it on to one of his former timeshare side-kicks. But in the end, Palmer had to virtually give the property away because the running costs were so high.

The same man who bought the chateau was himself later arrested by French authorities and accused of money launder-ing. It was alleged he'd purchased the chateau from Palmer at an 'illegal' knockdown price as part of a money-laundering scam. Palmer's former colleague got bail, immediately fled to Bali and never returned to Europe again. But he kept in close contact with Palmer. Within a year, the same man had left Bali and headed to Thailand where he set up a couple of timeshare resorts, using – some suspect – money from John Palmer.

In June 2002, Palmer was interviewed by police in Long Lartin Prison and accused of 'directing crime activities' on the Costa del Sol and the Canary Islands. Detectives told Palmer they'd arrested one of his senior timeshare executives when he arrived in the UK from Tenerife and that this same man was now 'helping them with their inquiries'.

Naturally, Palmer refused to comment. It struck him that the police were about three to five years out of date. He'd already wound down most of his 'business interests' in Tenerife. Detect-ives told Palmer they had evidence of castles, planes, yachts and luxury mansions and believed he was still sitting on a fortune in excess of €600 million.

Palmer laughed at mention of that figure but still refused to say a word on the record. He knew that back in Tenerife his loyal sidekick Scotty Miller was juggling a lot of balls on his behalf.

Palmer didn't realize it but Scotty Miller had just been beaten up so badly by a rival timeshare operator in Las Americas that he'd had to pretend he'd tried to kill himself because he didn't want to involve the police. Yet despite all this, Scotty remained steadfastly loyal to John Palmer, although the stress of it all was definitely getting to him. Mind-boggling bouts of insomnia had left Scotty looking like a shadow of his former self.

And he had a feeling his days were numbered.

CHAPTER THIRTY-THREE

THE FLYING SCOTSMAN

APARTMENT BLOCK, LAS AMERICAS, TENERIFE, JULY 2002

Scotty Miller always woke up at dawn in his third floor apartment, close to the headquarters of what remained of John Palmer's once booming Island Village timeshare empire. Scotty struggled out of bed and went to feed his tropical fish. His aquarium had always been 'the real love of my life', he'd told his boss John Palmer many times in such a broad Scottish accent that he often had to repeat himself at least three times. Scotty had blown almost a thousand pounds on the state-of-the-art tempered glass tank for his large selection of tropical fish 'friends'. One time Scotty had even admitted to Palmer that he often talked to his fish when he was feeling a bit low.

On this particular morning, Scotty watched the sunrise slowly ascending above the Atlantic Ocean from his balcony.

In some ways, he envied John Palmer's jail sentence. At least he didn't have to deal with this day-to-day shit, Scotty must have thought to himself. It was never-ending; aggravation with trigger-happy Russians; loan sharks circling because he owed them money; angry locals no longer afraid of the name 'John

272

Palmer'; and certain corrupt police officers demanding back-handers for information they'd already told other people.

Scotty Miller, now aged 39, had tried drink and drugs to drown out his ongoing sense of helplessness but none of it had made him feel any better. Scotty had been happy to run things for John Palmer a few years earlier because he needed the money. But Tenerife had changed beyond recognition.

Even the round-the-clock sunshine couldn't lift Miller's mood any more. He told one friend he'd grown to hate waking up every morning because it was always the same; sun, sun and more sun. 'I don't know what day of the week it is most mornings because it's always the fuckin' same,' Scotty told one of his oldest friends in Tenerife. He longed for some grey clouds and a splattering of rain to remind him of his childhood out on the streets of Glasgow. Back on his balcony that morning, Scotty lit a cigarette while watching the deep orange sunrise sending speckled rays of golden light across the living room of his apartment. *Just another day in fucking paradise*, he thought to himself. *Just another day in fucking paradise.*

A few minutes later, the only noise that could be heard from Scotty Miller's apartment was the desperate, flickering sounds of Miller's tropical fish twitching in a macabre dance of death on the floor of his living room surrounded by shards of glass from the aquarium, which had been smashed to pieces.

In the bedroom lay Scotty Miller, his half-naked body smeared in blood from a gaping wound in the carotid artery of his neck. This had been caused by a pointed or sharp object, possibly a piece of glass from the aquarium. It also looked as if someone had tried to mutilate his genitals.

Next to Scotty on the bedside table was a very convenient list of the names of the people he loved.

Local Policia National officers, who broke into Scotty Miller's flat later that morning, found a trail of blood, which suggested the wound in his throat had been inflicted while he was in the living room and then he'd stumbled into his bedroom before collapsing.

Scotty's friends and neighbours told police he suffered from depression. But the police were far from convinced it was suicide, so they opened an investigation to determine the real cause of Scotty Miller's death. Out on the streets of Las Americas many were already saying it had to be murder.

More than fifteen hundred miles away in Long Lartin Prison, John Palmer reacted to the news of Scotty Miller's death with a guarded mark of respect. 'Shame. He was a good kid.'

The hard, cold edge of John Palmer was never far from the surface. 'JP seemed to accept death as if it was nothin' special,' recalled one old associate. 'Maybe that's how he got through doin' what he did.'

Detectives eavesdropping on Palmer in prison were disappointed he wasn't more animated about Scotty Miller's death. They were beginning to wonder if he had discovered he was being monitored behind bars.

John Palmer and his associates eventually concluded that Scotty Miller had probably been murdered as a warning to others not to speak to the Spanish police, who were at the time trying to persuade timeshare workers to become informants to provide new evidence to launch further prosecutions against both Palmer and Tel.

Palmer reckoned the latest batch of Russians whom Billy Robinson seemed to be working for were the most likely culprits, which was convenient. Palmer had never forgotten how Misha the oligarch told him that Russians liked to make sure their murders always looked like suicide. A couple of criminals known to Palmer – who were in the money-laundering game in London – had been found splattered on pavements after supposedly jumping from high-rise apartments. Misha said they liked to call such deaths 'Russian Suicides'.

In Scotland, Professor Anthony Busuttil, a leading forensic pathologist and an expert in suicide, told the media that the method of suicide in Miller's case was 'exceptionally rare'. He explained: 'I see about three to four suicides a week and over a year you will only get one or two where people have cut their own throats.'

But eight weeks after Scotty Miller's death, Tenerife police closed the case and marked it 'suicide' after all. Apart from the forensic evidence, police on the island had concluded that Miller took his own life because of an alleged suicide attempt just a month before he died. On that occasion he'd been rushed to hospital with cuts to parts of his body. No one came forward to say Scotty had actually got those injuries when he was beaten up by timeshare rivals.

Tenerife police insisted Scotty must have mutilated himself after he was depressed over a recent break-up with a girlfriend, and because of the pressure of running John Palmer's fast-fading empire.

But many on Tenerife believed that Spanish detectives had 'conveniently' decided Scotty Miller's death was suicide because they were afraid of confronting the foreign gangsters, who'd taken over so much of John Palmer's territory. The autopsy report on Miller's death was never made public and many suspected that certain individual police officers knew a lot more than they were admitting.

Then, like the proverbial bad penny, the Curse of Brink's-Mat yet again reared its ugly head. On 14 May 2003, Brink's-Mat gang member 'Georgie Boy' Francis, 63, was gunned down at point-blank range as he sat in his car outside a courier business he ran in south-east London. He should have known better after being injured by another shooter seventeen years earlier, but 'Georgie Boy' had apparently believed he was untouchable.

Brink's-Mat insurance investigator Bob McCunn – who'd spent years tracking Palmer and many others in a bid to find the missing gold – later said he believed both Francis and earlier murder victim Brian Perry were probably 'quite literally fishing for gold and they got too close' and paid for it with their lives.

Murder squad detectives visited Long Lartin Prison to interview John Palmer about the death of George Francis. He immediately accused the police of deliberately trying to wind up other criminals into thinking he was an informant by making such a high-profile visit. Palmer told the officers he had nothing to say and suggested they speak to his lawyer next time they wanted to see him.

John Palmer always held hands with Christine Ketley during her visits to see him in prison. He said he couldn't wait to get out and move into their house in Essex, which was located next to a large country park in South Weald, a tiny hamlet with a population of just 1,829, near Ketley's family home in Brentwood. Palmer heartily approved of the property because it was completely isolated from other homes.

Ketley still occasionally visited Tenerife to oversee the couple's remaining legitimate businesses, including a restaurant. There was also a swish cocktail bar and another restaurant in the centre of Tenerife owned by the Crown Leisure Corporation, sole administrator and shareholder one 'S. L. Ketley'. In addition, there was one of the largest flats in the El Beril complex also in Ketley's name. She was also listed as the sole director or administrator of some real-estate businesses on the island, as well as being the 'final beneficiary' of a portfolio of companies based in the British Virgin Islands.

In Madrid, Spanish prosecutors were supposed to make a freezing order on all Ketley's assets in Tenerife but it never happened. Judge Garzón was so irritated he ordered his investigators to begin assembling a new timeshare fraud case specifically against Ketley, which would carry a custodial prison sentence if she was found guilty at any subsequent hearing.

In Long Lartin Prison, Palmer was recorded by NCIS investigators organizing money transfers to pay for an extension to be built on the couple's Essex property. Ketley also continued to receive a sizeable monthly sum to pay for the running costs of the house. Ketley even opened a legitimate money-lending business called Essex Pawn Stars, in Brentwood, near their home.

Back in Tenerife, Palmer's yacht, the *Brave Goose of Essex*, remained moored in a marina, untouched by Spanish or UK authorities, who were powerless to seize it. Palmer had long since fired the lowly paid Filipino crew after deciding there was no point in having them.

There was still outrage in the media that John Palmer's vast fortune still remained relatively untouched. But the latest twist in his battle to hold on to his fortune took even Palmer by surprise. The £33 million compensation order against Palmer was reinstated by three judges who were then overruled by a superior court judge on the basis that those judges had misunderstood and misapplied the law and Palmer's case had been wrongly decided.

This enabled Palmer to once again be allowed to keep the £33 million he'd been ordered to pay back. Most believed Palmer had at least six times that amount.

Norman Brennan, a serving police officer and director of the Victims of Crime Trust, later told reporters: 'Who said crime doesn't pay? It's never paid so well for John Palmer.'

Ironically, John Palmer's secret lover Saskia Mundinger had a lot more success in the High Court than all those appeal judges put together. In early 2004, Palmer was ordered to pay £3 million to the former German student after the court heard that Saskia – who was in her thirties and by this time lived in London – had been paid £60,000 a year by Palmer since the birth of their child following their affair in Tenerife. But Saskia decided she wanted a bigger chunk of Palmer's fortune. As a result, the High Court awarded her a total of two homes worth more than £1 million, £100,000 a year and £600,000 in security. Palmer also faced hundreds of thousands of pounds in legal bills.

Inside prison, John Palmer said he was 'gutted' by the legal ruling but privately admitted it was a small price to pay after that earlier £33 million confiscation order had been overturned.

As usual, Palmer was juggling. He was a past master at bouncing back from all types of adversity.

CHAPTER THIRTY-FOUR

BACK IN THE REAL WORLD

LONG LARTIN PRISON, WORCESTERSHIRE, SUMMER 2004

So while John Palmer cooled his heels in prison, his onetime Tenerife henchman Billy Robinson was tarnishing his reputation on the island by continuing to work for the latest gang of Russian timeshare invaders.

Billy and wife Flo even wrote letters to Palmer in prison to keep him informed about developments in Tenerife without mentioning Billy's new job.

John Palmer's main concern was that Billy Robinson might have blabbered about his activities in Tenerife. However, with Flo still holding the fort at the crumbling Island Village headquarters, it didn't make sense for Palmer to do anything just yet.

Then Palmer heard that Flo and Billy had splashed out a million pounds on a flashy new villa up in the mountains overlooking Las Americas. 'Cuban palm trees every fuckin' where, big garden, fuckin' great big pool and a bloody lagoon crammed with goldfish the size of Dover sole,' one of Palmer's oldest Tenerife associates told him during a visit to Long Lartin.

Palmer rolled his eyes. 'What's with all these tropical fish, eh? Scotty had a load of them as well but they didn't do him much good, did they?'

'Yeah, Flo's smothered herself in so much permatan she looks like one of her own fuckin' goldfish,' added Palmer's visitor. 'Billy's given her a one hundred thousand pound Merc convertible. Suddenly they're fuckin' loaded.'

And Palmer's associate added: 'And those two fuckin' dogs. What they called again?'

'Sid and Nancy,' Palmer replied without the hint of a smile.

'Yeah, Sid and fuckin' Nancy. Well, my missus was in the hairdresser with Flo last week and those fuckin' dogs went for some old girl's ankles and they had to be dragged out of the place. They should be fuckin' put down . . .'

John Palmer nodded his head slowly at that last remark.

Flo and Billy Robinson were indeed skating on very thin ice. When Flo tried to entice Billy's Russian boss to a pool party up at their house, he looked at her as if she was mad. When Jack Russell terrier Sid growled at the same Russian, he promptly kicked the dog so hard it flew across the room and landed in the corner with a nasty squelching sound.

Flo immediately scooped up her injured pooch and marched out of the Russians' office muttering something about 'fuckin' foreigners'.

At home that night, Flo tried to persuade Billy to quit his job with the Russians and come back to work at Palmer's crumbling Island Village resort. But Billy was earning four times his Palmer salary and besides, he knew he couldn't walk away from the Russians in one piece.

A few days later a friend of Flo's visited John Palmer in prison: 'Flo needs you to help her sort out the Russians, JP,' said the man. 'She wants Billy to come back and work for you.'

Palmer said nothing for a few moments while he mulled over the request.

'Too late, old son,' he finally said. 'Tell her that she and Billy are on their own. I can't bail 'em out no more. It ain't like the old days.'

Back in Tenerife, Sid's broken leg was now in a cast balanced on a stick between a couple of small wheels which enabled the dog to move around more easily, although he could no longer dive in the pool while chasing dragonflies.

Flo Robinson still fancied herself as a bit of a tarot reader. But she'd shuffled her cards (so to speak) very close to her chest in recent months. As one of the couple's oldest friends on the island later said: 'Flo should have looked into her own future and then she would have realized she and Billy needed to get off that fuckin' island as quickly as possible.'

In early 2005, John Palmer finally stepped out through Long Lartin Prison's high steel gates and back into the real world after serving four years for the timeshare fraud.

Palmer had told Christine Ketley not to turn up at the prison gates in case the press were waiting for him. An early morning departure had been agreed with the prison governor to help him avoid the expected media scrum. But there was little public interest in John Palmer by this time. The press considered him a bit of a burned-out old dinosaur of crime.

With no bullet-proof vest to keep him safe, Palmer simply put his head down against the wind and walked speedily towards a dark Mercedes with blacked-out windows waiting in the prison car park.

Twenty minutes later, Palmer was in his Bell helicopter as it lifted off from a nearby airfield and headed south towards the peace and quiet of the Essex countryside, where lover Christine Ketley was awaiting his return in their newly refurbished home. He was no doubt relieved to find one of his beloved bullet-proof vests on board the Bell after all those years.

Palmer's decision to live in the UK after his release from prison surprised a few people because there was a public campaign mounting against him, thanks in part to his exposure by heavyweight TV investigator Roger Cook, who continued to pursue him despite those earlier assassination threats.

Palmer was also aware that another bankruptcy probe was on the horizon because British and Spanish officials still refused to let Palmer off the hook when it came to his finances. Hundreds of Palmer's timeshare victims also sued him once again, this time for more than £3 million, but a few weeks after his release he was again declared bankrupt in the United Kingdom, this time with alleged debts of nearly £4 million.

Yet John Palmer probably still had hundreds of millions of pounds hidden away in a variety of 'unusual' locations.

Meanwhile, UK and Spanish law enforcement agents were busy transcribing thousands of pages of transcripts of recordings made during many years of surveillance on Palmer and his associates via mostly wire taps and spy planes. Everyone involved realized that the only way to properly nail Palmer was to transcribe everything and then study those transcripts thoroughly before presenting evidence to persuade prosecutors to launch a new case. One police detective involved in the operation later explained: 'It was a hell of a long process but we were told that we'd get him in the end. But it was hard to watch him still throwing his money around on helicopters and limousines when we knew where all that money had come from.'

*

In the middle of all this, John Palmer still found it hard to turn down a 'decent deal'. This time he was tempted into investing in a huge shipment of cannabis. Palmer knew that prison sentences for hash smuggling were much lower than for cocaine and it wasn't even considered a lethal substance in many countries.

Three months after his release from prison, Palmer got a call from an old-time professional ex-robber from south London, who'd known him since the Brink's-Mat days. He told Palmer he had a friend who wanted to put a proposition to him that could earn him millions.

Palmer initially replied that he wasn't interested and was about to put the phone down when his associate told him the name of the man who wanted to meet him: Howard Marks. Palmer was intrigued. After all, Marks was probably the most famous hash dealer the world had ever known and his life story read like something out of spy novel. He'd been educated at Oxford then got into the drugs game and even claimed to have worked as a spy for MI6 at one stage, as well as serving a long sentence in a US prison.

Palmer liked the sound of Howards Marks, even if he was in a business that Palmer probably should have avoided like the plague. So Palmer invited Marks to the Savoy Hotel in London for lunch.

Howard Marks's personal charm and wit could not be more at odds with the dour, quiet John Palmer but within minutes of arriving in the quaint riverside restaurant the two men were getting on like a house on fire. Marks was entertaining Palmer with war stories about life in a tough prison in the Deep South of the USA and the bumbling coppers he'd made to look stupid down the years. Palmer was intrigued by Marks because he was unlike any criminal he'd ever met before.

It wasn't until this unlikely couple were halfway through their main course at the Savoy that Howard Marks mentioned the 'deal of the century' which he wanted Palmer to help finance.

One of Palmer's oldest associate explained: 'Howard was offering JP 50 per cent of all the profit in exchange for a £200,000 initial investment. It sounded like a steal.'

Marks claimed the cannabis shipment would garner profits of at least £2 million, which meant £1 million for Palmer.

But Palmer was used to even bigger profits from timeshare, so he hesitated. As one of his associate later pointed out: 'A villa worth £200,000 on JP's timeshare complex could make him £1.5million in profit if sold in sections over fifty weeks of the year.'

Palmer demanded a bigger percentage share: 'I'd want 75 per cent for me, 25 per cent for you,' he said to Marks. 'What d'you reckon?'

'I reckon you're a greedy fuckin' cunt,' muttered Howard Marks, his 'happy hippy' expression having drained from his face faster than a sinking stone.

Before Palmer could respond, Howard Marks stood up, placed his napkin on the table and walked out of the restaurant.

Palmer's associate later explained: 'JP told me he blew the Howard Marks deal out of the water deliberately. He'd decided he didn't trust Marks. Afterwards, JP tried to contact Marks. JP said all he'd wanted to do was explain everything but Marks was so offended he refused to ever talk to JP again.'

Many years later Howard Marks hinted at his meeting with John Palmer when he said to me in his broad Welsh accent: 'Hmmm. John Palmer. Not a very pleasant individual.'

*

Towards the end of 2005, Tel was arrested on new terrorism charges, when he tried to slip back into Tenerife on 'business'. But once again Tel was quickly released and given bail. Palmer became even more convinced that he must have done a deal with various law-enforcement agencies in order to keep his freedom.

Following his latest release without charge, Tel tried to gain the upper hand by calling a news conference in Tenerife where he told the media all about his knowledge of the local under-world. It was a clumsy 'in plain sight' move by Tel that was intended to get the heat off his back and enable him to rejoin forces with his old partners, the Russians.

At an expensive restaurant in Santa Cruz – ironically, one of John Palmer's favourite watering holes – burned out, coke-addled Tel rattled away at a hundred words per minute to a group of bewildered reporters, some of whom didn't even real-ize who Tel really was. The press conference ended prematurely after paranoid Tel confronted two shady-looking reporters in sunglasses whom he accused of being real criminals.

Palmer's decision not to head back to Tenerife looked like an extremely smart move on his part. He was told by one of his few remaining police contacts on the island that Tel had done a deal with the DEA which was enabling him to side-step any charges. However, this agreement was put in jeopardy when Tel continued working as a gun runner for terror groups. It seemed Tel was using the DEA as protection to ensure he could continue all his criminal and terror activities without risking further arrest.

The DEA were so infuriated by Tel's double-dealing that agents proposed sending a snatch squad to Tenerife to grab Tel and smuggle him directly by plane to the notorious US terrorist internment camp at Guantanamo Bay. But in Madrid Judge

Garzón refused to give the Americans permission because so many of Tel's alleged crimes had been committed on Spanish soil where justice needed to be served.

This brief impasse between the Spanish and American authorities enabled Tel to flee and seek refuge with the Colombians. They offered him work scouting for 'secure' isolated locations to drop off cocaine shipments on West Africa's deserted coastline. The Colombians had targeted three poverty-stricken countries just a short hop from Tenerife.

In Essex, John Palmer shook his head with astonishment every time he heard more about the chaos in Tenerife. There seemed to be forces at work on the island that were from areas that were way beyond Palmer's remit. Palmer later admitted to one associate that his arrest and subsequent imprisonment in the UK probably helped save his life. He had little doubt he would have been murdered if he'd stayed in Tenerife.

Palmer had grown to really hate Spain, the country he'd used and abused for so long. He was sick of being connected to virtually every major crime committed in the southern half of Tenerife.

A classic example came when 31-year-old Brit John Joseph Shannon, born in Liverpool, and his partner Anarda De La Caridad Pérez Friman, also 31, of Spanish nationality and Cuban origin, were murdered in their rented villa in what police described as a 'timeshare-connected killing'. It was later claimed the couple were about to leave the island for a meeting with Palmer in the UK when they were killed. But this was later discounted by detectives as yet another 'Palmer rumour'.

John Palmer had always embraced new technology, going back to when he was one of the first people to own a mobile phone in the late 1980s, when they were the size of a brick. But the use of mobile phones had become so prevalent by 2005 that he'd concluded they were the biggest risk to his liberty.

He ordered everyone close to him to dump their pay-as-you-go phones on virtually a weekly basis. Palmer was convinced that Kenneth Noye had been arrested in Spain on those road-rage murder charges because police and MI6 had tracked other criminals' mobiles and then located a number that turned out to be Noye's, which ultimately helped pinpoint his exact location.

Before any meeting, Palmer insisted his associates throw all their phones into a big dustbin bag, which was then taken to a scrapyard and crushed into such tiny pieces that not even Scotland Yard would have been able to put those pieces together again. His attitude rubbed a lot of other criminals up the wrong way but later most of them had to reluctantly admit he was right.

By this time, John Palmer had the Russian mafia, the London underworld, the UK and Spanish police and even America's DEA on his tail, so his inbuilt paranoia was growing by the day. Not only did he wear his bullet-proof vest at all times but he'd insist on 'cleaning' any room he arrived in with a device that was supposed to pick up any wires. But the latest equipment being used by law enforcement was undetectable because it had been manufactured in plastic deliberately to avoid such metal-seeking devices.

At the end of the day, John Palmer was a middle-aged analogue criminal in a fast-moving digital age.

CHAPTER THIRTY-FIVE

WIRED

While Kenneth Noye languished in prison with a life sentence still hanging over his head, John Palmer quietly looked forward to a long and happy retirement. Palmer grew much closer to his now-teenage son James, by Christine Ketley, and even voiced regrets for some of his past actions. He told one associate he also wished he'd spent more time with his daughters.

That same associate later explained: 'A few recent close shaves had softened up JP a bit. He talked about the importance of family and how they were all that mattered. I started to wonder if he was seeing a shrink because he seemed to have become a far more reflective character.'

Palmer told one associate he didn't need most of his money and sometimes even felt bad about how he earned it in the first place. 'But then he'd grin and say he also wasn't gonna hand it back, either!' said that associate.

So it was no big surprise when one typical underworld cockroach came crawling out from under a large rock after deciding he needed John Palmer's help.

This character was a hood from a Birmingham council estate

288

just like Palmer. We'll call him 'Lem'. Many of Lem's relatives and friends had known Palmer when he was a youth. Lem was renowned as a champagne Charlie, who was very flash with his cash. Lem claimed to have close links to the players and management of a well-known English professional football club, which had at one time been in the Premiership. There were rumours Lem had even owned the club at one time through myriad typical camouflage companies.

At Lem's obligatory Marbella penthouse on the Costa del Crime, he kept seven cars including a Ferrari and a Bentley. And just like Palmer, Lem had left his wife for his secretary and the couple had just had a child. Lem's unofficial nickname 'Concorde' referred to the size of his nose, which had seen more cocaine up it than most people had had hot dinners.

Four years earlier, Lem's family had been victims of a kidnap attempt by the Russian Mob after he fell out with them over a 'business deal'. No wonder John Palmer labelled Lem as 'trouble' when he turned up at Palmer's home in Essex with a proposition to invest in a timeshare resort he planned to build in Brazil.

Lem waxed lyrically to Palmer about the opportunities in South America and compared it to Spain twenty or thirty years earlier. 'Cheap land and cheap labour and you can do anything you want if you bung the right people,' Lem told Palmer.

Palmer told Lem he needed a few weeks to mull over his business proposition. During that time Palmer had one of his recently retired tame Scotland Yard officers carry out some 'due diligence' checks on Lem. What he found out was far from encouraging.

Lem had not only ripped off other business partners in the past, but he also had a penchant for violence. One of his associates had been crippled for life after a 'disagreement' over the sale of a detached house in Palmer's childhood home of Olton.

Palmer also heard a rumour that Lem had been 'turned' by the much-feared DEA, whom Palmer knew still had him in their sights.

But instead of immediately shutting Lem out, Palmer decided to have him watched for a few weeks. It soon became clear that Lem was indeed playing a dangerous game. He was spotted having lunch with two former UK police detectives, who lived on the Costa del Sol. They were renowned for providing 'safe' transportation for drug deals.

Palmer eventually got one of his henchmen to tell Lem the Brazil timeshare deal was off. Lem said he didn't care because he had plenty of other investors available and he was going to fly out to Brazil anyway to finalize the timeshare deal within the next few days.

Lem and an associate then travelled to Brazil with two of their supposed investors, who wanted to view the section of the jungle where the proposed timeshare development was going to be built. All four men boarded a specially hired twin-engine Cessna 310 at Recife International Airport, where John Palmer had been arrested almost twenty years earlier.

The Cessna aircraft lost contact with air traffic controllers minutes before it was due to land at the coastal city of Ilhéus and was never seen again. Within hours, the Brazilian air force and police began searching a 400km-square area of the jungle for the missing aircraft.

A manager at the plane's charter firm later said: 'It was flying perfectly as it prepared to land. The pilot said he was making a visual approach to the airport, and that was the last we heard.'

In Essex, John Palmer did his customary shrug of the shoulders when he heard about the 'tragic accident' and told one associate: 'Brazil is a cesspit. I wouldn't invest my last penny there. Poor bastard never stood a chance.'

A few weeks after the crash, a story began circulating that John Palmer had had a violent disagreement with Lem shortly before he left the UK for Brazil. This fuelled another rumour that the crash was part of a deliberate plan to kill Lem because he'd become a liability.

Palmer later insisted to one associate that he'd had nothing to do with the plane crash and claimed it was more likely Lem had some serious financial problems and had faked his own death.

But some were now saying that Palmer had his own 'Kill List' to rival the one that had already been dubbed 'The Curse of Brink's-Mat'.

John Palmer wanted to maintain a low profile so he tried not to wind up too many people on Tenerife. Being based in rural Essex was certainly helpful but even so, he once again found himself being 'hung out to dry' and blamed for many violent crimes committed on the island. The death of a mother of four in Las Americas and two of her children was another classic example. Palmer was outraged by the brutal slaying. He knew instinctively this had all the hallmarks of the Russians or Eastern Europeans. But whichever way he turned, the finger of suspicion always pointed in his direction. He was convinced others were pulling the strings. They wanted to smear his name, so it took the heat off them.

Palmer later told one associate that the deaths of those innocent children had hit him very hard. He'd never agreed with so-called 'collateral damage' by criminals and he knew those dead children could so easily have been his own.

Despite his efforts to maintain a low profile, Palmer was still the subject of an intense surveillance operation by British and Spanish security services. Beechcraft spy planes often looped across Essex while monitoring Palmer's movements in his isolated house on the edge of a 500-acre country park. Other times, two-man teams of detectives shadowed Palmer's associates and family members. And a number of criminals were starting to come forward to help police nail Palmer once and for all because they were sick of his double-dealing games.

In late 2005, John Palmer sent Flo and Billy Robinson a message via what remained of his old crew in Las Americas, advising them to leave the island before 'it all goes tits up'. Flo and Billy believed the message meant their old boss Palmer was threatening them, so they mentioned it to their new Russian bosses. They assured the couple they were safe and reminded them that Palmer was no longer a big name on the island.

Not long after that last communication between Palmer and the Robinsons, Flo and Billy's adult son Liam received a number of death threats on his mobile phone.

At first Billy Robinson tried to laugh off the threats by telling his son they were probably from the jilted boyfriend of Liam's latest girlfriend. But Billy and Flo suspected they knew exactly where the threats were really coming from. Billy convinced Flo not to worry on the basis that if someone really wanted to harm their son, they wouldn't bother warning them first. But Flo was far from convinced her husband was right.

CHAPTER THIRTY-SIX

SID AND NANCY'S BIG ESCAPE

TEPPENYAKI RESTAURANT, SAFARI SHOPPING MALL, LAS AMERICAS, TENERIFE, 12 JANUARY 2006

Yappy Jack Russell terriers Sid and Nancy were sorely missed when 55-year-old Flo Robinson, husband Billy, 58, and a couple of work friends decided to meet for dinner at their favourite restaurant.

The couple adored their two dogs but it was Billy who'd insisted they leave them behind at home after Sid (the chippy one) had picked a fight with an Alsatian on the Golden Mile the previous day. Billy cracked a gag about Sid's bark being worse than his bite but no one else that evening seemed to appreciate his joke.

A crisp wind was blowing in off the Atlantic and there had even been talk that Tenerife might see its first snow for forty years over the coming days. Flo and Billy and their guests were all sitting outside because two of them were smokers.

Flo and Billy particularly liked the Teppenyaki restaurant because it was tucked away on the ground floor of the Safari shopping mall, far from the tourist bustle, on the edge of Las Americas.

But none of them noticed the skinny man wearing a helmet perched on a scooter parked thirty yards away.

As the four friends ate Japanese fusion tapas dishes including a 'Nippon' omelette with wafer-thin slices of succulent beef teriyaki, Billy and Flo entertained their guests with non-stop banter about life on Tenerife since their 'old friend' John Palmer had quit the island.

It was clear Billy and Flo were rather relieved to see the back of him. But they admitted they hated the Russians even more and told their friends all about that Russian 'lump' who'd almost killed terrier Sid when he kicked the handbag-sized dog across a room during a meeting with Flo a few months earlier.

Thirty yards up the street, the skinny man who'd been watching the outside of the restaurant while sitting on his scooter pulled out a cheap pay-as-you-go mobile and punched a number into it. Then he began talking quietly into the receiver while all the time still watching the restaurant. Others walking by later recalled the youth because he only took his helmet off momentarily while making the call and then put it straight back on.

Towards the end of the meal, the Robinsons and their friends giggled as they struggled to get Billy's new mobile phone to work. He'd wanted to call their son Liam to see how he was because Flo was still worried about the threatening phone calls that Liam had received over the previous few weeks.

Billy had bought the phone as a replacement for a perfectly good one which he'd felt obliged to throw away after a local police contact warned him that his mobile was being monitored by law-enforcement agents. Billy even surprised the other couple by mentioning they were often followed by national police detectives from Madrid, who'd been spending more and more time on the island in recent months.

Further up the street, the scooter driven by the youth had been replaced by a people carrier with blacked-out windows, which contained the vague outline of two men sitting in the front seats.

Just before the men drove off, Billy had spotted them in their minivan and cursed the police in front of the other three. He told Flo he had a good mind to go up and have a word with them.

Flo urged Billy not to bother and pointed out that it wasn't such a bad thing to have the police on their tail since there were some 'bad people' out there who might want to do them harm after their many years in the timeshare game.

At 10.30 p.m., Flo and Billy Robinson said their goodbyes to the other couple and headed off to the shopping centre car park to get their cars, which they'd arrived separately in from work earlier.

A few minutes later, Flo's convertible Mercedes and Billy's gunmetal-grey Porsche Cayenne edged out of the car park exit and headed north in convoy. The minivan with the two men followed at a safe distance. Billy spotted the vehicle immediately and nearly called Flo on the mobile to tell her he was right but didn't bother.

Flo, with Billy close behind her, headed east through the narrow streets at the back of town towards the Montana de Guaza mountains, which had a tiny covering of snow on their peaks.

The van with the blacked-out windows still hung back but remained close enough not to lose them.

Flo and Billy's cars eventually left the town perimeter to begin a steep climb up a hill that led across the valley towards the mountains. When Billy braked sharply in the Porsche as he took a right-hand turn behind Flo, he noticed the van was still behind them and gritted his teeth with irritation.

Up on the mountain road, Flo slowed down on three succes-sive hairpin bends before turning off down a narrow road. As Billy followed, he checked his rearview mirror and was relieved to see the van had continued on the main road. Maybe he'd been wrong about them after all?

Flo and Billy eventually turned off the narrow road on to a lane that led through an olive grove towards their beloved villa, in the tiny hamlet of San Miguel de Abona.

Just three hundred metres from the property, Billy's Porsche was overtaken by a speeding red 4x4 that swerved so sharply in front of him that it almost forced him off the road. The car then slammed on its brakes before a hand came out of the window and beckoned Billy to stop.

Billy pulled up sharply and jumped out of his Porsche. Ahead of him, Flo had just noticed what had happened in her rearview mirror. She braked hard and then started reversing quickly back towards them. Billy signalled with his hands for Flo to stay in her vehicle as a man emerged from the 4x4, looking apologet-ically in Billy's direction.

'Oh shit, it's the Feds,' Billy muttered to himself.

Flo – still sitting in her car – wished she'd brought Sid and Nancy with her after all.

At that moment, the black minivan from earlier appeared on the moonlit horizon in front of them. Billy squinted in its direction before recognizing the vehicle. Now he knew they were in trouble.

As Billy walked towards the man who'd got out of the 4x4, he continued looking at Flo in her car as if to say, '*Just stay there, love, I'll sort all this out.*'

As Billy approached the 4x4, he heard the sliding door at the side of the black van opening and two men emerged carrying weapons. They headed straight to Flo's Mercedes as the man from the 4x4 pointed a gun at Billy, who immediately put his hands up. He'd been through this routine many times before with the police.

It was only when he looked back at Flo's car that Billy must have realized this time it was different. The two men were dragging Flo along the dusty track towards the black van, which still had its side door open.

Billy begged them to let his wife go but ended up with the tip of the barrel of a gun making a dent in his forehead.

Behind him, Flo pleaded with the men as she was pushed into the back of the minivan.

Billy must have heard the muffled sound of Flo's screaming but couldn't see anything through the van's blacked-out windows. He was then grabbed and shoved towards the same side door of the van.

Inside the vehicle, Billy saw that Flo had collapsed on the floor and one of the men had her pinned down with his boot on her neck. Billy struggled to pull away from them, so they clumped him with a gun and he collapsed on the floor next to his hysterical wife.

No one knows exactly what happened then except that the couple were tortured inside that van to within an inch of their lives. No doubt Billy was forced to watch his wife being physically abused and then it was his turn. The beatings were brutal.

When Flo offered the men her diamond earrings worth £10,000 if they'd stop, the men ignored her and kicked her husband even harder.

The use of the van as a torture chamber was further evidence of the gang's professionalism. The only DNA evidence of what actually happened that night would have been in the van which was no doubt crushed into a small box of twisted metal within hours.

After being tortured for about fifteen minutes, Flo and Billy lay crumpled on the floor of the van next to each other. Both were then pulled out and dragged along the dusty ground. One man then leaned down next to Flo and calmly slit her throat before doing the same thing to Billy. Flo rolled over and died instantly. Next to her, Billy remained semi-conscious, so one of the men put his gun to Billy's head and pulled the trigger.

The assailants then stood and waited while the dead couple bled out before dragging Billy's corpse back to his Porsche Cayenne, where they positioned it in the back seat so it looked as if Billy was asleep. One man then got in the driver's seat, fired up the V6 engine and headed off back down towards the town.

The two men who'd arrived in the van lifted Flo's body, carried it across the road and threw it on the dusty ground next to her beloved Mercedes. There was no need to hide the corpse. The message was crystal clear.

A trucker who just happened to be driving along that narrow lane less than an hour later noticed a flock of dozens of seagulls pecking at something on the side of the road close to an abandoned Mercedes convertible. Moments after stopping to investigate, the trucker saw Flo Robinson's battered corpse on the ground and immediately rang the police.

Officers who attended the scene were slow to work out what had happened and presumed Billy Robinson had fled the scene after murdering his beloved wife, so they put out an APB alert on Billy, describing him as armed and dangerous.

CHAPTER THIRTY-SEVEN

COLLATERAL DAMAGE

LAS AMERICAS, TENERIFE, 13 JANUARY 2006

Early next morning police received a call from a factory worker who'd found Billy's Porsche on a bleak, deserted road behind the Las Chafiras industrial estate, on the edge of Las Americas. The man said he couldn't be sure because of the blacked-out windows but it looked as if there was a man asleep on the back seat.

The police swooped on the Porsche, guns drawn, expecting a shootout with a wife-killer. It wasn't until they ripped open the back door of the Porsche they realized Billy Robinson was dead.

Local police were baffled by the murders at first. Nothing had been stolen from either Billy or Flo, not even Billy's £100,000 watch. Detectives concluded that the killers had gone out of their way to emphasize how little they cared about the Robinsons and their wealth, which also probably meant that whoever ordered their death was so rich he or she simply didn't care. 'It was very personal,' one source said. 'It seems like an act of revenge. They wanted the Robinsons to suffer and those close to them to know that they had suffered.'

No trace of the killers was ever found on Tenerife. It's presumed they left the island within hours of the murders, although they would have first gone to a safe house to wash themselves and dispose of their clothes. It was likely they used a private plane to avoid all the usual customs checks.

Flo's beloved terriers Sid and Nancy were discovered that morning whimpering in a locked area in the kitchen of the villa, where they always stayed when Flo and Billy were out. The two dogs immediately scampered off in the direction of Flo's Mercedes convertible slung up on that lane just three hundred metres away. One police officer later recalled that the dogs yelped uncontrollably as they sniffed at patches of blood by the car. A dog handler had to eventually be called from Las Americas to retrieve them.

Initially, Tenerife police said little about the Robinson killings in public because they were embarrassed by the implications of the crime, which had stunned the island. Detectives even used an age-old excuse that they couldn't talk about the murders because the investigation was ongoing. Certain Tenerife police officers also knew that Judge Garzón would soon be breathing down their necks once more.

The Robinson murders sent shockwaves through southern Tenerife and beyond. Many presumed they'd been killed because they'd crossed the Russians. Others pointed out that the killings were rather convenient for John Palmer because they sent out a chilling message to other criminals not to cross him.

In Madrid, battle-hardened Judge Garzón was appalled by the ferocity of the Robinson slayings and ordered an elite police unit, Greco, to fly to the island as soon as possible to start clearing out all the organized crime elements on Tenerife. The brutal double murder had tipped the scales. Garzón knew something needed to be done immediately before Tenerife sank into a sea of criminality.

Garzón looked on the murders as John Palmer's fault, even if he wasn't responsible for the killings himself. Palmer had tainted the island for years with violence and crime and now this was his legacy.

Yet many Spanish politicians were dismissive of the Robinson killings, saying the news might harm Tenerife's already declining tourist trade. The Spanish media dubbed the Flo and Billy murders as 'typical British criminal behaviour'. Many island residents saw it as 'a British criminal problem' which they didn't want to get involved in.

The double murder of the Robinsons was headline news back in the UK because they finally exposed southern Tenerife as a lawless society. London journalists invaded the island looking for answers. But their inquiries in the bars and clubs of Las Americas were soon met with slammed doors and awkward silences.

A few days after the murders, the police announced that it was all the work of one of the burgeoning Eastern European criminal gangs that had infiltrated the island in recent years. A lot of Tenerife residents dismissed this as pure speculation by the police, who clearly didn't have a clue. Not surprisingly, many presumed the killings were connected to the timeshare business. The police eventually cottoned on to this and came up with a new explanation that the couple had been murdered by hitmen hired by rival operators.

The official trail went cold very quickly on the Robinson investigation. This suggested the police had already wound down their inquiries but in fact local detectives had simply stood aside following the arrival of Judge Garzón's specialist police unit, Greco.

Garzón was fed up with the local police but knew he had to tread carefully because of their close connections to many gangsters on the island. He gave his unit special dispensation to knock down as many doors as it took to get a breakthrough on the Robinson case.

Meanwhile, Tenerife's timeshare blog sites were soon crammed with allegations about the killings. Many implied that the Robinsons somehow 'had it coming'. One of the couple's oldest friends on the island commented: 'The way they [the Robinsons] lived and not keeping a low profile plus their connections, it was bound to go wrong one day.'

And Garzón's Greco unit was soon facing additional problems; the Robinson slayings had created a vacuum that had left the gate open for Albanian, Kosovan and Romanian gangsters to move into positions of power in southern Tenerife. Initially they homed in on control of drugs, cheap labour and organized begging rackets, but they also had plans for property and timeshare businesses.

As ever, John Palmer struggled to show much empathy when he heard about the Robinson murders back in the UK. Palmer tried to step back and take stock of the situation but it didn't really make it any easier to handle. He knew fingers were being pointed at him over the Robinson killings but that was nothing new. He'd got used to being blamed for every serious crime committed on Tenerife for the previous thirty-five years.

Palmer knew only too well that the police in Tenerife would struggle to solve the Robinson murders. In the back of his mind was a nagging feeling that perhaps the Robinsons had been architects of their own deaths.

But for now Palmer had other problems of his own to consider, revolving around his favourite subject – money. Despite having tens of millions of pounds, he couldn't get anywhere near most of it. But then neither could the authorities. In a sense, John Palmer was frozen in time at the centre of a bizarre three-way stand-off between himself, a bunch of revenge-obsessed villains and police officers determined to bring him to justice.

In the past, Palmer had often stuck to the old-fashioned underworld habit of creating secret stashes filled with cash buried around the south of England and there were still a few of them in Tenerife. They didn't contain all Palmer's money by any means, but they had enough in them to help him survive well into retirement.

However, raiding his own stashes of cash was never going to be enough for a workaholic like John Palmer, so he tried to get back into the money-laundering game by contacting his old Birmingham childhood associate GB, who was now reputed to be one of the wealthiest and most powerful money launderers in London, if not the world. But GB wouldn't even agree to meet in person because he believed Palmer was under constant police surveillance.

Palmer felt deeply insulted by this snub and left an angry message for GB on his phone. Palmer eventually received a visit from three of GB's henchmen who told Palmer that if he ever tried to contact GB again he would not live out the year.

Palmer hated being bullied but he knew from other contacts that he had little choice in the matter. GB and a couple of other launderers in London had sewn up all the wealthiest oligarchs and the Chinese and they had more influence in the UK capital than he'd ever had in Tenerife.

John Palmer was no longer the top dog.

Spanish investigators led by Judge Garzón were gradually uncovering more and more evidence of Russian and Eastern

European mafia activities in Tenerife. Garzón knew that the island's resident Russian oligarch Misha was still regularly in contact with his old St Petersburg school friend Vladimir Putin, now the President of the Russian Federation. It meant Garzón had to tread especially carefully because he didn't want to set off a diplomatic incident that would throw his entire investigation into jeopardy.

Then out of the blue on 26 August 2006, John Palmer's one-time business partner Misha arrived at police headquarters in Estepona, on the Costa del Sol, claiming that four masked men had broken into his nearby house and beaten, bound, gagged and blindfolded him before stealing valuable high-tech gadgets and a number of even more valuable Old Master paintings.

A few months later, on Christmas Eve 2006, Misha returned to the same police station and told officers that the previous night someone had kidnapped one of his guards and then entered the house to kill him. Misha told police he was only saved because he wasn't at home at the time.

Spanish detectives later recalled there were many inconsistencies in Misha's story. He had been extremely agitated and officers concluded he was most probably on cocaine at the time he went to the police station.

The following morning, Judge Garzón in Madrid was told that John Palmer's former Russian associate Misha had conveyed a message to the Spanish intelligence services saying he wanted to name a group of Russian mobsters and their connections to Vladimir Putin, as well as talk about his business dealings with John Palmer. Misha claimed Putin personally owned property in Spain and had even invested in the timeshare business he ran with Palmer in Tenerife.

Misha wanted a deal that would help save his life. He believed the raid on his house had been a warning to him to stop talking about his connections to Putin.

Judge Garzón didn't know whether to punch the sky with happiness or take a deep breath. Was the Russian billionaire trying to trick the authorities? What if Misha was just double-bluffing and wanted to get inside the Spanish investigation in order to find out what information they really had?

For the following five days, Misha was heavily debriefed but investigators were told not to offer him full-time protection until they were sure his motives were honourable. Garzón and his police agents even set up a dramatic fake raid on Misha's house in Estepona to convince his mafia friends back in St Petersburg that he was not helping them.

Meanwhile, Misha continued to plead with the Spanish for full-time protection and access to a safe house. They refused his request and pointed out that if they did this then everyone would just presume he was informing on his underworld associates and he'd probably be killed within days.

Misha stormed out of a meeting with his Spanish police controllers convinced he was about to lose his life. Nine days later, Misha decided to drive from Spain all the way to St Petersburg to confront his old mafia associates and try to get a face-to-face meeting with Putin. He'd decided not to fly because he wanted to get into the city before anyone even realized he was there. Misha felt a lot safer out on the open road in his BMW than sitting at home waiting for the inevitable knock on the door.

CHAPTER THIRTY-EIGHT

AN EYE FOR AN EYE

**MOTORWAY ROADWORKS, SAINT JULIENNE,
FRANCE, 8 JANUARY 2007**

Misha's BMW had to slow down for motorway speed restrictions
otherwise he might have been pulled over by the police. But as
Misha changed lanes, his BMW swerved into the slow lane of
the carriageway right into the path of a concrete mixer lorry.
According to a French police report, Misha's car was crushed
in a split second and careered off the edge of the motorway
and down a steep ravine. After Misha's body was identified a
few hours later, French police reported his death to the French
secret services. His BMW contained multiple documents nam-
ing certain individuals and outlining numerous Spanish bank
account details. It looked as if Misha was planning to try and
'buy' his life back by threatening to expose his former associates, including Putin himself. The French secret services soon
concluded that Misha's death was not an accident.

Palmer was, in the words of one old associate, 'completely
freaked out' by the news of Misha's death. The associate
explained: 'JP had dealt with this guy in both Russia and on

Tenerife. He'd even travelled on JP's Learjet. But it wasn't his actual death that upset JP. It was the way in which his enemies had managed to reach out and kill him, even in the middle of a foreign land.'

John Palmer could see himself being 'finished off' in just the same way. Palmer particularly loathed the way no one knew for sure if Misha had been assassinated. 'That really bugged JP,' said one associate. 'He said if he was going to be hit then he wanted the whole world to know he'd gone out with a bang.'

John Palmer had underestimated the power and influence of Misha's mafia bosses in Russia. Palmer still, in theory, had a share of two timeshare resorts in Tenerife with Misha but he hadn't been paid any of his pre-agreed commission since leaving Tenerife. Palmer didn't like people ignoring him and Misha's mafia bosses in St Petersburg were not returning calls and he felt disrespected. Like a lot of his businesses, he was feeling side-lined. It seemed as if his prison sentence followed by a decision to live back in the UK had given others an opportunity not to pay their dues to Palmer.

But Palmer knew only too well that travelling to Russia would be a huge mistake, so he kicked his heels and got increasingly bitter about the way he was being treated.

PART
THREE

THE CHILL FACTOR

FACTOR
2007–2015

Somebody's stickin' a red hot poker up our asses and I wanna know whose name is on the handle.

Mr Pink, *Reservoir Dogs*

CHAPTER THIRTY-NINE

WATCHING AND WAITING

MADRID, SPAIN, SPRING 2007

One of John Palmer's biggest problems was that Spanish Judge Garzón had studied him so closely over the previous ten years that he'd virtually got inside Palmer's head, second-guessing his every move.

Garzón had an entire wall in his Madrid office covered with Post-it notes and photos linking Palmer and Tel with dozens of major criminal enterprises and underworld figures. As one of Garzón's colleagues later said: 'He knew *everything* about Palmer, from what he ate for breakfast to his latest sexual conquests. He'd also pulled in a few of Palmer's oldest and most trusted associates and told them that they either helped him or they were going to prison.'

Garzón presented his case to each Palmer informant as a simple, clear-cut scenario. He told them all: 'Palmer will presume you're a rat whatever the truth of the matter, so you might as well get it all off your chest and help me bring him down, otherwise he'll be out there waiting for you.'

And if Palmer heard that an associate had been to see Garzón then as far as he was concerned that person had grassed him up, whatever the truth of the matter.

In the spring of 2007, John Palmer heard a strong rumour that Bill and Ben – the two brothers from that London crime family – were considering moving their entire operation to Tenerife. They were being hounded by the police in London, who wanted to bring them down in much the same way Garzón was after John Palmer. The brothers told mutual acquaintances they needed a new 'outlet' and that the island fitted the bill.

Palmer believed that if he encouraged the two brothers to move to Tenerife then other criminals might think twice about going after him. But John Palmer knew only too well how Bill and Ben operated.

One of Palmer's oldest associates had owned a very successful night club in west London back in the 1990s until the two brothers decided they wanted a piece of his action. Bill and Ben had strolled into his premises with big smiles on their faces, asked for the keys to the club and told the owner to 'fuck off'.

Palmer knew all about these sort of 'take-overs' from his days as a green young villain in Birmingham. It was a dog-eat-dog world out there and he knew he stood no chance of taking Bill and Ben on in a head-to-head battle.

These days their family were linked to drugs, extortion, robbery, money laundering, fraud and up to twenty-five murders. Masterminded by the eldest brother Bill – one of eight children born to Irish immigrant parents – the family was said to have made more than £200 million since their humble beginnings in the London slums in the early 1970s.

So John Palmer engineered a face-to-face meeting with the brothers, even though both parties were under round-the-clock surveillance by UK law-enforcement agencies at the time. There followed three dummy meetings in A-road laybys in the south-east of England with the deliberate intention of testing out the police's surveillance skills.

Once they'd cleared all these obstacles, Palmer met Bill and Ben at a pub in Suffolk. Each party brought with them two bodyguards as per an earlier agreement and the two brothers arrived in their own personal black cab, which they used to travel around the Home Counties.

All three sat at a table in the pub's garden despite the chilly weather so that any wires would have been drowned out by the noise of the passing traffic. No one knows what was exactly said between them but Palmer eventually shook the brothers' hands and then headed off back to his home in South Weald, fifty miles away.

It later emerged that Palmer had thrashed out a deal in which Bill and Ben and their family could take over all Palmer's remaining criminal activities on Tenerife in exchange for Palmer being allowed to finance robberies and other criminal enterprises inside the family's London territory. The brothers wanted Palmer's Tenerife businesses primarily as money-laundering 'tools'. Palmer insisted on retaining a couple of restaurants and other legitimate businesses but that was it. Palmer told the brothers he needed a few weeks' grace while he closed down all his other interests on the island.

One of Palmer's oldest associates later explained: 'The family were right under the cosh in the UK and saw Tenerife as the perfect place to run their operation without interference.'

Bill and Ben told Palmer they intended hiring a team of Spanish accountants to help them get their laundering and timeshare operation started.

John Palmer wasn't exactly overjoyed but he knew he was fortunate to have got through the previous six months in one piece. He also realized it was only a matter of time before the London crime family came back and made fresh demands. Here he was, a one-man band, with only a handful of henchmen and associates left to his name. Palmer was vulnerable and he knew it.

His bullet-proof vest continued to offer the most reliable protection but his use of one was so well known in the underworld by this time that criminals talked openly about how the best way to kill John Palmer was to shoot him in the legs and then aim at the head from close range.

But criminals as cunning as John Palmer always have something extra up their sleeve. After the meeting, Palmer handed the tapes from his pocket-sized recorder to a secretary to transcribe. During that meeting with Bill and Ben, he'd got them to open up about some of their previous activities. Palmer knew that on those tapes were references the brothers had made to murdering at least two of their rivals, including one of the victims of the so-called 'Curse of Brink's-Mat'. Palmer had a feeling that he was now sitting on a goldmine that might turn out to be the key to his survival.

John Palmer knew he needed to get in and out of Tenerife quickly to sort out a few things before Bill and Ben caused any chaos. It was going to be risky because Judge Garzón and many others were on his tail. But Palmer hadn't been charged with anything yet. He also wanted those classic cars back, which were gathering dust in the underground car park of his old skyscraper headquarters in Las Americas. And then there were the stashes of cash up in the mountains. A couple of those stashes were in quarries near to where Billy and Flo Robinson had lived until they were murdered.

'JP reckoned that unless he made a personal appearance on the island then the vultures would pick off his few remaining businesses without even bothering to ask first,' explained one of Palmer's oldest business associates.

In the good old days, John Palmer had always looked forward to arriving in Tenerife. But now, and against his better judgement, he was there to sort out some 'unfinished business'.

CHAPTER FORTY

UNLUCKY FOR SOME

As John Palmer's Gulfstream made a final twist and turn before levelling out for landing in Tenerife that morning, he thought back to the good old days when this was his empire and no one ever challenged him. Palmer looked down at the golden beaches and whitewashed tower-block hotels and wondered if he'd made a big mistake pulling out in the way he had and then inviting Bill and Ben – of all people – to take over.

Palmer was daydreaming along these lines as the Gulfstream slowed to a comfortable halt at the end of the run-way and turned towards his hangar in the far corner of the airport.

It was only then that Palmer noticed half a dozen police vehicles driving across the tarmac. At first he wondered why they were there but when they stopped outside the hangar, he realized they were all there for him.

Minutes later, four detectives working for Judge Garzón's Greco police unit climbed the steps to the Gulfstream and entered the cabin. Palmer and Christine Ketley were sitting next to each

316

other, glass of champagne in hand and Palmer's faithful worn-out brown leather bag on his lap.

'Señor Palmer.'

Palmer looked up and smiled. He knew what was coming.

Neither of them resisted and Palmer even managed to convince the detectives they didn't need to put them in handcuffs because they weren't going to run away.

Ten minutes later, John Palmer was shown into a cell at the police station attached to the airport. Christine Ketley was kept in a cell on the other side of the same building. All they knew was that they were going to be charged in the morning.

'Charged with what?' Palmer had asked, coolly.

He was told the allegations revolved around 'multiple criminal activities' said to have been carried out by Palmer and his so-called gang including 'timeshare fraud, money laundering, credit card fraud, threats, crimes against people's physical integrity and freedom, trafficking drugs, falsifying passports and possession of weapons'.

The police had wanted to keep Palmer's arrest secret for at least twelve hours to give them a chance to round up other suspects.

The following morning John Palmer and Christine Ketley were transferred by plane to Madrid where they were taken in separate vehicles to the city's Valdemoro Prison under a police escort, which included motorbike outriders and a helicopter hovering overhead. This was a big statement from the Spanish police. They'd finally brought the bad English *hombre* to justice and they wanted the world to know they'd done it.

This time Judge Garzón – the man who'd pursued Palmer for more than a decade – believed he had his man 'bang to rights'. Palmer was warned, though, that a Spanish trial would probably not take place for at least three to four years due to the complex nature of the charges.

Under Spanish law, Judge Garzón had until the following afternoon to decide whether John Palmer should be remanded in jail while the allegations against him were investigated.

The day after Palmer's detention, Judge Garzón's agents from Unit Greco announced through the Madrid media that Palmer's timeshare and property empire in the Canary Islands was worth at least €360m (£245m). They placed his overall wealth at around €600m.

Palmer was more infuriated by the figures being bandied around than his own incarceration because he knew that there were still people out there who thought he'd ripped off the Brink's-Mat gold-bullion gang.

A lot of the information in Garzón's Palmer file had come from Juan Cotino, director general of Tenerife's police investigation department. He'd spent years secretly investigating John Palmer and had uncovered a criminal netherworld that included the regular torture of his enemies by Palmer and his Clumpers. And while their victims' cries for help were heard, Palmer would often taunt them until he was satisfied he knew everything he wanted.

It was in Valdemoro Prison that John Palmer came face to face with Judge Baltasar Garzón for the second time in his life. The judge told Palmer he and UK authorities had enough evidence to put Palmer away for the rest of his life. Garzón also alleged that Palmer had continued his criminal activities during his previous term in prison following his 2001 Old Bailey conviction for fraud.

One of Palmer's oldest associates later recalled: 'JP was shown a dossier that was supposed to outline all the evidence against him. But he reckoned most of it was utter bollocks without any real substantiation.'

Judge Garzón made it clear to his prized prisoner John Palmer that he also was determined to prosecute his lover Christine Ketley. Garzón outlined all the directorships next to her name at Companies House as testament to her involvement. Ketley had six in the UK and seven in Spain at the time of her arrest. Spanish officials alleged assets that included a luxury flat by the sea in Tenerife, restaurant interests on the island, as well as the couple's Essex home, worth in excess of £1 million.

The Spanish also named UK businesses, including the pawn-broker's shop, a second-hand jewellery store and a beauty parlour. Ketley was, claimed Spanish prosecutors, 'totally inter-woven' into Palmer's 'organization'. Ketley denied all the charges. It was also revealed that Spain's tax authorities intended seizing a substantial slice of Palmer's vast fortune before much of it was hidden away.

An indictment filed at Madrid's National Court clearly stated that Spanish prosecutors wanted Ketley jailed for two years for criminal association and six years for fraud, with a further two years – and a €2 million fine – for money laundering. But despite all these allegations the Spanish were once again unable to even get Ketley's assets officially frozen.

Palmer urged his Spanish lawyer to push ahead with a request for bail because he wanted to get out of Spain as quickly as possible. His hatred for the country was now overwhelming. He'd sensed it was a bad idea to travel to Tenerife and now he was paying the price for ignoring his own instincts. If he could just get himself and Christine Ketley out of jail, he had no intention of ever walking on Spanish soil again.

*

Within days of arriving at Madrid' s Valdemoro Prison, John Palmer discovered that the spectre of his old nemesis Kenneth Noye was never far away. Noye had been incarcerated in the same jail less than ten years earlier while he was awaiting extradition on the road-rage murder charges. It must have felt to Palmer as if Noye was haunting him. Prison staff were continually asking him how Noye was and what he was up to and telling him what a nice chap Noye was.

Palmer genuinely feared for his safety inside Valdemoro and complained to the authorities about some prison officers, whom he said were still in contact with Kenneth Noye.

Then Palmer bumped into another notorious old-school British gangster who was in Valdemoro. This man had long been rumoured to have taken part in the Brink's-Mat robbery and was in regular contact with Brink's-Mat gang leaders 'Mad Mickey' McAvoy and Brian Robinson, who'd both served long sentences for their part in the gold-bullion raid. John Palmer didn't know whether to talk to his fellow inmate or avoid him. In the end they exchanged a few strained pleasantries but made sure they kept out of each other's space most of the time.

While in Valdemoro Palmer also got some feedback about his other criminal associates, including crime family brothers Bill and Ben. A bodybuilder who claimed he worked for them appeared in a London court and admitted dismembering a number of possible Brink's-Mat 'victims' on behalf of Bill and Ben. It was also said in open court that potential witnesses were often too terrified to testify against the crime family brothers. This self-confessed 'butcher' was eventually jailed for seven years for the relatively minor charge of money laundering but his account of working for the family sent a chill up the spine of even the hardest villain. It also reminded John Palmer that he still had a very big ace up his sleeve.

John Palmer believed he had the best Spanish lawyer and enough contacts inside the Spanish judiciary to be able to get bail sooner or later for himself and, more importantly, Ketley. Palmer's lawyer urged him not to try to bribe anyone. Judge Garzón eventually instructed his officials to make it clear to Palmer and his lawyer that they were willing to let the charges against Palmer drift along for years if he helped them nail down some very 'big fish'. At first, Palmer refused point blank to help. Then he realized that 'playing that game' might be his only option.

His main aim was to get Ketley released so she could return to Essex to look after their son James, now 16, who was attending Brentwood School, where he eventually passed eight GCSE's and four 'A' Levels with flying colours to prove he was most definitely not a chip off the old block. Ketley's release occurred within weeks of the couple's arrest and she was allowed to travel back to Essex to live as one of the conditions of her bail. In the UK underworld, many were saying that John Palmer had already started 'singing for his supper'.

But in truth, Palmer was playing an even more dangerous game. He was slowly drip-dripping information to Judge Garzón and his investigators in the hope he could manipulate his own release from prison without giving too much away to the Spanish.

No one to this day knows if it worked.

Back in London, Bill and Ben had changed their minds about moving their operation to Tenerife because they smelt a trap and had been hearing bad things about what was happening in the south of the island.

Palmer's arrest reminded them that he was a 'security risk'

and they were deeply concerned that he might be tempted to inform on them to the police in either the UK or Spain in exchange for a lenient sentence or maybe even an acquittal.

Palmer, meanwhile, continued to drip-feed information to Judge Garzón in the hope he could secure release on bail. But it was a slow process. Palmer would offer a titbit, Garzón's officers would then go off and check it out and then come back and ask for more. More often than not, Palmer would insist he had no more info on that specific subject and then they'd all be back to square one.

It felt to Garzón and his investigators that Palmer was blatantly playing games. In the end they demanded more detailed information otherwise Palmer would never be granted bail and could end up in prison for years before his case even got to trial.

No one knows how much information Palmer told the Spanish judge and his team but in early 2009, John Palmer's lawyer was informed by Judge Garzón's office that if he posted €100,000 bail money with the court then his client would be released until his trial was heard. For Palmer it must have felt like money well spent. Spanish law authorities even returned his passport after promises from his lawyer that he would base himself back at his house in Essex with Christine Ketley, and son James, who'd even joined the army cadets while still attending Brentwood school, as well as taking up Muay Thai kickboxing.

Garzón hadn't been entirely happy about Palmer's release on bail but had accepted it on the basis that Palmer had made a legally binding agreement to stay at the house in Essex and not travel anywhere abroad while awaiting trial. He also had to report to court authorities in Madrid every two weeks.

So John Palmer was quietly released back into the real world with just his passport and a small plastic carrier bag containing a few humble possessions.

Palmer was caught between a rock and a hard place in a sense. He knew that his release from prison clearly implied he'd helped the authorities with their inquiries. He needed to look as if he still believed in a future for himself and Christine Ketley, then the underworld might accept that he hadn't turned informant after all. So Palmer began working on his legitimate businesses in Essex, including the pawnbroking outfit that was in Christine Ketley's name. Palmer even started to enjoy gardening in the vast grounds of his latest home. It was the only place outside his house where he still felt safe enough not to have to wear his bullet-proof vest.

With foreign travel restrictions – apart from to Spain – imposed thanks to bail conditions, John Palmer was facing great difficulty when it came to his own free movement on his private aircraft. The horrors of 9/11 had also meant that much stricter flight-plan rules had been introduced worldwide. It was no longer possible for Palmer to fly incognito like he'd done in the past. Even the landing arrangements for private planes had tightened up. At Bristol airport, authorities had closed down the 'secret gate' entrance Palmer had always used in the far corner of the airfield after pressure from the UK police and customs.

So Palmer sold off his Gulfstream jet. He was tempted to hang on to the Bell helicopter for the time being because it was useful for short hops inside the UK. But shortly afterwards Palmer sold the chopper as well after deciding that he needed to look 'as poor as possible' to all the police agencies who still had him in their sights.

If Palmer needed to go somewhere abroad secretly, he'd charter a small boat from one of the small ports dotted along the coastline of south-east England. His favourite vessel was skippered and owned by a former policeman whom he'd first met when he was being investigated about the Brink's-Mat gold bullion.

Meetings could then be reached by car, even if they were on the other side of Europe. Britain's membership of the EU had made it easy to cross borders within the union without a passport, which in turn meant there were few concrete records of his movements.

Twenty thousand feet above Palmer's Essex home occasional operations by Beechcraft spy planes tried to keep an eye on Palmer, although these flights were starting to become much less frequent because of budgetary restrictions.

So the luxury lifestyle Palmer had once so enjoyed was now a thing of the past. No more limos sweeping him up to his private jet at the airport. No more €4,000 bottles of wine. John Palmer tried to make out he was a nobody now. Who on earth would want to do him over? His secrets were long gone, surely?

At night, John Palmer and Christine Ketley curled up in front of the fire and watched a few DVDs, but Palmer found it hard to concentrate. He'd focused on nothing but money for forty bloody years so the intricacies of box-set dramas were not easy for him to comprehend. Palmer had always struggled to engage people on an empathetic level. His attitude had always been: what's the point? Trying to relate to a false premise featuring actors just didn't hit the spot.

After so many years of excitement and extreme risk-taking, John Palmer was now virtually a prisoner in his own home, aware that everyone from his old enemies to young, ambitious, tech-savvy Scotland Yard and Spanish detectives had him in their sights.

Occasionally, Palmer carried out midnight 'raids' on his stashes of cash hidden deep in the Suffolk and Essex countryside. One old associate recalled: 'JP didn't trust no one by this stage, so he'd drive out to these isolated spots, pull out his tape recorder and listen to his own instructions on how to find the precise spot where he'd hidden a stash of cash years earlier.'

Once Palmer had found it, he'd pull open his scruffy brown leather case and stuff as many notes as possible into it. Then he'd leave the rest for another time.

But the 'other' side of John Palmer began to emerge even more around this time. The inner loneliness which he'd always suffered from was challenging his attitude to life. He wished he had more friends but knew deep inside himself why he'd never got close to other men. Palmer undoubtedly had regrets and he still wished new challenges would come along. A last hit of excitement before he finally disappeared into a mundane life for the final twenty or so years of his life.

John Palmer also knew that his precious bullet-proof vest wasn't going to be enough to protect him from his enemies. At his detached house in Essex, he spent tens of thousands of pounds on CCTV cameras and specialized state-of-the-art alarm systems. But then he refused to connect them directly to his local police station because he didn't trust the police to save him if there was a genuine threat to his life.

Palmer is also said to have strategically positioned a gun in every room in his house. It was a risky move with teenage son James living on the premises but, as he later said to one associate, what else could he do? Those who knew Palmer at this time say he became much more nervy and withdrawn. Palmer told his family he'd taken up gardening because he needed some exercise, ignoring the fact he had a gym in the basement of the property in Essex for precisely that reason.

But there was another reason why Palmer was so attached

to the garden of his house. He liked to talk on his latest high-powered GPS satellite mobile phone out of earshot of everyone, including Christine Ketley and their son James. Palmer had ensured that certain parts of his garden were not monitored by his CCTV cameras. Palmer was convinced that a lip reader could soon work out what he was talking about if that CCTV footage ever fell into the wrong hands. He also believed that such footage might help police build a case against him if they zoomed in on what phone numbers he was dialling. Palmer told one associate he'd turned the garden into his office because he didn't want to put his lover and son in the firing line if the police ever hauled them in for questioning. Some days, Palmer spent as much as two hours in the garden talking on his satellite phone while Ketley, James and any of their friends remained inside under strict orders not to come out of the house if 'JP' was on the phone.

Palmer told his family he preferred to hold all his meetings on his satellite phone rather than going out to meet anyone in person. One of his oldest associates explained: 'JP said he didn't even like driving anywhere, let alone flying. He said that's when he was at his most vulnerable.'

One of Palmer's oldest associates explained: 'JP wasn't even sixty years old but he seemed to have the weight of the world on his shoulders and wasn't keen on even leaving the house, apart from when he went out late at night to raid his stashes.'

Some of Palmer's associates at this time were beginning to wonder if Palmer was going a bit stir crazy. For so many years he'd been good at masking his real feelings and sorting all his problems, often with an iron fist. But now he seemed eaten up by a combination of fear, loneliness and vengeance.

*

When John Palmer heard that Bill and Ben had decided not to move their operation to Tenerife, he started to wonder what they were up to. He'd encouraged them set up their money laundering in Tenerife in exchange for certain agreements; indeed, he'd revealed a lot of his business practices on the basis they were going there. The brothers had even sent a posse over to the island, but now they were back-pedalling. Why?

Typically, John Palmer then started scheming and realized the key to his survival was those secret tape recordings of the face-to-face meeting he'd had with Bill and Ben. The transcriptions of those tapes confirmed that Palmer had been present when the two brothers confessed to two murders. Maybe the tapes could provide him with some much-needed leverage, so he placed them in an anonymous safe-deposit vault in Central London. It seemed the most sensible place to keep them out of harm's way.

Then, with more murders undoubtedly going to be committed in the name of Brink's-Mat, John Palmer decided it was time to cash in on the power that those tapes gave him.

Back at the same Suffolk pub where they'd met earlier, Palmer calmly informed Bill and Ben that he had them 'over a barrel'.

The two brothers tried not to look surprised or angry. But inside they were seething. John Palmer had just lived up to his reputation as the most duplicitous criminal they'd ever come across.

Palmer was using the tapes to tell the brothers to keep their distance.

Now John Palmer felt as if he was the one back in control. He wanted the brothers to appreciate that if he or his family were harmed in any way, the tapes would be immediately sent to New Scotland Yard. It was an extraordinarily risky move but Palmer believed it would guarantee him a long and safe retirement.

CHAPTER FORTY-ONE

MISSING THE BOAT

GUINEA-BISSAU, WEST AFRICA, SUMMER 2010

In the middle of all this, John Palmer heard on the grapevine that his sworn enemy Tel had been promoted by the Colombians and was now helping run a so-called 'narco-state' in West Africa called Guinea-Bissau. Tel was overseeing huge shipments of cocaine, often flown in on second-hand Boeing 707s bought for $100,000 cash, which were then unloaded before being abandoned in the swamps near the capital city of Bissau.

Palmer also heard that some of his old crew of Clumpers from Tenerife had been hired as security men by Tel in Guinea-Bissau. The entire country was now under the control of the Colombians, who'd bribed all the top politicians and public officials while at the same time winning over the poverty-stricken population by financing everything from schools to public swimming baths to football teams.

Palmer was sorely tempted to set up a meeting with Tel because he felt they had a lot of unfinished business to sort out. But he soon changed his mind when he got a message back from Tel's people saying he'd have to travel to Guinea-Bissau because Tel was on an Interpol wanted list. This was a downright lie because Tel still had immunity from prosecution through various law-enforcement agencies. But defying his own bail restrictions to secretly fly into a broken African country being propped up by drug barons did not seem a sensible move to Palmer.

A few weeks later, Palmer heard rumours that Tel had actually been operating as a double agent in Guinea-Bissau, which had enabled him to continue working for the Colombians without being rearrested in Europe on those earlier terrorism and money-laundering charges. Tel had apparently swapped information for freedom, which meant he was able to move around the world completely without restrictions, despite all his links to terrorism and crime. Tel was playing the ultimate deadly double game by providing American security services such as the DEA with a running commentary on terrorism in the whole of West Africa, as well as providing titbits about his old home turf of Lebanon.

In 2011, John Palmer's dodgy lawyer Giovanni Di Stefano, now aged 57, was finally unmasked as a fraudster. After he'd encouraged Palmer to defend himself at his own fraud trial with disastrous consequences, a lot of questions had been asked about Di Stefano's background and qualifications as a lawyer. It emerged that he had no genuine legal qualifications whatsoever and he'd duped 'desperate and vulnerable victims' into thinking he was a bona fide legal professional. And, despite all this, Di Stefano had even managed to win some of his cases which helped him earn a small fortune. He was eventually convicted of twenty-five charges including deception, fraud and money laundering between 2001 and 2011 and was sentenced to fourteen years in prison.

In Essex, Palmer wondered if Di Stefano had agreed to help

Scotland Yard with their inquiries into some of his most no-torious clients. Palmer sent a message to Di Stefano via a mutual acquaintance reminding him of their association. There has never been any concrete evidence that Di Stefano did help the police, though.

John Palmer, ever the pragmatist, tried to get back into the money-laundering game in London, only to quickly realize he'd been left far behind by the really big players such as GB, his former Birmingham associate. Palmer later admitted he was green with envy when it came to the so-called 'top players' – like GB – on the London money-laundering scene. By this time, they were 'cleaning' tens of billions of pounds worth of cash each year on behalf of mainly Russian and Chinese tycoons, as well as a handful of the UK's rich and famous.

Palmer was irritated with himself for not waking up to money laundering on this scale much earlier. His operation back on Tenerife had been chickenfeed compared with what was hap-pening in London.

However, John Palmer did manage to grab a bit of money-laundering 'work' from oligarch Boris Berezovsky, whom he'd originally met through the late Russian Misha, his former 'busi-ness partner'. Berezovsky had been cast aside by all the other Russian billionaires in London because of his erratic behaviour after falling out with Russian leader Vladimir Putin.

Around this time, Palmer also heard about more chilling examples of so-called 'Russian Suicides'. These included the death of a man who 'fell' off the balcony of his penthouse apartment in Central London. Palmer had earlier been told by Misha that Russian Suicides usually involved a henchman hold-ing a gun to your head and telling you that you had a choice: you either jumped or you got shot in the head. Most people opted for jumping just in case something broke their fall. But of course that never happened and they'd just end up splattered on the pavement.

Palmer sensed that London had turned into a very wealthy version of Tenerife. These money launderers were running it all without any apparent interference from the police because it was such a secretive and deadly world that no one ever spoke openly about what was going on.

Back in deepest Essex, John Palmer still couldn't resist an 'earner'. When one of his oldest financial associates approached him with a plan to sell cheap oil in the Caribbean, Palmer should have avoided it like the plague. But he liked the sound of a criminal enterprise operated thousands of miles from where he lived, which could earn him money without him even having to leave the house.

Palmer's associate outlined a plan to purchase a small oil tanker in California and then sail it down to Venezuela where untaxed oil could be purchased for knockdown prices that were one hundred times less than anywhere else in the world.

That oil would then be sold island by island across the Caribbean. The authorities could do little about it because it would be sold from the ship in international waters, which would then sail on to the next island before anyone could do anything about it.

Palmer saw it as nothing more than the equivalent of a modest tax-avoidance scheme.

But he soon began getting impatient when his £100,000 investment brought him no return for many months. When Palmer tried to contact his old associate, the man had changed phone numbers and moved to Central America.

Palmer laughed about it later because few people usually

survived if they tried to take him for a ride. He'd clearly changed. Palmer also decided there and then that unless it was a 'real earner' he was going to avoid all such 'business propositions' in the future.

With John Palmer holed up in his Essex house most of the time, his lover Christine Ketley began developing her own hobbies and interests. This included a revival of her interest in riding horses, which of course had been Palmer's wife Marnie's favourite pastime as well. Ketley went out most days riding at a nearby stables, while son James, now 19, was attending the University of Birmingham, where he eventually went on to get a 2:1 in Economics. This left Palmer on his own in the house, often for many hours. Afraid of getting bored, he recorded his own special daily schedule on his trusted handheld tape recorder. This included gardening, an hour doing weights in the basement gym, a host of other chores and usually at least an hour on the satellite phone at the other end of the garden where the CCTV cameras couldn't snoop on him.

Palmer even began calling up some of his old legal associates and asking them if he could join their bridge clubs. Other times, he'd try and persuade people to come round to his house for a game of cards. But Palmer eventually gave up trying. Most people were not too keen on reconnecting with him.

John Palmer's entire criminal career had been built around not trusting anyone. Now he was trying to make friends but it was too out of character. He was, in the words of one old associate, 'swimming uphill without a paddle'. That same associate added: 'The trouble was JP couldn't swim. He hadn't bothered learning to and now he was paying the price.'

John Palmer also lived in dread of Kenneth Noye ever being

released from prison. Most of the underworld by this time saw Noye as a liability. Everything Noye touched turned to dust. Many had labelled him as nothing more than a bad-luck charm, who should be avoided at all costs.

But Kenneth Noye wasn't exactly languishing in prison. He was working on all fronts to get his conviction overthrown. Noye wasn't the type of character to feel sorry for himself. In any case, he knew the names of the characters who'd been 'dissing' him behind his back.

Meanwhile, in Madrid, Palmer's arch law-enforcement foe Judge Baltasar Garzón announced his retirement right in the middle of a crucial period in the Palmer investigation. Palmer presumed the case against him and Ketley would start to fade away when he heard the news. But what he didn't realize was that Garzón only agreed to retire on condition he could continue to 'pull the strings' with the Palmer probe until any eventual criminal trial. Garzón still had Palmer in his sights and he was determined not to let go at any cost.

SUNNINGHILL, BERKSHIRE, 23 MARCH 2013

John Palmer's occasional money-laundering client Boris Berezovsky was found dead in a locked bathroom with a ligature around his neck at his mansion on the outskirts of London. Berezovsky's death was announced in a post on Facebook written by his son-in-law. Berezovsky's lawyer insisted his client committed suicide having fallen into debt after losing a protracted lawsuit against Chelsea Football Club owner Roman Abramovich, another one of Vladimir Putin's 'close' friends in

London. Berezovsky had spent the final few months of his life selling his possessions to cover his court costs.

Palmer wasn't surprised by Berezovsky's death. He'd been needling a lot of very rich and powerful people in London, St Petersburg and Moscow and it was only a matter of time.

But Berezovsky's death sparked widespread speculation in the mainstream British news media that Russian leader Putin might somehow have been involved. Thames Valley Police classified Berezovsky's death as 'unexplained' and launched a formal investigation into the circumstances behind it.

A post-mortem examination carried out by a Home Office pathologist later found the cause of death was consistent with hanging and there was no evidence of a violent struggle. However, following an inquest, the coroner recorded an open verdict, commenting: 'I am not saying Mr Berezovsky took his own life, I am not saying Mr Berezovsky was unlawfully killed. What I am saying is that the burden of proof sets such a high standard it is impossible for me to say.'

But Boris Berezovksy's death reminded John Palmer how vulnerable he and his family were in Essex. He'd returned to the UK because he thought it would be safer then Tenerife but Berezovsky's 'Russian Suicide' proved this was not the case.

Is this how it's going to end for me? Palmer must have asked himself.

CHAPTER FORTY-TWO

COMING UP FOR AIR

SOUTH WEALD, ESSEX, SPRING 2014

It sometimes felt to John Palmer as if he was one of those plastic ducks at a funfair shooting range. He'd get knocked down and then bounce back up, only to go down yet again. But the killings all around Palmer were having a detrimental effect on him.

Since his release on bail from prison in Spain, he had – through his lawyers – requested UK police protection on a number of occasions. He'd concluded that since he had the cops around his neck much of the time anyway, he might as well have some free 'in plain sight' protection. But the police were not keen to help. They detested Palmer's arrogance and overtly crooked wealth. They turned down his request officially because their budget did not stretch to such round-the-clock security operations. But behind the scenes a lot of detectives took an uncompromising attitude.

'Fuck him. He can't just dial us in as his personal bodyguards. Let the dogs have him.'

In the middle of all this, yet another person connected to John Palmer had their life ended prematurely. One of his former timeshare executives – to whom he'd sold his French chateau a

335

few years previously – had eventually moved to Thailand, where he apparently died of a massive heart attack in March 2014 after setting up a timeshare resort many believed was financed by John Palmer. Palmer told associates he was convinced the man had been murdered.

John Palmer might have felt out of the loop in deepest Essex but he still kept 'connections'. In late 2014, Palmer heard that a bunch of elderly villains – including one criminal he knew from the Brink's-Mat gold-bullion smelting days – were looking around for some financial 'help' to put together what they claimed would be the 'Crime of the Century'.

Palmer let it be known he might be interested in financing the robbery and arranged a meeting with the two ringleaders of the gang in the layby of an A-road near Colchester, in Essex. Palmer and his two Clumpers had changed cars twice during the twenty-mile journey from his house in Essex just in case they were being followed.

Palmer greeted one of the old codgers, Brian Reader, 75, like a lost-long old friend because the two had worked together with Kenneth Noye smelting the Brink's-Mat gold more than thirty years earlier. Reader briefly reminisced about the good old days but Palmer thought he seemed a bit reserved.

In fact, Reader didn't trust Palmer as far as he could throw him and had been against the meeting, which had been arranged by his fellow gang leader, old-school robber Terry Perkins, 66, who'd pulled off the historic Security Express heist thirty years earlier.

Palmer and the two OAP criminals sat in his car while they talked through the job and how much it would cost Palmer to finance, as well as what Palmer could expect as his return for his 'investment'. Reader and Perkins admitted they'd also been to see Bill and Ben, the two brothers from the London crime family, for some development money. Palmer immediately asked why they still needed his money. Both men said they didn't trust the brothers and would prefer not to do the job with them, as they might double-cross them after the raid.

'Then why do you go to them in the first place?' asked Palmer, feeling a tad uncomfortable.

Both men said they had no choice because the location of the robbery was right in the middle of the family's 'territory'.

'Where's that then?' asked Palmer.

Both men looked at each other before Reader answered: 'We can't tell you that, JP. The less people know the location the better. If you come on board then we'll tell you everything.'

'Fair enough,' answered Palmer, who promised both men he'd come back to them with a decision soon.

On the drive back to his house in South Weald, Essex, Palmer felt that something was not right about the robbery.

Within hours, John Palmer had decided not to give the old codgers any cash but he still felt the need to know more about the proposed raid. So for the following few weeks, Palmer gave the two gangster veterans the impression he was still interested in financing them by holding two more meetings, this time in laybys in Suffolk.

But Brian Reader and Terry Perkins were equally suspicious and had also picked up on the fact that Palmer might be leading them on. So they very politely declined to meet Palmer again after those two meetings in the Suffolk countryside.

Palmer sensed he'd been rumbled, so he started racking his mind for any clues that the old boys might have unintentionally given him about the actual job. Then he remembered they'd admitted the proposed heist was going to take place on the crime family's 'territory', which at one stage had stretched from Tottenham in north London to the Kings Road in Chelsea, west London – a vast swath of the capital.

Then, just after Christmas 2014, Bill and Ben picked up a rumour that John Palmer had been talking to the pensioner robbers. The two brothers immediately pulled the old-timers in for a meeting and doubled the amount they were prepared to give the gang for their 'development costs' ahead of the raid.

The brothers also warned the old-school gangsters that if they found out Palmer had been told any details about the location of the job then the two ringleaders would be 'in a lot of trouble'. The brothers said they didn't trust Palmer and pointed out to the old codgers that he was suspected of being a police informant as far back as during the Brink's-Mat gold-bullion smelting operation in 1984.

Bill and Ben then effectively took over the running of the old codgers' preparation for the raid. They even insisted that the gang allowed one of their most trusted henchmen to take part in the job because he had the keys to the outside of the building that housed the vault they intended to rob.

Meanwhile John Palmer suddenly had something much more dangerous to deal with.

CHAPTER FORTY-THREE

DOOMED

SANDPIT COTTAGE, SANDPIT LANE, SOUTH WEALD, ESSEX, EARLY APRIL 2015

John Palmer's new-found love of gardening had come in handy when it came to his two-acre estate in Essex. It was the one place he felt safe enough not to bother wearing his bullet-proof vest. It had got so potentially dangerous beyond the perimeter of his home that he was increasingly unprepared to travel anywhere unless it was important.

John Palmer's mentality was still entrenched in the 'old days' when police surveillance teams would sit at the end of country lanes 'keeping an eye' on villains like Palmer. He still had no idea that Beechcraft aeroplanes had been swooping 20,000 feet above his home, capable of listening to everything from a pin being dropped to a fried egg sizzling on the cooker.

One day in early April 2015, John Palmer had just finished some heavy digging at the far end of his beloved garden when he suddenly felt a severe chest pain. It got so bad he could barely walk. He then keeled over as he was approaching the big glass double doors at the rear of his house.

Luckily Palmer's son James and Christine Ketley were both

nearby at the time and rushed out. They helped Palmer into a car and drove him straight to the nearby Brentwood Community Hospital. That night Palmer's chest was cut open and surgery was performed on the muscles, valves and arteries of his heart.

The following morning, Palmer and Ketley were told by a heart specialist that Palmer was extremely lucky to have survived. The operation would leave Palmer feeling sore for a few weeks and the wounds in his chest might leave lasting scars, but it was a small price to pay for still being alive. John Palmer swore his closest family members to secrecy because he didn't want anyone to know about his brush with death in case the usual 'vultures' started circling.

On 8 April 2015 – twenty-four hours before his scheduled release from hospital – Palmer was watching *Sky News* on the hospital TV set that hung above his bed. The lead item was about a gang of professional robbers who'd got away with tens of millions of pounds' worth of gems after breaking into a vault the previous bank holiday weekend.

By the time the three-minute news report had ended, John Palmer's electronic heart-monitoring machine alongside his bed had set off an alarm, which then alerted one of the nursing staff to his bedside.

Struggling for breath, Palmer tried to calm himself down. But he felt dizzy and weak and the same two words kept going round and round in his head.

Hatton Garden.

John Palmer knew he should have gone to that vault in Hatton Garden and removed the tapes and transcripts of Bill and Ben boasting about how they'd murdered two rivals in cold blood. But Palmer's collapse and subsequent heart surgery had diverted him.

The moment he saw the TV news bulletin he knew someone had told the brothers about that safety deposit box he kept in the Hatton Garden vault, which had just been so skilfully robbed by a bunch of elderly old-school villains.

The following day, John Palmer was released from hospital as the blanket news coverage of the Hatton Garden Job, as it was now known, continued to catch half the world's imagination. The ace that he had kept up his sleeve for his own protection was gone. Palmer hoped the aftermath of the Hatton Garden raid would divert all those concerned, especially the two brothers Bill and Ben. But Palmer wasn't sure he stood any chance of surviving 2015.

Palmer soon heard from a contact inside Bill and Ben's London crime family that his safety deposit vault box had in fact been delivered to the two brothers by their handpicked robber named 'Basil' just hours after the break-in.

It later turned out the brothers had heard all about Palmer's deposit box from one of the staff who worked at the Hatton Garden vault, which just happened to be across the street from a building Bill and Ben's family had owned for the previous thirty years. It was another reason for Palmer to kick himself. He wouldn't have been so half asleep a few years earlier.

Palmer's world began to crumble all around him. Now he'd lost the one thing that would have helped guarantee him and his family's safety. Palmer found himself waiting for the proverbial knock on the door followed by the inevitable words: 'Game's up, John.'

It came in the form of a message from the brothers announcing they had 'something' that belonged to Palmer and they needed an urgent 'meet'.

Palmer knew he couldn't spend the rest of his life looking

over his shoulder, so he agreed to a meeting. He didn't have much left to lose, after all.

The following day, Palmer arrived at the same Suffolk pub where he'd met the brothers twice before, unsure whether he'd even get out of there alive.

The safety deposit box containing the tapes and transcripts was the ultimate elephant in the room. For at least five minutes, no one mentioned it as they made small talk, but they all knew that was why they were there.

The brothers ramped up the pressure by enabling long, awkward silences to fill the space between each inane sentence.

'So, we've got your box, old son,' said Bill, who then sat back and watched the reaction on Palmer's face as the words sank in.

'So I hear,' replied Palmer flatly.

Then Bill continued: 'We got a proposition to put to you, mate.'

Palmer nodded very slowly, without a nugget of enthusiasm.

'Don't worry, John boy. You can rest easy at night. No one's after you,' said Ben, cheerily.

Palmer tried not to look confused.

Then Bill outlined their 'proposition'. Palmer would pay them a monthly 'retainer' of *one and a half million pounds* to guarantee his safety. After they'd delivered their ultimatum, Palmer rolled his eyes because he knew he should have seen it coming.

'And of course if anything happens to you then we don't get no money, so this agreement will guarantee you a long and healthy life,' said Bill.

One and a half million a month? That's more than Wayne Rooney gets paid, Palmer must have thought to himself.

'You must be jokin',' said Palmer, after much deliberation.

Palmer didn't know what else to say, so he let his words hang in the air.

He knew they believed he had hundreds of millions of pounds hidden away all over the globe.

The two brothers each forced a cheesy smile and looked straight at Palmer, nodding slowly.

'This ain't no joke, John boy,' said Bill.

Palmer stayed quiet. It was better to let them do the talking.

'So how much *can* you stump up then?' asked Ben.

'Seven fifty?' replied Palmer.

'Nah, not enough, mate,' said Bill.

Five minutes later, Palmer agreed to pay the brothers a monthly 'retainer' of £1 million. First instalment was due at the end of June.

Palmer struggled to his feet and left the pub without exchanging another word.

He'd just commuted his own death sentence but it would probably end up costing him more cash than he could ever lay his hands on because so much of his money had either gone or been deposited in places he could never reach within years, let alone months.

But at least if the brothers killed Palmer, they wouldn't get their hands on any of his money. Almost as good was the fact that they also didn't know about his heart problems or they would no doubt have tried to hit him for a much bigger one-off payout or just killed him.

So while Hatton Garden's so-called 'ghost robber' Basil was getting more media coverage than anyone since the Kray twins, John Palmer had just made the ultimate sacrifice to stop himself and his family from getting killed.

And it was all down to the contents of one safe deposit box.

One of John Palmer's oldest associates later summed it up: 'JP had believed that box held the key to his survival. Now it was in the hands of the very people who would have been sent to prison if its contents had ever been seen by the police. Talk about risky!'

If Bill and Ben had said to Palmer *we're gonna kill you*, then at least he could have got his life in order and said his farewells to his family. But this way, they were making his life a misery and he'd most likely end up broke as well. And of course, he didn't know where he stood. They could well have been lying. Mind you, why would they bother? So there he was, trapped in no-man's-land, not knowing which way to turn and who to trust.

It must have felt to John Palmer that in many ways he would be better off dead.

Within days, Palmer further increased security at his Essex home by installing extra CCTV cameras beside the entrance and along the length of his driveway all the way up to the main house. When the police monitoring Palmer's home saw all the new safety measures, they concluded someone must have been after him and it looked like an imminent threat.

But they did nothing.

Soon after Palmer's meeting with Bill and Ben, he and Christine Ketley were informed through their lawyers that new additional charges would be brought against them in Spain, including timeshare fraud and money laundering. Palmer's lawyer warned him that these extra allegations could mean an additional fifteen years in prison if Palmer was found guilty.

Palmer was stunned because he'd thought that Judge Garzón's retirement in 2012 meant the case against them both would probably fade away.

As Palmer told one associate at the time: 'They're gonna

hammer me. I might as well be dead than face all this shit all over again.'

In the underworld, many were convinced that the extra charges against Palmer and the others had been ordered so as to exert more pressure on him to reveal additional details about his money-laundering and drug-smuggling associates.

John Palmer felt as if he was back on the criminal treadmill. Bill and Ben were breathing down his neck and now law enforcement were twisting the thumb screws by threatening another big court case and even heavier prison sentences.

Hatton Garden ringleaders Brian Reader and Terry Perkins and the rest of their gang who pulled off the so-called Crime of the Century had left themselves 'wide open' when it came to the aftermath of the now world-famous raid. They made numerous basic errors, which suggested they were not up to speed with new technology and all of them – with the notable exception of Bill and Ben's man 'Basil' – were rounded up by police on 18 May, just over a month after the bank-holiday raid.

Word on the London underworld grapevine was that 'Basil' had 'gone awol' since the job. He'd been the so-called lockman whom Bill and Ben had insisted joined Reader and Perkins' gang because he had the keys to the front doors of the building that contained the basement vault.

Back in Essex, John Palmer tried his hardest to avoid all contact with anyone even remotely connected to the Hatton Garden Job. He didn't want any more aggravation.

Palmer's main priority was to find the first £1 million instalment of the money he had to pay Bill and Ben by the end of June. Palmer might still have had a 'sizeable' amount of cash but laying his hands on it was not going to be easy.

As the days and weeks ticked down towards the deadline, Palmer became increasingly agitated about the deal he'd agreed with the two brothers.

Then Palmer received a 'friendly' message from Bill and Ben reminding him that the money was due on the last day of the month.

The pressure was mounting on John Palmer and his already battered heart seemed to be taking an almighty pounding.

So he slipped out of Sandpit Cottage early one morning and stashed a bag containing audio tapes of dozens of underworld meetings he'd had over the previous forty years in a secret hiding place no one other than him would ever find.

It was time to take action for a 'rainy day'.

CHAPTER FORTY-FOUR

WATCHING THE DETECTIVES

SANDPIT COTTAGE, SANDPIT LANE, SOUTH WEALD, ESSEX, 21 JUNE 2015

Christine Ketley laid on a special Father's Day lunch at the couple's Essex house for the first time ever. Guests of honour were three of Palmer's children – James, Ella and Sarah. There had originally been talk of them all going out to a local restaurant but Palmer had overruled that and insisted the meal took place at home.

Palmer's children no doubt harboured dreams that their father was in the process of turning his criminal life around. The lunch itself went on long into the afternoon and Palmer was said by those present to be 'in very good form' during the meal. His recent heart problems combined with the disintegration of his empire seemed to have turned Palmer into a more considerate, thoughtful character.

But the day after the celebrations, Palmer sank back into a dark cloud of introspective depression, no doubt caused by a combination of his multimillion-pound debt to Bill and Ben and understandable anxiety over his own health following open heart surgery.

Furthermore, Palmer still hadn't sorted out all his remaining businesses in Tenerife. His prized collection of classic sports cars remained languishing in the underground car park of his former headquarters. And then there were the stashes of cash he'd buried all over southern Tenerife. And after seven years on police bail, there was still no court date despite the recent additional charges.

In the underworld, many yet again speculated that John Palmer had done a deal with the Spanish and British police. There were even rumours of his involvement with the Hatton Garden Job.

SANDPIT COTTAGE, SANDPIT LANE, SOUTH WEALD, ESSEX, 23 JUNE 2015

John Palmer had got very used to being shadowed by 'the feds', as he and many others now called the police. So the two men digging in Weald Country Park close to the dense shrubbery and woodland bordering Palmer's two-acre property didn't bother him particularly when he noticed them from his bedroom window that morning. In some ways, he liked having them there because they'd hopefully put off any of his enemies.

Palmer even found it faintly amusing to think that the two tall men aged between thirty and forty – who so clearly looked like policemen – would even bother keeping an eye on him so blatantly. It wasn't as if he was up to much any more, was it? Dog walkers and joggers also out in the park that morning noticed the men as well because they seemed to be digging up a lot of bushes and everyone presumed they were park workers.

Their presence no doubt reminded Palmer how Kenneth Noye had killed that undercover policeman in his garden all those years earlier during the Brink's-Mat gold-bullion smelting operation. Palmer had always wondered why Noye lashed out at the officer but as he watched the two 'feds' in the parkland shrubbery next to his house, he actually understood why Noye did it.

Palmer must have felt sorely tempted to grab one of the guns he'd hidden around the house and go out there and shove it right down one of those cops' throats. But then again, Palmer knew that – despite Kenneth Noye's later acquittal – it was highly unlikely he'd get away with such actions.

The presence of those two policemen that day also reminded Palmer that he needed to destroy a lot of incriminating paperwork, in particularly the 'cooked books' of a beauty salon business, through which he'd laundered money. Bundles of paperwork had been sitting untouched in his shed for months and he feared they could provide the tax man with yet more evidence against him, not to mention 'the Feds'.

SANDPIT COTTAGE, SANDPIT LANE, SOUTH WEALD, ESSEX, 24 JUNE 2015, 12.30 P.M.

Just after midday the following day, John Palmer noticed another policeman digging away with a shovel close to where the other men had been the previous day. This character was younger, in his early twenties and about five foot ten inches, slim, with short dark-blond hair. He was wearing light-blue jeans and a light-coloured baggy sweat top.

At around the same time, dog walkers in the park noticed two middle-aged women joggers stop and chat with the same young man briefly before trotting off back towards the middle of the parkland.

That lunchtime, Christine Ketley sat down to a light meal with John Palmer and their son James before Ketley announced at about 3 p.m. that she was off to go horse riding. James's girlfriend then turned up at the house because James had promised to help her with college homework.

After finishing his meal, Palmer stepped out of the double glass doors at the back of the house and walked up the garden alongside the driveway towards the barn where he kept his quad bike. Moments later, Palmer attached a trailer to the back of the vehicle before gingerly firing it up, careful not to exert himself too much in case he brought on any more heart problems.

Palmer drove the quad bike out of the barn and stopped at a pile of leaves and branches, which he then began loading on to the bike's flat-bed trailer.

Less than a hundred yards away, the same man Palmer had noticed digging on the parkland earlier that day was strolling casually through the undergrowth along a pathway that was mainly used by riders from the local stables. He was following a route alongside a fence that separated the park from the main road. It led directly to John Palmer's land. He was whistling as he walked. One rider later said: 'He didn't seem to have a care in the world.'

CHAPTER FORTY-FIVE

GARDENING LEAVE

SANDPIT COTTAGE, SANDPIT LANE,
SOUTH WEALD, ESSEX, 24 JUNE 2015, 4.00 P.M.

John Palmer drove past the kitchen window of his house on his quad bike and waved in the direction of James and his girlfriend, who were sitting together at the kitchen table. Just then, Palmer's satellite phone rang and he stopped the quad bike and got off it. Inside the house, James watched his father knowing that no one was allowed to go in the garden when he was on the phone.

When one of Palmer's Dobermann dogs leapt up at the window and began barking noisily, Palmer was relieved he'd told James to keep the dogs inside because they often made so much noise in the garden that he couldn't hear himself speak on the mobile.

Still on the phone, Palmer walked down towards where the dustbins were kept, safe in the knowledge it was out of range of the CCTV cameras, which fed into a special webcam monitor in the house.

Peering through a small hole in the fence and watching Palmer's every move was the same young man from earlier.

He'd spent days studying the layout of Palmer's garden and the surrounding parkland. He'd even been supplied with a sketch of the garden with the location of each CCTV camera and the areas where the cameras did not reach.

The man watched Palmer finish his phone call and then get back on his quad bike and drive over to collect leaves and wood to put on a bonfire. A few seconds later, Palmer stopped by the bonfire and put the rubbish on it before driving off again on his quad bike towards the other end of the garden.

Palmer then got off the quad bike, walked across to a small garden shed and entered it. Moments later he emerged with large bundles of paperwork in his arms. He dumped it all on to the back of the trailer. Then Palmer got back on his vehicle, drove it to the bonfire and began feeding the flames with the documents.

Palmer was about to make a phone call when he glanced back at the window where son James and his girlfriend had been earlier, but they'd gone down to the basement gym to work out. Just then one of Palmer's two dogs leapt up at the window, barking noisily in the direction of his master. Palmer smiled but said nothing.

Back behind that fence just a few yards away, the young man's eyes snapped around in all directions. He was picking up sounds and sights that most people wouldn't even notice. Even a lump of horse manure on the pathway had been earlier expertly avoided.

The man already knew the far corner of the garden near the dustbins was the only area the CCTV cameras did not cover. He glanced through the hole in the fence once again while crouching down, watching and waiting for the perfect moment as light rain began pitter-pattering on the green foliage in the dense shrubbery and woodland next to the house.

Back in the garden, John Palmer had just fed his fourth trailer-load of leaves and paperwork on to the fire when his GPS mobile rang once again. On the other side of the fence, the man heard Palmer's voice as he answered it.

Watching through that hole in the fence, the man removed a self-loading revolver containing smooth-bore .32 calibre bullets from his inside pocket. He then glanced at his watch before expertly screwing a silencer on to the end of the barrel.

Palmer walked to the spot away from his bonfire not covered by the CCTV cameras, so he could speak without fear of surveillance. It wasn't a long call this time and Palmer had just flipped off his phone when the young man leapt silently over the fence and pointed his gun directly at Palmer.

For a few moments, both men stood and stared at each other.

The muffled sound of the dogs barking could be heard in the distance.

Then the younger man squeezed the trigger.

CHAPTER FORTY-SIX

DOG EAT DOG

SANDPIT COTTAGE, SANDPIT LANE, SOUTH WEALD, ESSEX, 24 JUNE 2015, 6.00 P.M.

Three bullets pierced John Palmer's body, sending him crashing to the ground. Only a dull thud could be heard with each shot, thanks to the silencer. Those bullets contained wires which had been specifically designed to fragment and inflict maximum damage on internal organs, as well as ensuring that external bullet wounds would not be clearly visible.

Inside the house, John Palmer's two Dobermanns were barking so loudly that neither James nor his girlfriend downstairs in the gym heard any shots.

In the garden, John Palmer lay crumpled on the ground trying to breathe. Then he began crawling across the grass towards the decking near the dustbins. The shooter watched him for a few moments. Then he glanced casually down at Palmer's back and squeezed tight on the trigger three more times.

Inside the house the two dogs were still barking loudly and James Palmer's girlfriend said she was worried about his father. James repeated that no one was allowed in the garden when his father was on the phone and working, so the couple carried on with their gym exercises.

Outside, the shooter's eyes quickly panned 360 degrees to check for witnesses as the sweet, musty smell of cordite wafted through the air. He knew there were people inside the property but no one had stirred.

Before the shooter departed, he checked the ground for any evidence he might have left behind. Then he casually jumped over the fence and began strolling through the undergrowth and back on to the pathway used by riders before allegedly picking up a stolen bicycle he'd left leaning against a tree and heading on to the main road.

The killer is believed to have then cycled three-quarters of a mile along the entire length of Sandpit Lane before slinging his bike up against a lamppost and jumping into a waiting car. Less than half an hour later that same vehicle most likely crossed the Thames estuary on the Dartford Bridge between Essex and Kent. It then made its way down towards the Channel ports of Dover and Folkestone and the badlands of Europe and beyond.

Job done.

Back at the house, John Palmer's two dogs were frantically clawing and barking at the same double doors their master had used earlier. James's girlfriend insisted they should step outside and check on Palmer, so they locked the dogs in the sitting room and headed into the garden hesitantly.

Moments later they found Palmer's bloody body sprawled out on the decking near the dustbins. James rushed to his father's side, straddled him and frantically pressed up and down on his chest to administer CPR. There was no response. James then tried to breathe air between his father's limp, bluey lips but he knew he'd already gone.

With the bonfire still crackling in the background, James pulled out his own mobile phone and dialled 999.

Some claim John Palmer's face was frozen in a death smile as he lay there on the decking. Maybe he was relieved it was finally all over? His empire had crumbled. He was half the man he'd once been. His reputation was in tatters because he'd lost the respect of the underworld he had so brutally dominated for so long.

CHAPTER FORTY-SEVEN

DEAD MEN TELL NO TALES

SANDPIT COTTAGE, SANDPIT LANE, SOUTH WEALD, ESSEX, 24 JUNE 2015, 7 P.M.

Emergency services who attended the scene within a few minutes of that phone call from John Palmer's son James immediately performed such violent CPR that the body was left with so many bruises and dents that no one noticed the minute bullet holes which had pierced his skin. And, of course, if Palmer had been wearing one of his beloved bullet-proof vests they might have stopped to check his corpse more carefully.

But the paramedics did notice the evidence of Palmer's earlier heart surgery and presumed he must have fallen so heavily from his quad bike that the wounds had ripped open on impact with the ground. They concluded he died from natural causes, linked to his heart problems. So the paramedics didn't even bother carrying out a full examination of the body.

Two young police officers attending the scene also completely failed to notice that Palmer had been shot. They had no idea he was a criminal, let alone a legendary underworld figure. The officers didn't check his name for any criminal history.

And the incompetence didn't end there, either. The two

young constables also failed to call an inspector to the scene, whose job would have been to confirm their assessment and check Palmer's antecedents on the police's national computer.

As a result of all this, what detectives refer to as 'the golden hour' was completely lost. This is the period immediately after a murder when the best, freshest clues are most likely to be found. The police had thrown away an opportunity to catch his killer through their own ineptitude.

When news of John Palmer's death by natural causes reached the media, it was greeted by a stunned underworld. No one could quite believe he'd died such a 'normal' death.

No doubt the young man who carried out the hit and the people who'd commissioned him would have been confused and suspicious about the claims of death by natural causes from the police and media. Maybe it was all a cunning trick by detectives to give themselves extra time to track down the killer?

At their London headquarters, crime family brothers Bill and Ben were utterly bemused when they heard John Palmer had died of natural causes. His death meant they wouldn't be getting their £1 million a month retainer. And he'd even cheated them of the satisfaction of knowing he'd died violently at their hands or those of another criminal. Initially, the brothers must have wondered if it was all a trick by Palmer and he'd hotfooted it to a desert island.

One of Palmer's oldest associates later recalled: 'We was stunned. Remember, JP had kept his heart problems secret, so it was only when we was later told he'd just been for surgery in hospital that it seemed to make sense.'

Palmer's brush with death and his subsequent heart surgery had to a degree prepared his family for the inevitable, although it had happened a lot quicker than they expected. Naturally,

Christine Ketley and their son James were distraught. They even questioned why the police had to bother with a post-mortem since it was so obviously his heart that was the cause. The police themselves were by this time going through the motions because of Palmer's notoriety, but no one believed it was anything other than death by natural causes.

When Scotland Yard detectives and Judge Garzón in Spain voiced concern about the circumstances behind the death of John Palmer, they were told by Essex police that there was no mystery and it was a very straightforward case. It appeared that John Palmer had managed to dodge the ultimate bullet with his name on it, only to die at the hands of mother nature.

Meanwhile, Palmer's corpse remained refrigerated at a local morgue until well-known criminal pathologist Dr Benjamin Swift was available to examine it. Swift was called on to the case because by this stage police wanted to make absolutely sure there were no doubts about the cause of death.

Palmer's family were warned that this might take four or five days as Swift was on holiday, so they should not make any funeral arrangements for the time being.

Outside John Palmer's house, two young plain-clothes police officers in an unmarked estate car politely checked out the credentials of anyone who called at the property.

When Christine Ketley answered the intercom on the black metal gates at the entrance to the estate, she told reporters she was not Christine Ketley and even claimed such a person did not live at that address. But her name was clearly on the electoral roll and the house deeds.

On a table inside the detached double-fronted property, John Palmer's face stared out from the front page of a newspaper.

'Fraudster dies at his home,' the headline read.

CHAPTER FORTY-EIGHT

POINT BLANK

FORENSIC PATHOLOGY UNIT, UNIVERSITY OF LEICESTER, 30 JUNE 2015

Five days after his death, John Palmer's corpse finally gave up the secrets that everyone close to him had suspected all along. A post-mortem examination carried out by forensic pathologist Benjamin Swift found Palmer had been shot six times in the back, chest and arms. When the news went public there was hell to pay.

Essex Police chiefs were hauled into Scotland Yard to explain themselves. Palmer's name was so synonymous with police corruption that there were suspicions that the police might have deliberately misdiagnosed the cause of death in order to give his killer more time to escape.

When it became clear this was not the case and Essex Police had quite simply been inefficient, the force's serious crime squad was given a no-holds-barred brief to immediately launch a major murder investigation.

By the time Essex Police actually admitted Palmer's death now 'bore all the hallmarks of a professional hit' it seemed to be a classic case of too little too late.

Detective Chief Inspector Stephen Jennings was the officer leading the investigation and he told reporters: 'Due to John's significant criminal history there are people or groups of people who may have wished to do him harm. Therefore our search is not just for the gunman but for a person or group of people who may have commissioned the killing.'

Scotland Yard and the underworld rolled their eyes and looked skywards. '"Tell us something we don't know" was how we all reacted,' said one of Palmer's oldest associates.

The police even suggested Palmer had been very nervous about his upcoming court proceedings in Spain and this may have also contributed to his murder. The same associate recalled: 'What were they suggesting? He'd topped himself? Fuckin' coppers were in pieces. They'd screwed up big time and now they were plodding around like ducks on ice, all over the place.'

Jennings refused to comment on whether Palmer was a police informant at the time of his death but he did refer to possible links between Palmer and 'criminal groups and specific crimes in the UK, including the £14 million Hatton Garden raid'.

Sky News's veteran crime correspondent Martin Brunt wasn't surprised when he heard that John Palmer had been murdered by a hitman. It was a classic old-fashioned contract killing. No one else hurt. And a massive payday for the assassin who pulled it off. As Brunt later said: 'When I heard heart attack I couldn't believe my ears. Then they said they'd got it wrong and the whole case seemed to be falling apart before the investigation had even properly begun.'

Not surprisingly, Essex Police were highly embarrassed by the 'Keystone Cop' allegations thrown at them as a result of their officers' 'misdiagnosis' following the discovery of Palmer's body in his own garden. By initially insisting Palmer had died of heart failure, detectives had allowed Palmer in a sense to humiliate them, even after his death.

A couple of days after the revelation that Palmer had been murdered finally came out, the police arrived at Sandpit Cottage with a warrant to search the premises. Palmer's lover Christine Ketley was so surprised she called one of Palmer's lawyers to ask what she should do but in the end she agreed on the basis she had nothing to hide. There was no trace of any paperwork, arms or anything else, which might point to a motive for the killing.

But police did retrieve the last known image of John Palmer taken by his hated CCTV cameras as he drove along the side of his garden on his quad bike towing a trailer crammed with leaves and paperwork. There was a moment on the footage when Palmer looked up to the camera and smiled, almost as if he knew these would be his last few minutes on earth . . .

In many of England's prisons a cheer went up when it was revealed that Palmer had been, after all, killed by a hitman. Palmer's old associates and enemies were soon offering spicy information about him in exchange for shorter sentences.

Naturally, police investigating Palmer's death went to see Kenneth Noye inside prison. He said he would cooperate with them if his road-rage murder life sentence was 'looked at'. That request was immediately refused and Noye told his lawyers to inform the police not to come and ask him any more questions about John Palmer.

Essex Police knew their reputations were on the line if the killer of John Palmer slipped through their hands, so they tried to ensure there would be no cock-ups this time. Detectives immediately began working around the clock, steadily and effectively gathering intelligence information. It was a complex, well-organized operation known only to a select band of senior officers because there were genuine fears that certain corrupt officers might put a spanner in the works.

London's Crimelands were ablaze with rumours. Many said Palmer had had it coming for years. But they also pointed out that whoever had 'iced' Palmer would himself most likely be the underworld's next murder victim.

In London, Palmer's former mistress Saskia and their son only learned about Palmer's murder through the newspapers. She told one reporter: 'John has been portrayed as a bad man. But with us he was a very kind, lovely man.'

Meanwhile Essex detectives began examining all available surveillance material that had been gathered on Palmer in recent months for any potential clues. Some claimed the police played a role in Palmer's death by simply stepping back when they knew there was an imminent threat to his life. The police themselves denied this but in gangsterdom it remained a popular theory.

It would take months to study all the intel gleaned from the surveillance operation on Palmer and none of it was ever deemed significant in relation to the actual murder inquiry. One senior Scotland Yard source later explained: 'Detectives held back a lot of their findings because they wanted to use the info to help them catch even bigger fish than John Palmer.'

Among the material examined by Essex police for possible connections to the Palmer murder were seventy pages of transcripts of the conversations recorded by police monitoring the Hatton Garden gang in the aftermath of the raid. There were no mentions of the two crime family brothers or John Palmer. However, the same Scotland Yard source pointed out: 'The police could easily have edited those references out because they didn't want anyone to know what they were up to at such an early stage in their investigation. Maybe detectives intended to use those tapes later in court and they didn't want a feud breaking out between Palmer's associates and the London crime family brothers.'

Palmer's murder had left the underworld in complete disarray.

CHAPTER FORTY-NINE

THE USUAL SUSPECTS

Bill and Ben – the two London crime family brothers – continued to be stunned by Palmer's murder. They'd lost a fortune and decided to put out feelers to try to find out who was behind it, or so they wanted the underworld to believe. They were also angry with Palmer for not telling them he'd just had heart surgery. In a way he'd made them look fools even after his own death, just as he had the police.

The brothers also feared that other criminals would try to put them in the frame for Palmer's murder. And of course they couldn't say anything about their £1 million a month 'arrangement' with Palmer because that would have meant admitting the existence of Palmer's secret tapes containing undeniable evidence linking the brothers to two murders.

One man who helped the police in the aftermath of the Palmer murder was immediately given a secret identity and a twenty-four-hour police guard in an undisclosed location in case any gangsters tried to track him down. The same man's information was eventually discounted as a pack of lies, which had been deliberately told to the police to get them off the scent of the real killer. There had even been a false rumour spread that the same man had a £100,000 bounty on his head for helping the police to add authenticity to the man's so-called connections to the Palmer murder case.

In a top-security prison north of London, a criminal suspected of being connected to people who might have commissioned the hit on Palmer was given a twenty-four-hour guard in solitary confinement. Police believed a contract had been taken out to kill the man inside prison. He'd refused to help detectives but they knew that they needed to keep him safe just in case he ever changed his mind.

And Palmer's onetime intended target, TV investigator Roger Cook, said after hearing about the murder: 'Hopefully, after twenty-one years, the £20,000 bounty he put on my head in 1994 has died with him.'

BRENTWOOD, ESSEX, AUGUST 2015

The day before John Palmer's very low-key funeral, a man was arrested on suspicion of Palmer's murder but then given police bail on condition he did not travel to the Brentwood area of Essex, where Christine Ketley still lived, and the funeral itself.

Those who attended the service later said the atmosphere was 'tense' between Ketley and Palmer's relatives, who'd wanted him buried in a family plot in Birmingham next to his mother, whom he'd loved so much.

Police officers mingled with mourners at the funeral, much to the irritation of many present that day. At the small wake afterwards in a local pub, most mourners only stayed for one drink and then left.

Two months later, the same man questioned about the killing of John Palmer was told no further action would be taken against him and allegations against him were dropped. Many believed the arrest of the man was just a clumsy attempt by the police to put certain individuals under intense pressure to try to find out who'd really killed Palmer.

In the autumn of 2015, there were rumours in the underworld that the criminal who actually commissioned the hit on John Palmer had himself been 'dealt with' in Amsterdam by two Colombian hitmen on a motorbike, but this has never been officially confirmed.

In late 2015, it was also alleged by the *Times* newspaper in London that John Palmer had been protected from further prosecution by a 'clique' of high-ranking corrupt Metropolitan Police officers who were themselves eventually exposed by a police probe called Operation Tiberius.

In early 2016, six of the elderly men involved in the Hatton Garden vault raid were jailed for a total of forty years after pleading guilty to stealing the contents of those safety deposit boxes. Another man was given a suspended sentence of twenty-one months.

Among those found guilty was John Palmer's Brink's-Mat gold bullion associate Brian Reader, now aged 77. He received a prison term of six years and three months for his role in the raid.

To many, Palmer's death and the jailing of Reader marked the end of an era.

In March 2016, John Palmer's lover Christine Ketley appeared on BBC TV's *Crimewatch* programme alongside the couple's son James Ketley and they both made a fresh appeal for information about Palmer's murder. Ketley admitted Palmer had 'made mistakes in his life' but insisted he 'had paid for those mistakes'.

She added she had been 'proud' that Palmer appeared to be adjusting to 'normal life'.

Police received no tangible leads as a result of that TV appeal.

In the summer of 2016, detectives hunting the killer of John Palmer contacted me to ask for help. It was a measure of how desperate detectives had become. I was unable to help Essex Police but was deeply disturbed by their approach because it suggested they had no real leads or suspects.

Senior investigating officer Stephen Jennings later tried to water this down by pointing out to the media that Palmer had at least 16,000 enemies because that was how many people had been scammed out of their money by his timeshare empire. Jennings also referred to '700 lines of inquiry' and how 'over 200 individual statements from witnesses have been taken'.

But none of this seems to have thrown up any real clues.

On 17 October 2016 – more than a year after John Palmer's murder – his will was blocked by Spanish authorities determined to claw back some of the millions of pounds alleged to have been stolen from those timeshare investors in Tenerife and on the Spanish mainland.

But this development was even more significant because for the first time, it was publicly admitted by the police in both Spain and the UK that they had wired Palmer's cell in Long Lartin Prison, as well as monitoring all his phone calls and a lot of his movements in a secret surveillance operation that had first started back in 1999.

At Palmer's inquest on 18 December 2016, senior Essex coroner Caroline Beasley-Murray concluded to the court: 'In light of all the evidence that has been heard before the court, mainly from DCI Jennings, I'm sure that Mr Palmer was unlawfully killed.'

Yet again it seemed that all investigations into John Palmer's cold-blooded murder had completely 'missed the boat'.

CHAPTER FIFTY

AS LONG AS YER ARM

GUINEA-BISSAU, WEST AFRICA, LATE 2016

Over in the tinpot country of Guinea-Bissau – just a short hop from Tenerife – Tel continued to thrive thanks to his Colombian drug-cartel bosses, who'd turned this poverty-stricken nation into a thriving narco-state. In an interview with local journalists, Tel grandly spoke about how Guinea-Bissau was fighting ISIS infiltration in its society and insisted that the notorious terror group was the greatest threat to world peace.

Tel referred to Russia's role in bringing peace back to war-torn Syria. There were even rumours in West Africa and the Middle East that Tel was playing matchmaker between the Colombians and ISIS, who wanted a clear route through the Middle East for their cocaine.

Tel claimed to one reporter in Guinea-Bissau that ISIS fighters used drugs during battles. He also appeared to be very knowledgeable when it came to arms trafficking in Syria, Iraq, Libya, Yemen and various African countries.

Many who read Tel's claims believed that he was simply flexing his muscles on behalf of the Colombians, who needed guarantees from ISIS that their main cocaine-trafficking routes would not be disrupted by the terror group.

Tel – now projecting himself as an international diplomat – called on Western countries to 'clearly differentiate Muslims from terrorists and that anyone who supports the jihadists should go to jail, unceremoniously, no matter whoever and whatever'. Tel told one reporter he feared for Europe's future because of the vast amount of immigration from war-torn Africa and the Middle East and how it would inevitably lead to more and more terrorism attacks. Tel even demanded tighter border controls in Europe without mentioning he was still officially on Europe's Most Wanted list.

By the end of 2016, silence within the underworld seemed to have forced Essex Police detectives to unofficially wind down their investigation into John Palmer's death. After much intense work, including checks on at least four other murder cases, police told Palmer's family they couldn't find a specific motive or the actual identity of his killer.

So the John Palmer inquiry joined a string of other unsolved killings including many of those slayings connected to the Brink's-Mat gold bullion heist. As one detective later admitted: 'An inpeneterable wall of silence existed around John Palmer even after his death.'

There is no doubt that John Palmer's estimated 16,000 time-share fraud victims revelled in his death. But many remained extremely disgruntled because so few of them could ever expect to get their money back.

Some criminals in Spain and the UK believe to this day intelligence on John Palmer was leaked by the DEA and other law-enforcement agencies to rival criminals, which may have led to Palmer's murder.

'The law [police] don't care if we live or die. It's another one out of the way whenever we get popped,' said one of Palmer's oldest associates. 'Let's face it, the police were happy to see the back of John Palmer.'

I have been told by one UK Customs source that copies of UK and Spanish surveillance reports on Palmer may well have fallen into the hands of criminals close to some of Palmer's long list of enemies. These reports were supplied by a unit of crooked Dutch policemen, who'd been taking bribes from criminals for years and one of whom was even suspected of carrying out another contract killing on behalf of gangsters. But this has never been corroborated.

In early February 2017, a 50-year-old British man was questioned by Essex Police about the murder of John Palmer. The man, originally from Tyneside, was said to live on Spain's Costa del Sol and had voluntarily visited detectives in Essex. He was released without charge following his interview.

POSTSCRIPT

Shortly after completing this book, I bumped into a retired judge, who'd helped me with a few of my previous books on some of Palmer's most notorious contemporaries. He told me that Palmer didn't go to his grave with his multimillion-pound fortune still intact. The judge said: 'He avoided effective confiscation orders brilliantly for many years thanks to his lawyers and the ineptitude of many within the British legal system. But Palmer made a secret settlement a couple of years before he died that saw him left with a mere fraction of his so-called fortune still intact.'

The judge claimed the confiscation order remained a secret because police and prosecutors wanted to 'squeeze' Palmer for information by threatening to expose the settlement in public if he refused to help them. That would have put him directly in the firing line of numerous underworld enemies.

The judge explained: 'I don't know what he told authorities but in the end even John Palmer discovered that crime doesn't pay.'

*

Recently, I got a call from a retired gangster associate of Palmer's who contributed to this book. This character's 'speciality' had been clumping Palmer's enemies in Las Americas whenever they crossed him in the clubs and bars close to Palmer's timeshare empire. 'It's a different place now JP has gone,' said his associate. 'The Russians came in and scared the shit out of everyone and then they were followed by the Eastern Europeans, who'd shoot their own children. Now they're running everything from the brothels to the timeshare scams to the drugs. JP got out at the right time.'

Palmer's associate also said: 'At least when JP was top man he kept a lid on most of the violence. People wouldn't dare step out of line and, as a result, the whole place stayed relatively peaceful and safe. Now it's a shitty, rundown slum of a place. People get mugged for their shopping, literally. And no one dares complain in case the foreign criminals chop their heads off.'

Palmer's associate also mentioned the rumours about Palmer's murder that still dominate the underworld. 'It looks to many of us like an "inside job",' he said. 'Whoever did it knew JP wouldn't be wearing his bullet-proof vest and the exact location of those CCTV cameras in his garden. Tells you everything, don't it?'

ACKNOWLEDGEMENTS

It's inevitable that somewhere in *Killing Goldfinger* I've missed out a few 'faces' and maybe even a few of the facts. So, to those individuals I say sorry, although I'm not sure if any of them will mind!

Then there are the retired police officers – some of them ex-Flying Squad detectives – who helped me on behalf of their serving colleagues, because these days Scotland Yard officers don't tend to talk frankly and openly to journalists. Again, I can't name them for obvious reasons but their contribution to this book has been immeasurable.

Most of the dialogue represented here was constructed from available documents and court records, some was drawn from tape-recorded testimony and some was dramatically reconstructed via the memory of participants. Historic references were carefully researched from archive material.

Fear has driven most of these informants to hide behind anonymous descriptions of themselves. I apologize for using the word 'associate' so frequently but it was the most accurate word to use because John Palmer did not have any friends as such.

One of these very same 'associates' cried off three interviews with me and then claimed he was afraid John Palmer wasn't dead and would come back and kill him if he cooperated with me. Such is the power and influence of Palmer, even from beyond the grave. This same informant is convinced Palmer is living in the heart of a jungle in a big bamboo castle like Marlon Brando's Captain Kurtz in *Apocolypse Now*. It sounds intriguing but highly unlikely.

Meanwhile, I just hope you enjoyed reading *Killing Goldfinger* as much as I have enjoyed writing and researching it.

Wensley Clarkson
London, 2017

APPENDIX

KENNETH NOYE remains a criminal enigma. He's outlived most of his friends and enemies and has pushed hard to get released from his life sentence for the road-rage murder. In fact, he may well have left prison by the time you read this.

TEL continues to flourish, thanks to his Colombian 'friends' and deals he's apparently struck with law-enforcement agents across the globe. He remains 'close' to the government of Guinea-Bissau, the Colombians' favourite narco-state.

BILL AND BEN still run their criminal empire in the heart of London, despite round-the-clock police surveillance teams.

GIOVANNI DI STEFANO – otherwise known as the Devil's Disciple – remains in prison following his conviction.

JUDGE BALTASAR GARZÓN retired from his job inside the Spanish justice system but is still unofficially involved in helping clean up Palmer's onetime kingdom of Tenerife.

MICKEY McAVOY and **BRIAN ROBINSON** have never been implicated in any crimes since the Brink's-Mat robbery, having kept a low profile following their release from prison in 2000.

GB – one of the UK's richest money launderers – continues to rake in millions of pounds every week, thanks to London's ever-increasing popularity among the mega-rich.

THE PROFESSOR disappeared shortly after his clash with John Palmer. Later, he fled his home near Cali, Colombia, after hearing that a team of Nazi hunters were on his trail.

DIESEL the bodyguard continues to smother his body in baby oil and was last heard of working as a male stripper in Benidorm.

ELVIS THE EEL returned to the UK after working as one of Palmer's troupe of entertainers. He retired from showbusiness and now runs an antique shop in a small town on the coast of southern England.

BOBBI – the south London robber turned drag queen – was last heard of entertaining tourists on the Costa del Sol with his Marilyn Monroe impersonations.

MARNIE PALMER recently sold the family home at Battlefield and moved into a flat nearby. She had no involvement in her husband's criminal activities and has always maintained a dignified silence about Palmer.

CHRISTINE KETLEY still lives in the Brentwood area of Essex and has only once spoken in public about her murdered lover. Palmer had always been extremely careful not to involve her in any of his criminal activities away from the timeshare business.

JAMES KETLEY says his father was a laugh and nothing like the nasty gangster he has been portrayed as. He no doubt cherishes many fond memories of him and had no involvement in Palmer's criminal activities.

APPENDIX

ROGER COOK never moved home and refused to be intimidated by Palmer, despite John Palmer's plan to have him killed by a hitman.

SASKIA MUNDINGER now lives quietly in London and continues to receive a generous financial settlement from John Palmer's estate.

THE CURSE OF BRINK'S-MAT still lingers in the air like a malignant force encouraging murder and mayhem. It's highly unlikely that John Palmer will be its final victim.

THE *BRAVE GOOSE OF ESSEX* remains in port in Tenerife. Its rotting woodwork is a chilling testament to the way owner John Palmer is gradually fading from the minds of the islanders.

THE ISLAND VILLAGE TIMESHARE RESORT no longer has any connection to John Palmer and is currently run as a package-holiday hotel.

TENERIFE itself has suffered hardships since it was ripped apart by the likes of John Palmer and Tel. Today the southern half of the island is gradually rebuilding itself but timeshare resorts are no longer encouraged.

PALMER'S CLASSIC CAR COLLECTION was allegedly destroyed when a fire swept through the underground car park in Tenerife where they were stored. Millions of pounds' worth of cash and gold bullion bars are rumoured to have been hidden in them. Did someone empty the cars of their hidden treasure before setting them ablaze?

PALMER'S TAPES of hundreds of meetings with criminals over the previous forty years remain hidden in one of the numerous places where he kept his stashes of cash. Whoever finds them will be sitting on a veritable gold mine.

And finally . . .

SID AND NANCY lived for a couple more years following the brutal slayings of Flo and Billy Robinson but friends say they never chased dragonflies again.

Anybody who can help the John Palmer murder inquiry is asked to contact the Brentwood Major Investigation Team on Essex Police 101.

If, on the other hand, you wish to remain anonymous you can call Crimestoppers on 0800 555 111.

THE LAST WORD

'Remember the golden rule,' was the motto John Palmer liked to quote, *'he who has the gold makes the rules.'*

Not always.